The Discipline of Law

'What is the argument on the other side? Only this, that no case has been found in which it has been done before. That argument does not appeal to me in the least. If we never do anything which has not been done before, we shall never get anywhere. The law will stand still whilst the rest of the world goes on: and that will be bad for both'.

Denning LJ in *Packer v Packer* [1954] P 15 at 22.

The Discipline of Law

by The Rt Hon
LORD DENNING
Master of the Rolls

London
BUTTERWORTHS
1979

England London	Butterworth & Co (Publishers) Ltd 88 Kingsway, WC2B 6AB
Australia Sydney	Butterworths Pty Ltd 586 Pacific Highway, Chatswood, NSW 2067 Also at Melbourne, Brisbane, Adelaide and Perth
Canada Toronto	Butterworth & Co (Canada) Ltd 2265 Midland Avenue, Scarborough M1P 4S1
New Zealand Wellington	Butterworths of New Zealand Ltd 77–85 Customhouse Quay
South Africa Durban	Butterworth & Co (South Africa) (Pty) Ltd 152–154 Gale Street
USA Boston	Butterworths (Publishers) Inc 19 Cummings Park, Woburn, Mass 01801

ISBN Casebound   0 406 17604 3
Limp   0 406 17605 1

Typeset by Scribe Design, Chatham, Kent
Printed in Great Britain by Billing & Sons Limited
Guildford, London and Worcester

Preface

In speaking of the Discipline of Law, I use the word in the sense given in the Shorter Oxford Dictionary of 'Instruction imparted to disciples or scholars'. But I have no disciples: and scholars are few. Yet I use the word so as to show that I wish to impart instruction — instruction, that is, in the principles of law as they have been, as they are, and as they should be.

My theme is that the principles of law laid down by the Judges in the 19th century — however suited to social conditions of that time — are not suited to the social necessities and social opinion of the 20th century. They should be moulded and shaped to meet the needs and opinion of today.

In pursuit of this theme I have taken some of the principles where progress has been most marked: and in which I myself have taken some part. Not, I hope, out of conceit, but because I happen to be well acquainted with them. I have put forward proposals which have had a mixed reception. Some of them have come to be accepted during my time. Some have been rejected. Others have not been accepted as yet. Most of them have found their way into the Law Reports. So recently I determined to collect them together in a book. I have arranged them, chapter by chapter, according to the subject in hand. I have quoted extensively from my judgments and connected them together by a running commentary in the hope that these proposals may be discussed in the Law Schools: and perhaps in future years find acceptance. But this book is outside my judicial work. All I write now must be treated with reserve. For I am still serving as a Judge:

and must and will keep an open mind. Views which are formed in my library may well be found to be wrong. Many a time have I changed my mind after hearing argument. Reasoning has been found to be fallacious. First impressions have been found to be wrong. Outlook has been distorted by prejudice. All these are swept away in the judgment-seat. For like the centurion in the Gospel: 'I also am a man set under authority' (Luke 7:8). Restless under authority, irked by it — when I feel it to be wrong — nevertheless it is my duty to abide by it — unless I can persuade my brethren that it is working injustice. Then when authority is shown to be wrong, the time will come when it will be overthrown: or at any rate it should be. If not by the Judges, then by Parliament — at the instance of the Law Commission. Where I have failed they may succeed.

Denning.

November, 1978

Contents

Contents

Contents

PART SEVEN. THE DOCTRINE OF PRECEDENT

Table of Cases

Table of Cases

Part one

The construction of documents

Introduction

In the daily practice of the law, the most important subject is the construction of documents. Yet it is the subject on which opinions are still much divided. There are the 'strict constructionists' on the one hand: and the 'intention' seekers on the other hand. The strict constructionists go by the letter of the document. The 'intention' seekers go by the purpose or intent of the makers of it.

In the 19th century the strict constructionists dominated the legal scene. They stood by the 'golden rule' laid down by the House of Lords in 1857 in *Grey v Pearson*[1]. The Lord Chancellor there said that the Courts should 'adhere as rigidly as possible to the express words that are found and to give those words their natural and ordinary meaning'. That rule still has many adherents today.

In the 20th century the 'intention' seekers have been gaining ground: but very slowly. They have been reinforced of late by the method of interpretation used by the European Court at Luxembourg. The legal system there is so broadly conceived that the Judges have recourse to what they call the 'schematic' method of interpretation. They look to the scheme or design and then fill in the gaps.

In this first part I trace the development of these rival methods and present them for your consideration. I would simply ask: Which method is to be preferred?

1. (1857) 6 HL Cas 61.

1 Command of language

1 The tools of trade

To succeed in the profession of the law, you must seek to cultivate command of language. Words are the lawyer's tools of trade. When you are called upon to address a judge, it is your words which count most. It is by them that you will hope to persuade the judge of the rightness of your cause. When you have to interpret a section in a Statute or a paragraph in a Regulation, you have to study the very words. You have to discover the meaning by analysing the words – one by one – to the very last syllable. When you have to draw up a will or a contract, you have to choose your words well. You have to look into the future – envisage all the contingencies that may come to pass – and then use words to provide for them. On the words you use, your client's future may depend.

The reason why words are so important is because words are the vehicle of thought. When you are working out a problem on your own – at your desk or walking home – you think in words, not in symbols or numbers. When you are advising your client – in writing or by word of mouth – you must use words. There is no other means available. To do it convincingly, do it simply and clearly. If others find it difficult to understand you, it will often be because you have not cleared your own mind upon it. Obscurity in thought inexorably leads to obscurity in language.

Sometimes you may fail – without your fault – to make yourself clear. It may be because of the infirmity of the words themselves. They may be inadequate to express the

5

meaning which you wish to convey. They may lack the necessary precision. 'Day' and 'Night' are clear enough at most times. But when does day begin and night end? Some may say at sunrise. Others would say at dawn. Then when does 'dawn' begin? No one can tell exactly. Or a word may mean one thing to one person and another thing to another. Take 'punctual payment' or 'prompt payment'. To one it may mean immediate payment. To another it may permit of a little latitude and it may suffice if payment is made within a day or two. The difference between the two will remain unless it is settled by the House of Lords[1]. Yet again a word may mean one thing in one context and another thing in another context. Thus 'money' may be limited to the money in your purse and cash at bank or it may include money owing to you for dividends or rents[2]. Yet again a word may mean one thing in one situation and another in another. Take the words 'insulting behaviour'. Blowing a whistle on the Centre Court at Wimbledon may be 'insulting behaviour'; but blowing it at the Cup Final at Wembley would not. It depends on the meaning which you yourself choose to give to 'insulting'. The difference is not to be settled by authority, but by individual choice[3]. Constantly you will find ordinary people giving different meanings to the same word. This gives full scope to the lawyer.

2 Acquiring skill

How then can you acquire this command of language so much to be desired? Forgive me here if I give of my own experience. When I was young, I did not think much in words. At Oxford I studied Mathematics. No need for words there. The tools I used then were numbers, letters and symbols. They were lifeless things without meaning or sound — the necessary tools of the scientist but not of the lawyer. But when I was called to the Bar, I had to become proficient with words. I did it by drawing on my reserves of English

1. *Maclaine v Gatty* [1921] 1 AC 376.
2. *Perrin v Morgan* [1943] AC 399.
3. *Brutus v Cozens* [1973] AC 854.

literature. These I had acquired at the Elizabethan Grammar School to which I went daily. I had read much of Shakespeare and many of our poets and novelists whilst still at school. All my prizes from the age of 11 were for English. I have them still, bound in handsome leather, with the school crest and the date AD 1569. The titles in succession are the Great Authors, Macaulay, Carlyle, and Milton. Reading these and others provided the essentials: a wide vocabulary of words, and an understanding of the meaning attached to them by the masters of the language. Come to think of it, that is how the makers of the great Oxford Dictionary set about their task to discover meanings. They compiled it 'from over five million quotations derived from English works of literature and records of all kinds'. Then glance at the Dictionary itself to see the result. It shows that the meaning of a word may change from decade to decade, from place to place, even from one person to another. It may depend on the subject-matter under discussion or the context in which it is used. So you have a challenging task ahead if you are to acquire command of language: and to say what meaning any particular word has in any particular case.

Next, I had to practise continually. As a pianist practises the piano, so the lawyer should practise the use of words, both in writing and by word of mouth. Again, forgive a personal reminiscence. In chambers, if asked to advise, I took infinite pains in the writing of an opinion. I crossed out sentence after sentence. I wrote them again and again. Seek to make your opinions clear at all costs. Make them positive and definite. Not neutral or vacillating. My pupil master told me early on of the client's complaint: 'I want your opinion and not your doubts', and of Sir George Jessel's characteristic saying: 'I may be wrong and sometimes am, but I am never in doubt'.

3 Addressing the Court

Apart from writing, there is addressing the Court. Speaking needs even more practice: and even more experience. I was no good at first. I was too shy; also too nervous. Others are different. Many friends of mine − who have since become eminent − started as President of the Union at Oxford or Cambridge. At Oxford I joined the Union but never spoke there. I only learnt by actual experience − by the small briefs which come the beginner's way − by addressing a jury, for whom you must make things simple and clear − like a dock brief at Quarter Sessions at Winchester with only half-an-hour before the case comes on − or a two-guinea brief in the Marylebone County Court before a testy judge. He could be very rude if you made the slightest mistake. Remember also that, whatever the tribunal, you must give a good impression. Your appearance means a lot. Dress neatly, not slovenly. Be well-groomed. Your voice must be pleasing, not harsh or discordant. Pitch it so that all can hear without strain. Pronounce your consonants. Do not slur your words. Speak not too fast nor yet too slow. All these things are commonplace but they are so often forgotten that I warn you against the mistakes I see made daily. No hands in pockets. It shows slovenliness. No fidgetting with pencil or with gown. It shows nervousness. No whispering with neighbours. It shows lack of respect. No 'ers' or 'ums'. It shows that you are slow-thinking, not knowing what to say next. Avoid mannerisms like the plague. It distracts attention. Don't be dull. Don't repeat yourself too often. Don't be long-winded. All these lose you your hearers: and once you have lost them, you are done for. You can never get them back − not so as to get them to listen attentively.

One thing you will not be able to avoid − the nervousness before the case starts. Every advocate knows it. In a way it helps, so long as it is not too much. That is where I used sometimes to fail. My clerk − as a good clerk should − told me of it. I was anxious to win − and so tense − that my voice became too high-pitched. I never quite got over it, even as a King's Counsel. No longer now that I am a Judge. The tension is gone. The anxiety − to do right − remains.

2 The interpretation of statutes

1 Finding the intention

In almost every case on which you have to advise you will have to interpret a statute. There are stacks and stacks of them. Far worse for you than for me. When I was called in 1923 there was one volume of 500 pages. Now in 1978 there are three volumes of more than 3,000 pages. Not a single page but it can give rise to argument. Not a single page but the client will turn to you and say: 'What does it mean?' The trouble lies with our method of drafting. The principal object of the draftsman is to achieve certainty – a laudable object in itself. But in pursuit of it, he loses sight of the equally important object – clarity. The draftsman – or draftswoman – has conceived certainty: but has brought forth obscurity; sometimes even absurdity.

Books and books have been written upon the interpretation of statutes. All for the old hand. Not one for the beginner. Maxims are given to help. They are called 'Rules of Construction'. Have recourse to them when they suit your case, but do it with discretion. You will sometimes discover that if you find a maxim or rule on your side, your opponent will find one on his side to counteract it.

Beyond doubt the task of the lawyer – and of the judge – is to find out the intention of Parliament. In doing this, you must, of course, start with the words used in the statute: but not end with them – as some people seem to think. You must discover the meaning of the words. I have known statutes where there is no discernible meaning. Then we can say with the King in *Alice in Wonderland:* 'If there's no meaning in it, that saves a world of trouble, you know, as we needn't try to find any'. But in most cases there is some meaning: so we have to go on as the King did: 'And yet I don't know', he went on, 'I seem to see some meaning in it after all'.

At one time the Judges used to limit themselves to the bare reading of the Statute itself — to go simply by the words, giving them their grammatical meaning, and that was all. That view was prevalent in the 19th century and still has some supporters today. But it is wrong in principle. The meaning for which we should seek is the meaning of the Statute as it appears to those who have to obey it — and to those who have to advise them what to do about it; in short, to lawyers like yourselves. Now the Statute does not come to such folk as if they were eccentrics cut off from all that is happening around them. The Statute comes to them as men of affairs — who have their own feeling for the meaning of the words and know the reason why the Act was passed — just as if it had been fully set out in a preamble. So it has been held very rightly that you can inquire into the mischief which gave rise to the Statute — to see what was the evil which it was sought to remedy. You can for this purpose look at the Reports of Royal Commissions, of Departmental Committees and Inquiries, Law Reform Committees — and the like. So can the Judges. But oddly enough the Judges cannot look at what the responsible Minister said to Parliament — at the object of the Statute as he explained it to the House — or to the meaning of the words as he understood them. Hansard is for the Judges a closed book. But not for you. You can read what was said in the House and adopt it as part of your argument — so long as you do not acknowledge the source. The writers of law books can go further. They can give the very words from Hansard with chapter and verse. You can then read the whole to the Judges. That is what happened in a recent case about the Ombudsman[1]. Parliament gave him power to investigate complaints of 'maladminist-ration': but deliberately did not define it in the Statute.

1. *Bradford City Council v Lord Commissioner* (1978) July (unreported).

The only person who attempted a definition was Mr. Richard Crossman, the Lord President of the Council. He made a speech in Parliament giving illustrations of what 'malad--ministration' means. His illustrations became the guide-lines for the Ombudsman himself and his advisers. They were known as the 'Crossman Catalogue'. They were quoted in full in a public address given by the Ombudsman and also by the professors and text-writers. In that form they could be, and were, read by the Judges: and helped them as much as they did the Ombudsman.

2 'Ironing out the creases'

The first case in which there was an opportunity to advocate a new approach to the interpretation of statutes was *Seaford Court Estates Ltd v Asher*[1]. I was a very junior Lord Justice of Appeal of only six months' standing. Lord Greene MR was presiding with Asquith LJ and me. It was a case where the rent of a flat had been increased from £175 a year to £250 a year. The increase was because the landlord agreed to provide the hot water for the flat. The tenant freely agreed to pay the £250 but then tried to get it reduced to £175. He had no merits at all. His argument depended on giving a literal meaning to the word 'burden' in the Rent Act 1920. It was a situation which Parliament never foresaw and for which it had made no provision. We reserved judgment for four weeks. I prepared my judgment and showed it to Lord Greene. He agreed with it and said so in his own judgment. Lord Justice Asquith also agreed with it. So it had backing of the first order. This is what I said:

'The question for decision in this case is whether we are at liberty to extend the ordinary meaning of 'burden' so as to include a contingent burden of the kind I have described. Now this court has already held that this sub-section is to be liberally construed so as to give effect to the governing

1. [1949] 2 KB 481.

11

principles embodied in the legislation . . . and I think we should do the same.

'Whenever a statute comes up for consideration it must be remembered that it is not within human powers to foresee the manifold sets of facts which may arise, and, even if it were, it is not possible to provide for them in terms free from all ambiguity. The English language is not an instrument of mathematical precision. Our literature would be much the poorer if it were. This is where the draftsmen of Acts of Parliament have often been unfairly criticized. A judge, believing himself to be fettered by the supposed rule that he must look to the language and nothing else, laments that the draftsmen have not provided for this or that, or have been guilty of some or other ambiguity. It would certainly save the judges trouble if Acts of Parliament were drafted with divine prescience and perfect clarity. In the absence of it, when a defect appears a judge cannot simply fold his hands and blame the draftsman. He must set to work on the constructive task of finding the intention of Parliament, and he must do this not only from the language of the statute, but also from a consideration of the social conditions which gave rise to it, and of the mischief which it was passed to remedy, and then he must supplement the written word so as to give 'force and life' to the intention of the legislature. That was clearly laid down by the resolution of the judges in *Heydon's* case, and it is the safest guide today. Good practical advice on the subject was given about the same time by Plowden. . . . Put into homely metaphor it is this: A judge should ask himself the question: If the makers of the Act had themselves come across this ruck in the texture of it, how would they have straightened it out? He must then do as they would have done. A judge must not alter the material of which it is woven, but he can and should iron out the creases.

'Approaching this case in that way, I cannot help feeling that the legislature had not specifically in mind a contingent burden such as we have here. If it had would it not have put it on the same footing as an actual burden? I think it would. It would have permitted an increase of rent when the terms were so changed as to put a positive legal burden on the land-lord'.

The case went to the House of Lords and our decision was upheld but it was there put by the majority of the House on traditional grounds. Lord MacDermott (who dissented) took the literal meaning. He thought I had stated the principles 'rather widely'[1].

3 'A naked usurpation of the legislative function'

The new approach did not last long. Only a year later it was roundly condemned by the House of Lords. It was in *Magor and St Mellons Rural District Council v Newport Corporation*[2]. The Newport Corporation had expanded its boundaries by taking in goodly parts of the two Magor and St. Mellons Rural Districts — taking in the richest parts paying a large amount of 'rates. The Act provided for reasonable compensation to the two District Councils. Then the Minister made an Order amalgamating the two District Councils into one. On that account the Newport Corporation sought to reduce the compensation to nothing. This seemed to me most unjust. The Newport Corporation sought to rely on the literal meaning of the Order. They succeeded in all Courts. I protested in the Court of Appeal, saying:

'This was so obviously the intention of the Minister's Order that I have no patience with an ultra-legalistic interpretation which would deprive (the appellants) of their rights altogether. I would repeat what I said in *Seaford Court Estates Ltd v Asher*. We do not sit here to pull the language of Parliament and of Ministers to pieces and make nonsense of it. That is an easy thing to do, and it is a thing to which lawyers are too often prone. We sit here to find out the intention of Parliament and of Ministers and carry it out, and we do this better by filling in the gaps and making sense of the enactment than by opening it up to destructive analysis'.

1. [1950] 1 All ER 1018 at 1029.
2. [1951] 2 All ER 839.

My protest carried some weight with Lord Radcliffe. He had the best mind of anyone of his time. He rejected the strict literal view saying: 'I regard this as an injustice'[1], but all the others insisted upon it. Lord Simonds was a dominating intellect but cast in a most conservative mould. He rejected my proposition that it was 'the duty of the Court to find out the intention of Parliament — and not only of Parliament but of Ministers also'. He said that it 'cannot by any means be supported. The duty of the Court is to interpret the words which the legislature has used'. That is the traditional view expressed, as usual, by Lord Simonds in his most dogmatic fashion. He went on to pour scorn in these words:

'. . . The court, having discovered the intention of Parliament and of Ministers too, must proceed to fill in the gaps. What the legislature has not written, the court must write. This proposition, which restates in a new form the view expressed by the Lord Justice in the earlier case of *Seaford Court Estates Ltd v Asher* (to which the Lord Justice himself) refers), cannot be supported. It appears to me to be a naked usurpation of the legislative function under the thin disguise of interpretation. And it is the less justifiable when it is guess-work with what material the legislature would, if it had discovered the gap, have filled it in. If a gap is disclosed, the remedy lies in an amending Act'.

So injustice was done. The new approach was scotched. It took a long time to bring it to life again. Yet gradually it came. Even in the House of Lords, some Law Lords began to say — quite contrary to Lord Simonds — that it was their task to find out the intention of Parliament: and that they would adapt the words of the statute — put a strained construction on them if need be, to carry out that intention. Thus in *Nimmo v Alexander*[2] Lord Wilberforce said:

'If I thought that Parliament's intention could not be carried out, or even would be less effectively implemented, unless one particular (even though unnatural) construction were

1. [1951] 2 All ER 839 at 849.
2. [1968] AC 107 at 130.

14

placed on the words it has used, I would endeavour to adopt that construction'.

And in *Kammins v Zenith Investments Ltd*[1] Lord Diplock drew a clear distinction between the 'literal approach' and the 'purposive approach', and used the purposive approach to solve the question.

There remained only one further push needed. It was provided by Sir David Renton in the Report of his Committee[2]:

'We see no reason why the Courts should not respond in the way indicated by Lord Denning. The Courts should, in our view, approach legislation determined, above all, to give effect to the intention of Parliament. We see promising signs that this consideration is uppermost in the minds of the members of the highest tribunal in this country'.

4 A voice from the past

Thus encouraged, I soon found occasion to restate the principle I had stated nearly thirty years before. It was in *Nothman v Barnet Council*[3]. Men and women teachers were entitled, under their contracts, to continue in employment until the age of 65. A lady of 61 was dismissed. She claimed compensation for unfair dismissal. The Employment Appeal Tribunal held that, if she had been a man, she would have been entitled: but as she was a woman she was not. They regretted it. They said that they felt they were bound by the literal meaning of the words. This is how I summarised their viewpoint and commented on it:

'The Employment Appeal Tribunal realised this was most unjust, but felt they could do nothing about it. I will give their words . . . .

"The instant case provides as glaring an example of discrimination against a woman on the grounds of her sex as

1. [1971] AC 850 at 881.
2. Cmnd. 6053, para. 19.2.
3. [1978] 1 WLR 220.

there could possibly be. The facts of this case point to a startling anomaly".

'Yet they thought the judges hand their hands tied by the words of the statute. They said . . . :

"Clearly someone has a duty to do something about this absurd and unjust situation. It may well be, however, that there is nothing we can do about it. We are bound to apply provisions of an Act of Parliament however absurd, out of date and unfair they may appear to be. The duty of making or altering the law is the function of Parliament and is not, as many mistaken persons seem to imagine, the privilege of the judges or the judicial tribunals".

'I have read that passage at large because I wish to repudiate it. It sounds to me like a voice from the past. I heard many such words 25 years ago. It is the voice of the strict constructionist. It is the voice of those who go by the letter. It is the voice of those who adopt the strict literal and grammatical construction of the words, heedless of the consequences. Faced with glaring injustice, the judges are, it is said, impotent, incapable and sterile. Not so with us in this court. The literal method is now completely out of date. It has been replaced by the approach which Lord Diplock described as the "purposive approach" . . . . In all cases now in the interpretation of statutes we adopt such a construction as will "promote the general legislative purpose" underlying the provision. It is no longer necessary for the judges to wring their hands and say: "There is nothing we can do about it". Whenever the strict interpretation of a statute gives rise to an absurd and unjust situation, the judges can and should use their good sense to remedy it — by reading words in, if necessary — so as to do what Parliament would have done, had they had the situation in mind'.

Since that case there have been others where the literal meaning was adopted by the Employment Appeal Tribunal and rejected by the Court of Appeal: such as when an airline pilot on international routes claimed compensation for unfair dismissal. The Employment Appeal Tribunal held that it had no jurisdiction because he was a man who 'ordinarily worked' outside Great Britain. The Court of Appeal reversed this decision holding that, despite the literal words, it was sufficient if his base was in Great Britain. This was *Todd v British Midland Airways*[1].

Very recently the House of Lords have considered again the rules of interpretation of statutes. It was in *Stock v Frank Jones (Tipton) Ltd*[2]. Although it contains some views which look as if there were a return to the rules of 'strict construction', nevertheless there is an encouraging sentence by Viscount Dilhorne when he said:

'It is now fashionable to talk of a purposive construction of a statute, but it has been recognised since the 17th century that it is the task of the judiciary in interpreting an Act to seek to interpret it "according to the intent of them that made it" (Coke 4 Inst 330)'.

So Lord Coke was an intention seeker: and not a strict constructionist. It was natural for Viscount Dilhorne to support Lord Coke. He is a direct descendant of that bold Chief Justice. A strong pair.

Since that case the Court of Appeal have yet again shown themselves ready to supplement the Order of a Minister so as to fill in the gaps which the draftsmen had left[3]. So the new approach is gaining ground.

5 The Treaty of Rome

I venture to suggest that this new approach is much to be desired: because it brings our method of interpretation into line with those adopted by the European Court. I compared the two methods — our English traditional method with the European method — in *Bulmer Ltd v Bollinger SA*[4]:

'The first and fundamental point is that the Treaty concerns only those matters which have a European element, that is to

1. (1978) 122 Sol Jo 661.
2. [1978] 1 WLR 231.
3. *Lewis v Dyfed and Burnham Committee*, November 1978 (unreported).
4. [1974] 4 Ch 401 at 411.

say, matters which affect people or property in the nine countries of the common market besides ourselves. The Treaty does not touch any of the matters which concern solely England and the people in it. These are still governed by English law. They are not affected by the Treaty. But when we come to matters with a European element, the Treaty is like an incoming tide. It flows into the estuaries and up the rivers. It cannot be held back. Parliament has decreed that the Treaty is henceforward to be part of our law. It is equal in force to any statute. . . .

'. . . What then are the principles of interpretation to be applied? Beyond doubt the English courts must follow the same principles as the European Court. Otherwise there would be differences between the countries of the nine. That would never do. All the courts of all nine countries should interpret the Treaty in the same way. They should all apply the same principles. It is enjoined on the English courts by section 3 of the European Community Act 1972, which I have read.

'What a task is thus set before us! The Treaty is quite unlike any of the enactments to which we have become accustomed. The draftsmen of our statutes have striven to express themselves with the utmost exactness. They have tried to foresee all possible circumstances that may arise and to provide for them. They have sacrificed style and simplicity. They have forgone brevity. They have become long and involved. In consequence, the judges have followed suit. They interpret a statute as applying only to the circumstances covered by the very words. They give them a literal interpretation. If the words of the statute do not cover a new situation – which was not foreseen – the judges hold that they have no power to fill the gap. To do so would be a "naked usurpation of the legislative function". . . The gap must remain open until Parliament finds time to fill it.

'How different is this Treaty! It lays down general principles. It expresses its aims and purposes. All in sentences of moderate length and commendable style. But it lacks precision. It uses words and phrases without defining what they mean. An English lawyer would look for an interpretation clause, but he would look in vain. There is none. All the way through the Treaty there are gaps and lacunae. These have to be filled in by the judges, or by Regulations or directives. It is the European way.…

'Likewise the Regulations and directives. They are enacted by the Council sitting in Brussels for everyone to obey. They are quite unlike our statutory instruments. They have to give the reasons on which they are based: article 190. So they start off with pages of preambles, "whereas" and "whereas" and "whereas". These show the purpose and intent of the Regulations and directives. Then follow the provisions which are to be obeyed. Here again words and phrases are used without defining their import. Such as "personal conduct". . . . In case of difficulty, recourse is had to the preambles. These are useful to show the purpose and intent behind it all. But much is left to the judges. The enactments give only an outline plan. The details are to be filled in by the judges.

'Seeing these differences, what are the English courts to do when they are faced with a problem of interpretation? They must follow the European pattern. No longer must they examine the words in meticulous detail. No longer must they argue about the precise grammatical sense. They must look to the purpose or intent. To quote the words of the European Court . . ., they must deduce "from the wording and the spirit of the Treaty the meaning of the community rules". They must not confine themselves to the English text. They must consider, if need be, all the authentic texts, of which there are now six . . . . They must divine the spirit of the Treaty and gain inspiration from it. If they find a gap, they must fill it as best they can. They must do what the framers of the instrument would have done if they had thought about it. So we must do the same. Those are the principles, as I understand it, on which the European Court acts'.

6 International Convention

The time soon came for these principles to be tested. It was

19

in *Buchanan & Co v Babco Ltd*[1]. A load of whisky was being carried in a trailer from Glasgow all the way across Europe to Tehran. It was stolen in England. The exporters had to pay £30,000 excise duty on it. Was that 'a charge in respect of the carriage of the goods' so as to be payable by the carriers within the Convention?

To my mind, the words in their literal meaning did not make the carriers liable and so I sought to overcome the literal meaning by adopting the European method. I said:

'This article 23, paragraph 4, is an agreed clause in an international convention. As such it should be given the same interpretation in all the countries who were parties to the convention. It would be absurd that the courts of England should interpret it differently from the courts of France, or Holland, or Germany. Compensation for loss should be assessed on the same basis, no matter in which country the claim is brought. We must, therefore, put on one side our traditional rules of interpretation. We have for years tended to stick too closely to the letter – to the literal interpretation of the words. We ought, in interpreting this convention, to adopt the European method .... Some of us recently spent a couple of days in Luxembourg discussing it with the members of the European Court, and our colleagues in the other countries of the nine.

'We had a valuable paper on it by the President of the court (Judge H. Kutscher) which is well worth studying: "Methods of interpretation as seen by a judge at the Court of Justice, Luxembourg 1976". They adopt a method which they call in English by strange words – at any rate they were strange to me – the "schematic and teleological" method of interpretation. It is not really so alarming as it sounds. All it means is that the judges do not go by the literal meaning of the words or by the grammatical structure of the sentence. They go by the design or purpose which lies behind it. When they come upon a situation which is to their minds within the spirit – but not the letter – of the legislation, they solve

1. [1977] QB 208.

the problem by looking at the design and purpose of the legislature — at the effect which it was sought to achieve. They then interpret the legislation so as to produce the desired effect. This means that they fill in gaps, quite unashamedly, without hesitation. They ask simply: what is the sensible way of dealing with this situation so as to give effect to the presumed purpose of the legislation? They lay down the law accordingly. If you study the decisions of the European Court, you will see that they do it every day. To our eyes — shortsighted by tradition — it is legislation, pure and simple. But, to their eyes, it is fulfilling the true role of the courts. They are giving effect to what the legislature intended, or may be presumed to have intended. I see nothing wrong in this. Quite the contrary. It is a method of interpretation which I advocated long ago in *Seaford Court Estates Ltd v Asher* . . . . It did not gain acceptance at that time. It was condemned by Lord Simonds in the House of Lords in *Magor and St Mellons Rural District Council v Newport Corporation* . . . as a "naked usurpation of the legislative power". But the time has now come when we should think again. In interpreting the Treaty of Rome (which is part of our law) we must certainly adopt the new approach. Just as in Rome, you should do as Rome does. So in the European Community, you should do as the European Court does. So also in interpreting an international convention (such as we have here) we should do likewise. We should interpret it in the same spirit and by the same methods as the judges of other countries do. So as to obtain a uniform result. Even in interpreting our own legislation, we should do well to throw aside our traditional approach and adopt a more liberal attitude. We should adopt such a construction as will "promote the general legislative purpose" underlying the provision. This has been recommended by Sir David Renton and his colleagues in their most valuable report on *The Preparation of Legislation* . . . . There is no reason why we should not follow it at once without waiting for a statute to tell us.

'Looking at paragraph 4 of article 23 in this light, it seems to me that there is a gap in it – or, at any rate – in the English version of it. It speaks only of the charges incurred "in respect of the carriage of the goods", but says nothing of the charges consequent on the loss of the goods. I think we should fill that gap . . .'.

The case went to the House of Lords[1]. The House did not agree with what I had said. They said that we must apply the English method of interpretation in the context of an international convention. Both the majority of three and the minority of two claimed to be applying the English method: but they came to completely opposite conclusions. Their difference arose out of the different meanings they gave to the three words 'in respect of'. The majority gave them a broad meaning. The minority gave them a narrow meaning. I ask the question: why choose the broad meaning rather than the narrow? Lord Salmon was influenced by what 'reason and justice seem to demand'. That is very much the new approach for which I plead. Whenever there is a choice, choose the meaning which accords with reason and justice.

So I leave this question of statutory interpretation open for discussion: which is better? The old grammatical approach or the modern purposive approach – the traditional English approach or the modern European approach?

1. [1978] AC 141.

3 The interpretation of wills and other unilateral documents

1 The ghosts of dissatisfied testators

A similar controversy has surrounded the interpretation of wills. The Chancery Judges used always to say that their object was to ascertain the intention of the testator, but they went on in the same breath to declare that his intention could only be ascertained from the words he used. The result of this double-thinking was that they ignored his intention and construed the words of the will. They construed them literally. As a result the law books became full of reported cases as to the meaning of such common words as 'money', 'children' and so forth: which successive judges slavishly followed.

I would have hoped that the House of Lords in *Perrin v Morgan*[1] put an end to that mistaken approach. It was certainly the hope of Lord Atkin who said: 'I anticipate with satisfaction that henceforth the group of ghosts of dissatisfied testators who, according to a late Chancery Judge, wait on the other bank of the Styx to receive the judicial personages who have misconstrued their wills, may be considerably diminished'.

2 'No jurisdiction to achieve a sensible result'

My hopes were dashed, however, by *Re Rowland*[2] . A young doctor and his wife went to the South Seas. Before leaving

1. [1943] AC 399.
2. [1963] Ch 1.

they made mutual wills. He made a bequest 'in the event of my wife's death preceding or coinciding with my own death'. She likewise. They went out in a small vessel which disappeared without trace except that after some days one body was found and some wreckage. The inference was that the vessel had gone down suddenly with all hands: and all drowned. Did their deaths 'coincide'? I held that they did. But my two Chancery colleagues held they did not. I ventured to take, as I thought, a more sensible view:

'One way of approach, which was much favoured in the nineteenth century, is to ask yourself simply: what is the ordinary and grammatical meaning of the word "coincide" as used in the English language? On that approach, the answer, it is said, is plain: it means "coincident in point of time". And that means, so it is said, the same as "simultaneous" or "at the same point of time". So, instead of interpreting the word "coincide", you turn to interpreting the word "simultaneous". And at that point you come upon a difficulty because, strictly speaking, no two people ever die at exactly the same point of time. Or, at any rate, no one can ever prove that they do . . . .

'. . . . I asked Mr. Knox whether deaths are simultaneous when an aircraft crashes on a mountainside and all its occupants are killed. He said they were not, because one might have died a little while after the others. To be simultaneous there would have to be proof that they died instantaneously at the same instant, and such proof would rarely be available.

'I must confess that, if ever there were an absurdity, I should have thought we have one here. It is said that when an aircraft explodes in mid-air, the deaths of the occupants coincide; but when it crashes into a mountainside, they do not! The supporters of this argument invoke as their authority "the ordinary man". He would, I suggest, be amazed to find such a view attributed to him. Yet it is the argument, as I understand it, which urges that in this case the deaths of Dr. Rowland and his wife did not coincide. It seems to me that the fallacy in that argument is that it starts from the wrong place. It proceeds on the assumption that, in

24

construing a will, "It is not what the testator meant, but what is the meaning of his words". That may have been the nineteenth century view; but I believe it to be wrong and to have been the cause of many mistakes. I have myself known a judge to say: "I believe this to be contrary to the true intention of the testator but nevertheless it is the result of the words he has used". When a judge goes so far as to say that, the chances are that he has misconstrued the will. For in point of principle the whole object of construing a will is to find out the testator's intentions, so as to see that his property is disposed of in the way he wished. True it is that you must discover his intention from the words he used: but you must put upon his words the meaning which they bore to him. If his words are capable of more than one meaning, or of a wide meaning and a narrow meaning, as they often are, then you must put upon them the meaning which he intended them to convey, and not the meaning which a philologist would put upon them. And in order to discover the meaning which he intended, you will not get much help by going to a dictionary. It is very unlikely that he used a dictionary, and even less likely that he used the same one as you. What you should do is to place yourself as far as possible in his position, taking note of the facts and circumstances known to him at the time: and then say what he meant by his words.

. . . .

'I decline, therefore, to ask myself: what do the words mean to a grammarian? I prefer to ask: What did Dr. Rowland and his wife mean by the word "coincide" in their wills? When they came to make their wills it is not difficult to piece together the thoughts that ran through their minds: the doctor might well say: "We are going off for three years to these far-off places and in case anything happens to either of us we ought to make our wills. If I die before you, I would like everything to go to you: but if you die before me, I should like it to go to my brother and his boy". She might reply: "Yes, but what if we both die together. After all, one of those little ships might run on the rocks or something and

25

we might both be drowned: or we might both be killed in an aeroplane crash". "To meet that", he would say, "I will put in that if your death coincides with mine, it is to go to my brother and his boy just the same". He would use the words "coinciding with", not in the narrow meaning of "simultaneous", but in the wider meaning of which they are equally capable, especially in this context, as denoting death on the same occasion by the same cause. It would not cross Dr. Rowland's mind that anyone would think of such niceties as Mr. Knox has presented to us. I decline to introduce such fine points into the construction of this will. I would hold that Dr. Rowland, when he made his will, intended by these words "coinciding with" to cover their dying together, in just such a calamity as in fact happened: and that we should give his words the meaning which he plainly intended they should bear'.

But that was a dissenting opinion. Russell LJ for the majority applied the strict traditional line:

'The testator's language does not fit the facts of the case, so far as they are known. To hold otherwise would not, in my judgment, be to construe the will at all: it would be the result of inserting in the will a phrase which the testator never used . . . . There is no jurisdiction in this Court to achieve a sensible result by such means'.

Those words bear the same imprint as in the traditional interpretation of statutes: the Court must not fill in the gaps, no matter how sensible it may be. The Court had no jurisdiction to do it. Mark the words 'no jurisdiction'. No jurisdiction to achieve a sensible result. Is it really so? May it not be there is something wrong with the means employed if it produces a non-sensible result?

3 Unusual common-sense

I did not give up hope. Three years later we had another will to interpret. It was *Re Jebb*[1]. This time I had a good

1. [1966] Ch 666.

common lawyer sitting with me, Winn LJ; and a Chancery lawyer who was endowed with unusual common-sense, Danckwerts LJ. A grandfather aged 86 made a will leaving his residuary estate, among others, to the 'child or children of my daughter Constance Jebb'. Now the daughter was aged 47 and not married. She had no child of her own body but she had an adopted child Roderick. It was a legal adoption by order of the Court. The grandfather knew all about the adoption. He had seen the child in his pram. The Chancery Judge who tried the case held that on the authorities 'child' meant a legitimate child of the mother's body and did not include an adopted child. On appeal we all rejected that method of interpretation. The will did benefit the adopted child. I said:

'In construing this will, we have to look at it as the testator did, sitting in his armchair, with all the circumstances known to him at the time. Then we have to ask ourselves: "What did he intend?" We ought not to answer this question by reference to any technical rules of law. Those technical rules have only too often led the courts astray in the construction of wills. Eschewing technical rules, we look to see simply what the testator intended.

'Looking at this will in the light of the surrounding circumstances it seems to me quite plain that when the testator spoke of the "child or children of my said daughter", his intention was to refer to the adopted child, Roderick, or any further adopted children that she might have. He did not contemplate that she might marry and have a child of her own. But if the extreme improbability had taken place that she had married and had a legitimate child, I think that child would be included too'.

4 Palm Tree Justice in the Court of Appeal

This decision appalled my good friend Dr. John Morris of Magdalen College, Oxford. He was – and is – one of the most distinguished law teachers and writers of our time. He was a great authority on the interpretation of wills. He wrote

27

an article condemning the decision[1]. The heading is 'Palm Tree Justice in the Court of Appeal' and concludes in words reminiscent of Lord Simonds[2]:

'By departing from the established rules of law the Court of Appeal seems to have usurped the function of the legislature. The decision will require the re-writing of the whole of the chapter on gifts to children in the text-books on wills, unless the editor has the courage to say that it is manifestly wrong.... If this new addition to the construction of wills comes to prevail, it will not be sufficient just to re-write the chapter on gifts to children in the text-books on wills. The text-books themselves will have to be scrapped, and construction reduced to the level of guesswork. It is submitted that rules of law binding on the Court cannot be evaded merely by calling them "technical" '.

Dr. Morris's views made great impact. This can be seen by a case in the next year. It is *Sydall v Castings Ltd*[3]. It was not a will but a document of similar nature, a group life assurance scheme. Mr. Sydall's employers had a scheme by which, on a workman's death, money was payable to his 'dependants' or 'relations'. Mr. Sydall died and £300 was payable. He had four grown-up children by his old wife. But he had separated from her and had formed a permanent association with a lady with whom he lived and had a baby girl, Yvette, aged three years. The trustees wanted to pay some of the £300 for the benefit of the baby girl: but the Court held that none was payable. They did it frankly on the grounds that she was illegitimate. I protested saying:

'I would hold, therefore, that according to the ordinary meaning of the words, Yvette is a "relation" of her father and a "descendant" from him. She should, therefore, be included among those qualified for benefit.

'But we are pressed by counsel to give the words an extra-ordinary meaning. "Relations", it is said, includes only legitimate relations. And "descendant" means only a

1. See 82 LQR 196.
2. Ibid., p. 202.
3. [1967] 1 QB 302.

legitimate descendant. For this purpose reliance is placed on a passage in Jarman on *Wills* .... If this contention be correct, it means that because Yvette is illegitimate, she is to be excluded from any benefit. She is on this view no "relation" of her father: nor is she "descended" from him. In the eye of the law she is the daughter of nobody. She is related to nobody. She is an outcast and is to be shut out from any part of her father's insurance benefit.

'I have no doubt that such an argument would have been acceptable in the nineteenth century. The judges in those days used to think that if they allowed illegitimate children to take a benefit they were encouraging immorality. They laid down narrow pedantic rules such as that stated by Lord Chelmsford in *Hill v Crook:* "No gift, however express, to unborn illegitimate children is allowed by law". In laying down such rules, they acted in accordance with the then contemporary morality.

'Even the Victorian fathers thought they were doing right when they turned their erring daughters out of the house. They visited the sins of the fathers upon the children – with a vengeance. I think we should throw over those harsh rules of the past. They are not rules of law. They are only guides to the construction of documents. They are quite out of date. We no longer penalise the illegitimate child. We should replace those old rules by a more rational approach. If they are wide enough to include an illegitimate child we should so interpret them .... So here the words "relations" and "descendant" in a group assurance scheme are wide enough to include illegitimate children and we should so interpret them'.

Russell LJ took the traditional view. He said:

'I see no sufficient ground for departing from the normal rule of construction. In my judgment "descendant" is to be construed as decendant in the legitimate line'.

So little Yvette – because she was illegitimate – took nothing. Quite contrary to what her father would have wished and contrary to what the trustees desired.

29

5 'I am a Portia man'

In justification of his view Russell LJ quoted a passage from Shakespeare. It is worth recording because there are lessons to be drawn from it — as there often are from Shakespeare.

'I may perhaps be forgiven for saying that it appears to me that Lord Denning MR has acceded to the appeal of Bassanio in the *Merchant of Venice*.

Bassanio
"And, I beseech you,
Wrest once the law to your authority:
To do a great right, do a little wrong."

But Portia retorted:

"It must not be; there is no power in Venice
Can alter a decree established:
'Twill be recorded for a precedent,
And many an error, by the same example,
Will rush into the State: it cannot be." '

Then said Russell LJ:

'I am a Portia man'.

Now the decree of which Portia spoke was not a precedent on the construction of words — such as the Court had in *Sydall*'s case. It was a decree by which the bond-holder could enforce a penalty without mercy. Shylock said: 'I crave the penalty and forfeit of my bond'. The law of Venice knew nothing of relief in equity against penalties or forfeitures. Hence Shylock's warm approval of Portia's doctrine:

'A Daniel come to judgment: yea a Daniel! —
O wise young judge, how do I honour thee!'

I cannot believe that Russell LJ would be a 'Portia man' if it meant aligning himself with Shylock — in support of a strict law of penalties which could not be relieved by equity. To be truly a 'Portia man' the lawyer should follow the way in which Portia avoided an unjust decree. Not to let the words of the deed be the masters: but so construe them — adapt them as the occasion demands — so as to do what justice and equity require. This is how she turned the tables on Shylock:

'Tarry a little; — there is something else.
This bond doth give thee here no jot of blood;
The words expressly are a pound of flesh.
Take then thy bond, take thou thy pound of flesh;
But, in the cutting it, if thou dost shed
One drop of Christian blood, thy lands and goods
Are, by the laws of Venice, confiscate
Unto the state of Venice.
. . . .
For, as thou urgest justice, be assur'd
Thou shalt have justice, more than thou desir'st'.

It is in this dénouement that I would follow the example of Portia — I too am a Portia man.

So I leave the subject with this question: Are we to construe wills according to their grammatical construction as propounded in previous cases? or are we to mould them in accordance with the intention of the testator in the particular case, irrespective of earlier precedents? My Chancery friends tell me that the Chancery Judges nowadays go by the intention of the testator. That is why 'construction summonses' have become very few: and hardly any are reported.

4 The construction of contracts

1 *Consensus ad idem*

The construction of contracts is virtually a different subject. When construing a statute or a will, you are considering the intentions of one body only — be it Parliament or a testator. When construing a contract, be it in writing or by word of mouth, you are considering the intentions of two parties — who have agreed together on the terms that shall bind them. As the maxim goes, there is *consensus ad idem*. But in discovering that intention, you are not to look into their actual minds. The parties are not even allowed to give evidence as to what they intended — except in special cases where there is a claim for rectification. You have to go by the outward expression of their intentions — as conveyed by the words set out in writing or by the spoken words they used. So once again we come back to the meaning of the words.

2 The old strictness

Long ago the Courts were just as strict about the written words of a deed or a contract as they were about a statute or a will. They went by the grammatical meaning. They refused to look at outside aids. They refused to fill in any gaps. They refused to imply any terms. Thus, before the start of the Civil War, Paradine let a house and stables to Jane for 21 years. During the War, Prince Rupert in 1642 went into the tenant's house and stables and quartered his cavalry

32

there for three years. The tenant claimed to be excused from paying rent for those three years. But the Court held him bound to pay. It said:

'When the party by his own contract creates a duty or charge upon himself, he is bound to make it good, if he may, notwithstanding any accident by inevitable necessity, because he might have provided against it by his contract'.[1]

In short, it was for the party to anticipate every contingency that might befall and insert a term to protect himself. If he did not do so, he was bound by his written word. The Court would not write in any exception or implication to protect him.

Similarly with contracts for the sale of goods. The Courts applied the maxim *caveat emptor* rigidly. They did not imply any condition as to quality or merchantability as we do nowadays. No warranty was to be implied. The buyer had to stipulate for an express warranty or he failed. Thus in 1603 a goldsmith, Chandelor, sold a precious stone to Lopus for £100. He told Lopus that it was a bezoar-stone (which is a stone sometimes found in the stomach of an animal). Lopus afterwards discovered that it was not a bezoar-stone but a fake – but Chandelor did not know it. Lopus claimed damages. His claim was dismissed. The Court said: 'Everyone in selling his wares, will affirm that his wares are good, or the horse which he sells is sound: yet if he does not warrant them to be so, it is no cause of action'[2].

3 The great advance of the implied term

That attitude was all very well in those days. Very few people could read or write. Neither party to a contract could give evidence. Nothing was admissible to add to, vary or contradict a written contract. But it was bound to change. Simple justice demanded that the buyer or the consumer should be protected, even though he did not insert an express term on

1. *Aleyn* p. 27.
2. *Chandelor v Lopus* (1603) Cro Jac 4.

his own behalf. So the Courts filled in the gaps. They did this by means of the doctrine of 'implied terms'.

This was a great advance in legal theory. Even though there was no express term, nevertheless the law itself — which means the Court itself — implied a term. It wrote into the contract a term which the parties had not written: and upon which they had never agreed. It did this so as to do what reason and justice required. This legal theory can be traced back at least to *Gardiner v Gray*[1] when Gray showed Gardiner samples of some waste silk and offered to sell him some. The bargain was made. A sale note written: '12 bags of waste silk 10s 6d a lb'. On delivery the 12 bags were found to be inferior to the samples and of poor quality. Gardiner sued for damages. He sought to show an express warranty that the bags should be equal to the samples: he failed because it was not on the written sale note. In earlier times that would have been the end of the case. But Gardiner also alleged an implied warranty that the silk should be of a good and merchantable quality. On this, he succeeded. Lord Ellenborough said:

'Without any particular warranty, this is an implied term in every such contract . . . . The purchaser cannot be supposed to buy goods to lay them on a dunghill'.

The important point in that case was that the warranty was imposed or imputed by law. It was imposed because it was just and reasonable. Not because the parties had agreed to it, either expressly or impliedly.

Thenceforward the law as to implied warranties proceeded rapidly. As each case came before the Courts — so the Court implied a term to meet the situation. It spelled each term out with a particularity which the parties could never have agreed — even if they had spent days and days upon it. The terms differed according to whether the goods were specific goods or unascertained goods or whether the warranty was that they were reasonably fit for the purpose or merchantable — and so on. These cases were all collected together by

1. (1815) 4 Camp 144.

the Queen's Bench in *Jones v Just*[1]. Eventually these terms were given even greater force of law by being written into the Sale of Goods Act 1893 as now amended by the Supply of Goods (Implied Terms) Act 1973.

4 A dangerous misunderstanding

Now underlying the very phrase 'implied term' there lurked a dangerous misunderstanding. Was it implied in *fact*? or implied in *law*? In other words, was it a term agreed in fact? or a term imposed by law? The Courts in the 19th century were dominated by the legal theory that a contract was an agreement between two minds agreeing on the same terms – *consensus ad idem*. According to that theory, the only philosophical basis for introducing an implied term was that it was a term to which the two parties had impliedly agreed themselves – that is, agreed in fact. Carrying that theory to its logical conclusion, it followed that just as the express terms were those to which they had expressly agreed, so implied terms were those to which they had impliedly agreed – on which the two minds were agreed but had not expressed. To the judges of that time, no other justification was possible: for it was beyond the province of the Court to make a contract for the parties.

It was that line of thought which dominated the theory of 'implied terms' from 1889 onwards because in a celebrated case called *The Moorcock*[2], Lord Justice Bowen said:

'I believe if one were to take all the cases, and they are many, of implied warranties or covenants in law, it will be found that in all of them the law is raising an implication from the presumed intention of the parties with the object of giving to the transaction such efficacy as *both parties must have intended that at all events it should have*'.

That dictum led to the aphorism that you cannot imply a term simply because it is *reasonable* to do so, but only when

1. (1868) LR 3 QB 197.
2. (1889) 14 PD 64 at 68.

35

it is *necessary*. That was said by Scrutton LJ in *Reigate v Union Manufacturing*[1] and has been treated as gospel truth ever since. It assumes that everyone knows the meaning of 'reasonable' and 'necessary' so that everyone gives those words the same meaning – a very doubtful proposition!

5 'The officious by-stander'

This led in turn to the introduction into the Courts of a new personage – 'the officious by-stander'. He is a fictitious character – just as fictitious as 'the reasonable man' in negligence cases. But he has become the 'deus ex machina' – the god who is let down on to the stage so as to solve every problem of an implied term. He was brought on to the stage by Lord Justice Mackinnon who painted this picture of him in *Shirlaw v Southern Foundries*[2] :

'Prima facie that which in any contract is left to be implied and need not be expressed is something so obvious that it goes without saying; so that, if while the parties were making their bargain, an officious by-stander were to suggest some express provision for it in their agreement, they would testily suppress him with a common "Oh, of course" '.

In short, the 'officious by-stander' insisted on a term implied in *fact*.

6 Should he be sent off the field?

Quite recently I suggested that the 'officious by-stander' had held up the game too long. That it was time he was sent off the field. He insists on the Court finding – on the facts – a common intention in the minds of both parties. In other words, a term implied in fact. That limits the role of the Court too much. I suggested that we should get back to the

1. [1918] 1 KB 592 at 605.
2. [1939] 2 KB 206 at 227.

earlier and sound doctrine of an implied term — that is a term implied in law. The Court imputes or imposes a term whenever it is reasonable to do so — in order to do what is fair and just between the parties. This is a view which I put forward in *Greaves v Baynham*[1] and expressed more fully in *Liverpool City Council v Irwin*[2]. The City Council built a tower-block fifteen storeys high and let the flats out to tenants. The Council retained control of the lifts and staircases themselves. These fell badly out of repair — so that the tenants could not use the lifts and had to walk up the stairs in the dark. The Council were careful not to insert any covenant to repair in the tenancy agreements. They did not want to commit themselves to any obligation to repair. Was there an implied term that they should repair? My colleagues in the Court of Appeal thought not. I held the other view. I said:

'The lifts, staircases, and so forth, were not let to the tenants. The council kept them in their own control. The question arises: were they under any contractual duty to the tenant to keep them in repair?

. . . .

'It is often said that the courts only imply a term in a contract when it is reasonable and necessary to do so in order to give business efficacy to the transaction . . . (Emphasis is put on the word "necessary" . . . .) Or when it is obvious that both parties must have intended it: so obvious indeed that if an officious bystander had asked them whether there was to be such a term, both would have suppressed it testily: "Yes, of course" . . . .

'Those expressions have been repeated so often that it is with some trepidation that I venture to question them. I do so because they do not truly represent the way in which the courts act. Let me take some instances. There are stacks of them. Such as the terms implied by the courts into a contract for the sale of goods . . . : or the hire of goods . . . : or into a

1. [1975] 1 WLR 1095.
2. [1976] 1 QB 319.

contract for work and materials . . . : or into a contract for letting an unfurnished house . . . : or a furnished house . . . : or into the carriage of a passenger by railway . . . : or to enter on premises . . . : or to buy a house in course of erection . . . . 'If you read the discussion in those cases, you will see that in none of them did the court ask: what did both parties intend? If asked, each party would have said he never gave it a thought: or the one would have intended something different from the other. Nor did the court ask: Is it necessary to give business efficacy to the transaction? If asked the answer would have been: "It is reasonable, but it is not necessary". The judgments in all those cases show that the courts implied a term according to whether or not it was reasonable in all the circumstances to do so. Very often it was conceded that there was some implied term. The only question was: "What was the extent of it?" Such as, was it an absolute warranty of fitness, or only a promise to use reasonable care? That cannot be solved by inquiring what they both intended, or into what was necessary. But only into what was reasonable. This is to be decided as matter of law, not as matter of fact. Lord Wright pulled the blinkers off our eyes when he said in 1935 to the Holdsworth Club:

"The truth is that the court . . . decides this question in accordance with what seems to be just or reasonable in its eyes. The judge finds in himself the criterion of what is reasonable. The court is in this sense making a contract for the parties — though it is almost blasphemy to say so". (*Lord Wright of Durley, Legal Essays and Addresses* (1939), p. 259)

'In 1956, Lord Radcliffe put it elegantly when he said of the parties to an implied term:

"their actual persons should be allowed to rest in peace. In their place there rises the figure of the fair and reasonable man. And the spokesman of the fair and reasonable man, who represents after all no more than the anthropomorphic conception of justice, is and must be the court itself": see *Davis Contractors Ltd v Fareham Urban District Council* [1956] AC 696, 728.

. . . .

'Is there a term to be implied in this tenancy about the lifts and staircases and other common parts? Mr. Francis said there was no contractual obligation on the landlord at all. He repeated the old cliches about "necessary to give business efficacy" and the "officious bystander", and said there was no term to be implied at all.

'. . . . No one has ever doubted that the landlord is under an implied contractual obligation to the tenant in respect of those common parts . . . . The only question to my mind is the extent of the obligation. Is it confined to safety from personal injury? Or does it extend to fitness for use? To my mind it is the obligation of the landlord to take reasonable care, not only to keep the lifts and staircase reasonably safe, but also to keep them reasonably fit for use by the tenant and his family, and visitors. Suppose the lifts fall out of repair and break down. Can the landlord say to the tenant: "It is not my obligation to repair the lifts. You must repair them yourselves or walk up and down the 200 steps. It's up to you". If the electric light bulbs blow out on the staircase, can the landlord say: "I am not going to replace them, now or at any time. You must go up and down in the dark as best you can". Mr. Francis suggested that so long as nobody suffers personal injury, no one can complain. Not even the tenants. But that as soon as someone does suffer personal injury, he can bring an action for damages under the Occupiers' Liability Act 1957. I cannot accept this suggestion. It is clearly the duty of the landlord, not only to take care to keep the lifts and staircase safe, but also to take care to keep them reasonably fit for the use of the tenant and his visitors. If the lifts break down, the landlord ought to repair them. If the lights on the staircase fail, the landlord ought to replace them.

'I am confirmed in this view by the fact that the Law Commission, in their codification of the law of landlord and tenant, recommend that some such term should be implied by statute . . . . But I do not think we need wait for a statute. We are well able to imply it now in the same way as judges have implied terms for centuries. Some people seem to think that now there is a Law Commission the judges should leave it to them to put right any defect and to make any new development. The judges must no longer play a constructive role. They must be automatons applying the existing rules. Just think what this means. The law must stand still until the Law Commission have reported and Parliament passed a statute on it: and, meanwhile, every litigant must have his case decided by the dead hand of the past. I decline to reduce the judges to such a sterile role. They should develop the law, case by case, as they have done in the past: so that the litigants before them can have their differences decided by the law as it should be and is, and not by the law of the past. So I hold here that there is clearly to be implied for the common parts some such term as the Law Commission recommend. The landlord must take reasonable care to keep the lifts, staircase, etc. safe and fit for use by the tenants and their families and visitors'.

The House of Lords[1] upheld my view that the City Council were under an 'implied obligation' to take reasonable care to keep the means of access safe: but they declined to accept my general proposition about 'implied terms' and they refused to kill off the 'officious by-stander'. Lord Wilberforce said[2] of my judgment that he could not 'go so far as to endorse his general principle; indeed, it seems to me, with respect, to extend a long, and undesirable, way beyond sound authority'.

So there the matter rests. But it leaves a legacy of problems on which Judges give divided answers: as was shown in *Shell v Lostock*[3]. If we had killed off the 'officious by-stander' – and replaced 'necessary' by 'reasonable' – the Court might, I think, have come to a unanimous view.

In the circumstances I wonder if the Law Commission might be invited to consider this question: Is it right only to imply a term when it is 'necessary' to effectuate the intent of

1. [1977] AC 239.
2. Ibid., at 253.
3. [1976] 1 WLR 1187.

the parties? or is it permissible to imply it when it is 'reasonable' so to do in order to do what is fair and just as between the parties?

7 'Presumed intent' becoming fashionable

At the same time, I would draw your attention to a parallel doctrine which seems to be becoming fashionable. It might be called the doctrine of 'presumed intent'. Instead of asking whether the parties impliedly agreed on a term, the Court recognises that they never agreed on it at all: because they never envisaged that such a situation would arise. In such cases the Court seeks to find their 'presumed intent', that is, what they presumably would have agreed if they had envisaged the situation. It then presumes that the parties would have agreed upon a fair and reasonable solution: and the Court then declares what that fair and reasonable solution is. This whole process is said to be merely 'the construction of the contract'. The Court construes the contract so as to give effect to the presumed intent.

8 The foresight of a prophet

This doctrine had been simmering for some time before I joined the Court of Appeal, but it came to the boil in *British Movietonenews v London and District Cinemas*[1]. During the war in 1941 film distributors agreed to supply their newsreels to cinemas for ten guineas a week. These were newsreels to support the war effort. After the war ended there was in 1946 an entirely new situation. The newsreels were no longer devoted to the war effort. New regulations were made accordingly. The cinema company said they were no longer bound to take the war films at ten guineas a week. Delivering the judgment of a unanimous Court I said, referring to earlier judgments:

'The judgments, if I may say so, are so valuable that they

1. [1951] 1 KB 190.

should be read in full, and I will not venture to read extracts from them . . . . The judgments show that, no matter that a contract is framed in words which taken literally or absolutely, cover what has happened, nevertheless, if the ensuing turn of events was so completely outside the contemplation of the parties that the court is satisfied that the parties, as reasonable people, cannot have intended that the contract should apply to the new situation, then the court will read the words of the contract in a qualified sense; it will restrict them to the circumstances contemplated by the parties; it will not apply them to the uncontemplated turn of events, but will do therein what is just and reasonable.

'This principle is the same principle as that which underlies the *ejusdem generis* rule and the suspension clauses in frustration cases . . . . It is a recognition of the fact that parties with their minds concerned with the particular objects about which they are contracting are apt to use words, phrases or clauses which, taken literally, are wider than they intend or, I may add, cover situations which they never contemplated. Recognising this fact, the court refuses to apply them literally to an uncontemplated turn of events.

'This does not mean that the courts no longer insist on the binding force of contracts deliberately made. It only means that they will not allow the words, in which they happen to be phrased, to become tyrannical masters. The court qualifies the literal meaning of the words so as to bring them into accord with the true scope of the contract. Even if the contract is absolute in its terms, nevertheless if it is not absolute in intent, it will not be held absolute in effect. The day is done when we can excuse an unforeseen injustice by saying to the sufferer "It is your own folly. You ought not to have passed that form of words. You ought to have put in a clause to protect yourself". We no longer credit a party with the foresight of a prophet or his lawyer with the draftsmanship of a Chalmers. We realise that they have their limitations and make allowances accordingly. It is better thus. The old maxim reminds us that *Qui haeret in litera, haeret in cortice*, which, being interpreted, means: He who clings to the letter, clings to the dry and barren shell, and misses the truth and substance of the matter . . . .

'Applying these principles, the supplemental agreement says that it is to apply, "during the continuance of the Cinematograph Film (Control) Order 1943". Those words, taken literally, mean that the supplemental agreement is in full force and effect today, for the order still continues and may for aught one knows, continue for a long time yet. But the parties cannot have contemplated that the order would ever last so long. It was an order made in wartime to deal with war conditions, and they must have contemplated that it would be cancelled at or shortly after the end of the war. They cannot have contemplated that it would be continued in peacetime to deal with dollar shortages – certainly not that it would still be continuing five years after the war had ended. That being so, the court should not apply the agreement in this uncontemplated turn of events'.

9 'Presumed intent' takes hold

When the case reached the House of Lords, Viscount Simon gave the leading speech. He had appointed me a Judge eight years before. He was very critical of my judgment but wrote me a letter to soften the blow. Speaking for all the House he said of my judgment that in it 'phrases occur which give us some concern'[1]. He then proceeded to enunciate the doctrine of 'presumed intent' in these words:

'The parties to an executory contract are often faced, in the course of carrying it out, with a turn of events which they did not at all anticipate – a wholly abnormal rise or fall in prices, a sudden depreciation of currency, an unexpected obstacle to execution, or the like. Yet this does not in itself affect the bargain they have made. If, on the other hand, a consideration of the terms of the contract, in the light of the circumstances existing when it was made, shows that they never agreed to be bound in a fundamentally different

1. [1952] AC 166 at 181.

43

situation which has now unexpectedly emerged, the contract ceases to bind at that point – not because the court in its discretion thinks it just and reasonable to qualify the terms of the contract, but because on its true construction it does not apply in that situation. When it is said that in such circumstances the court reaches a conclusion which is "just and reasonable" (Lord Wright in *Constantine*'s case) or one "which justice demands" (Lord Sumner in *Hirji Mulji v Cheong Yue Steamship Co Ltd*), this result is arrived at by putting a just construction upon the contract in accordance with an "implication ... from the presumed common intention of the parties" (Lord Sumner in *Bank Line Ltd v Arthur Capel & Co*).

'If the decisions in "frustration" cases are regarded as illustrations of the power and duty of a court to put the proper construction on the agreement made between the parties, having regard to the terms in which that agreement is expressed, and to the circumstances in which it was made, including any necessary implication, such decisions are seen to be examples of the general judicial function of interpreting a contract when there is disagreement as to its effect'.

10 Frustration and 'presumed intent'

That is the classic formulation of the doctrine of 'presumed intent'. It has often been applied in the Court of Appeal. For instance in *The Eugenia*[1] the Suez Canal was blocked and a vessel had to go round by the Cape. The question arose whether the charterparty was frustrated. I applied the ruling of Lord Simon in the *British Movietonenews*[2] case saying:

'This means that once again we have had to consider the authorities on this vexed topic of frustration. But I think the position is now reasonably clear. It is simply this: if it should happen, in the course of carrying out a contract, that a fundamentally different situation arises for which the parties made no provision – so much so that it would not be just in the new situation to hold them bound to its terms – then the contract is at an end.

1. [1964] 2 QB 226.
2. [1951] 1 KB 190.

44

'It was originally said that the doctrine of frustration was based on an implied term. In short, that the parties, if they had foreseen the new situation, would have said to one another: "If that happens, of course, it is all over between us". But the theory of an implied term has now been discarded by everyone, or nearly everyone, for the simple reason that it does not represent the truth. The parties would not have said: "It is all over between us". They would have differed about what was to happen. Each would have sought to insert reservations or qualifications of one kind or another. Take this very case. The parties realised that the canal might become impassable. They tried to agree on a clause to provide for the contingency. But they failed to agree. So there is no room for an implied term.

. . . .

'We are thus left with the simple test that a situation must arise which renders performance of the contract "a thing radically different from that which was undertaken by the contract", see *Davis Contractors Ltd v Fareham Urban District Council* by Lord Radcliffe. To see if the doctrine applies, you have first to construe the contract and see whether the parties have themselves provided for the situation that has arisen. If they have provided for it, the contract must govern. There is no frustration. If they have not provided for it, then you have to compare the new situation with the situation for which they did provide. Then you must see how different it is. The fact that it has become more onerous or more expensive for one party than he thought is not sufficient to bring about a frustration. It must be more than merely more onerous or more expensive. It must be positively unjust to hold the parties bound. It is often difficult to draw the line. But it must be done. And it is for the courts to do it as a matter of law . . .'

11 Exemption clauses and 'presumed intent'

In the latest discussions on exemption and limitation clauses, the tendency is to apply the doctrine of 'presumed intent' rather than that of 'fundamental breach'. In *Photo Production Ltd v Securicor Ltd*[1], a security guard deliberately set fire to a factory which he was employed to guard. The security company sought to escape liability by relying on an exemption clause or alternatively a limitation clause. I suggested that the doctrine of 'presumed intent' should be applied in this way:

'It is important to notice that, in order to decide whether the exemption or limitation clause applies, you must construe the contract, not in the grammatical or literal sense, or even in the natural and ordinary meaning of the words – but in the wider context of the "presumed intention" of the parties – so as to see whether or not, in the situation that has arisen, the parties can reasonably be supposed to have intended that the party in breach should be able to avail himself of the exemption or limitation clause. That was pointed out by Lord Wilberforce in *Suisse Atlantique* [1967] 1 AC 361, 434, coupled with his illuminating observation in *Reardon Smith Line Ltd v Yngvar Hansen-Tangen (trading as H.E. Hansen-Tangen), The (Diana Prosperity)* [1976] 1 WLR 989, 996:

"When one speaks of the intention of the parties to the contract, one is speaking objectively – the parties cannot themselves give direct evidence of what their intention was – and what must be ascertained is what is to be taken as the intention which reasonable people would have had if placed in the situation of the parties. Similarly when one is speaking of aim, or object, or commercial purpose, one is speaking objectively of what reasonable persons would have in mind in the situation of the parties".

'In other words, in order to ascertain the "presumed intention" of the parties, you must ask this question: If the parties had envisaged the situation which has happened, would they, as reasonable persons, have supposed that the exemption or limitation clause would apply to protect the wrongdoer?

1. [1978] 1 WLR 856.

. . . .

'. . . Although the clause in its natural and ordinary meaning would seem to give exemption from or limitation of liability for a breach, nevertheless the court will not give the party that exemption or limitation if the court can say: "The parties as reasonable men cannot have intended that there should be exemption or limitation in the case of such a breach as this". In so stating the principle, there arises in these cases "the figure of the fair and reasonable man"; and the spokesman of this fair and reasonable man, as Lord Radcliffe once said, is and "must be the court itself": see *Davis Contractors Ltd v Fareham Urban District Council* [1956] AC 696, 728 – 729.

'Thus we reach, after long years, the principle which lies behind all our striving: the court will not allow a party to rely on an exemption or limitation clause in circumstances in which it would not be fair or reasonable to allow reliance on it: and, in considering whether it is fair and reasonable, the court will consider whether it was in a standard form, whether there was equality of bargaining power, the nature of the breach, and so forth.

'This solution follows the lead given by the legislature in the Supply of Goods (Implied Terms) Act 1973, section 4 [providing a new section 55 (4) of the Sale of Goods Act 1893], which says that, in a contract for the sale of goods, an exemption clause shall "not be enforceable to the extent that it is shown that it would not be fair or reasonable to allow reliance on the term". And somewhat similarly, sections 3 and 11 of the Unfair Contract Terms Act 1977. . .

. . . .

'Whilst the judge was, I think, right to apply the test of reasonableness, I do not agree with his application of it. I would point out that, whilst the owner of the premises insured against fire (save for £25,000), Securicor insured against liability for the acts of their servants (save for £10,000). So to my mind the insurance factor cancels out: and we are left with the question as between the two parties. Is it fair or reasonable to allow Securicor to rely on this

47

exemption or limitation clause when it was their own patrol-man who deliberately burned down the factory? I do not think it is fair and reasonable'.

12 Inflation and 'presumed intent'

More recently still there arose a case where a Water Company in the year 1929 agreed to supply water to a hospital 'at all times hereafter' at a fixed rate of seven pence (that is, old pence) per 1,000 gallons. Fifty years later that sum was absurdly small. Owing to inflation the payment in 1977 was only one-twentieth of what it was in 1929. The hospital authorities claimed that they were entitled to have the water at the extremely small rate to the crack of doom. We rejected the claim. My colleagues decided the case on traditional grounds, but I suggested that it could be decided by reference to the doctrine of 'presumed intent'. It was the *Staffordshire Area Health Authority v South Staffordshire Waterworks Company*[1] :

'Now I quite agree that, if the strict rule of construction were in force today, Mr. Justice Foster would be right. There is a great deal to be said for his view that the words "at all times hereafter" are plain and that they mean "forever or in perpetuity". . . .

'But I think that the rule of strict construction is now quite out of date. It has been supplanted by the rule that written instruments are to be construed in relation to the circum-stances as they were known to or contemplated by the parties: and that even the plainest words may fall to be modified if events occur which the parties never had in mind and which they cannot have intended the agreement to operate.

. . . .

'We were taken through six cases which considered contracts which contained no provision for determination. On going through them, they seem to show that, when a person agrees

1. (1978) 122 Sol Jo 331.

48

to supply goods or services continuously over an unlimited period of time in return for a fixed monthly or yearly payment, the courts shrink from holding it to be an agreement in perpetuity. The reason is because it is so unequal. The cost of supply of goods and services goes up with inflation through the rooftops: and the fixed payment goes down to the bottom of the well so that it is worth little or nothing. Rather than tolerate such inequality, the courts will construe the contract so as to hold that it is determinable by reasonable notice. They do this by reference to the modern rule of construction. They say that in the circumstances as they have developed — which the parties never had in mind — the contract ceases to bind the parties forever. It can be determined on reasonable notice.

. . . .

'From those cases it is possible to detect a new principle emerging as to the effect of inflation and the fall in the value of money. In the ordinary way this does not affect the bargain between the parties. As I said in the case of *Treseder-Griffin v Co-operative Insurance Society* [1956] 2 QB at page 149:

"In England we have always looked upon a pound as a pound, whatever its international value. Creditors and debtors have arranged for payment in our sterling currency in the sure knowledge that the sum they fix will be upheld by the law. A man who stipulates for a pound must take a pound whenever payment is made, whatever the pound is worth at that time".

'But times have changed. We have since had mountainous inflation and the pound dropping to cavernous depths. In the recent case of *Multiservice Bookbinding Ltd v Marden* [1978] 2 WLR at page 544, Mr. Justice Browne-Wilkinson departed from some of the things I said in *Treseder-Griffin* for that very reason — because of 20 years' experience of continuing inflation. The time has come when we may have to revise our views about the principle of nominalism, as it is called. Dr. F. A. Mann in his book on the legal aspects of money, third edition at page 100, said:

49

"If the trend of inflation which has clouded the last few decades continues, some relief in the case of long-term obligations will become unavoidable".

'That was written in 1971. Inflation has been more rampant than ever since that time. Here we have in the present case a striking instance of a long-term obligation entered into 50 years ago. It provided for yearly payments for water supplies at seven old pence a 1,000 gallons. In these 50 years, and especially in the last 10 years, the cost of supplying the water has increased twenty-fold. It is likely to increase with every year that passes. Is it right that the hospital should go on for-ever only paying the old rate of 50 years ago? . . . . So here the situation has changed so radically since the contract was made 50 years ago that the term of the contract "at all times hereafter" ceases to bind: and it is open to the court to hold that the contract is determined by reasonable notice'.

13 Family arrangements and 'presumed intent'

Apart from the contract proper, the doctrine has proved to be of much help in deciding 'family arrangements'. In these cases husband and wife — mother and daughter, or the like — often make loose arrangements for the future. But then things happen which they did not contemplate — such as a separation or a divorce — and the Court has to decide what is to be done. In *Appleton v Appleton*[1] a husband had done work on the wife's house. They separated. The question was whether he was entitled to be paid for it. With assent of my colleagues I said:

'As the husband pointed out to us, when he was doing the work in the house, the matrimonial home, it was done for the sake of the family as a whole. None of them had any thought of separation at that time. There was no occasion for any bargain to be made as to what was to happen in case there was a separation, for it was a thing which no one contem-plated at all.

1. [1965] 1 WLR 25.

'In those circumstances, it is not correct to look and see whether there was any bargain in the past, or any expressed intention. A judge can only do what is fair and reasonable in the circumstances. Sometimes this test has been put in the cases: What term is to be implied? What would the parties have stipulated had they thought about it? That is one way of putting it. But, as they never did think about it at all, I prefer to take the simple test: What is reasonable and fair in the circumstances as they have developed, seeing that they are circumstances which no one contemplated before? I should have thought that, inasmuch as the registrar found that the husband had done up to about one-half of the work of renovation, the husband should be entitled to something. He should get so much of the enhanced value of both of the properties as was due to his work and materials that he supplied. He should be given credit for a just proportion on any realisation of the house. A percentage of the proceeds ought to go to him commensurate to the enhancement due to his work in improving the properties and getting a better price on that account .... The husband is entitled to a percentage of the proceeds of sale, if and when the house is sold'.

In *Hardwick v Johnson*[1] the mother-in-law, at a cost of £12,000, provided a house for her son and his wife. They were to pay her £7 a week, if they could manage it. The son left. The mother-in-law sought to turn out her daughter-in-law. The Court applied the doctrine of 'presumed intent'. I said:

'No doubt if the marriage had turned out successfully, the couple would have gone on living in the house, the mother would not have insisted on receiving £7 a week, and on her death they would have inherited the house. But the marriage did not turn out successfully. It has broken down. A situation has arisen which they did not envisage. The son has left the house, leaving the daughter-in-law and the child there.

1. [1978] 1 WLR 683.

So we have to consider once more the law about family arrangements. In the well-known case of *Balfour v Balfour* . . . Atkin LJ said that family arrangements made between husband and wife "are not contracts . . . because the parties did not intend that they should be attended by legal consequences". Similarly, family arrangements between parent and child are often not contracts which bind them . . . . Nevertheless these family arrangements do have legal consequences: and, time and time again, the courts are called upon to determine what is the true legal relationship resulting from them. This is especially the case where one of the family occupies a house or uses furniture which is afterwards claimed by another member of the family: or when one pays money to another and afterwards says it was a loan and the other says it was a gift: and so forth. In most of these cases the question cannot be solved by looking to the intention of the parties, because the situation which arises is one which they never envisaged, and for which they made no provision. So many things are undecided, undiscussed, and unprovided for that the task of the courts is to fill in the blanks. The court has to look at all the circumstances and spell out the legal relationship. The court will pronounce in favour of a tenancy or a licence, a loan or a gift, or a trust – according to which of these legal relationships is most fitting in the situation which has arisen: and will find the terms of that relationship according to what reason and justice require. In the words of Lord Diplock in *Pettitt v Pettitt* . . . . :
". . . . the court imputes to the parties a common intention which in fact they never formed and it does so by forming its own opinion as to what would have been the common intention of reasonable men as to the effect"
of the unforeseen event if it had been present to their minds.

'The present case is a good illustration of the process at work. The correspondence and the pleadings show that the parties canvassed all sorts of legal relationships. One of them was that there was a loan by the mother to the couple of £12,000 which was repayable by instalments of £28 a month. Another suggestion was that there was a tenancy at £7 a week. Another suggestion was that there might be an implied or constructive trust for the young couple. Yet another suggestion was that there was a personal licence to this young couple to occupy the house.

'Of all these suggestions, I think the most fitting is a personal licence . . . .

. . . .

'So the position is that it was a personal licence to the son and daughter-in-law at £7 a week. But now comes the crucial question. Was this licence revocable by the mother? And in what circumstances? What term is the court to spell out about revocability?

In May 1975 the mother's solicitor, being uncertain of the legal position, wrote letters determining the tenancy, if there was one; determining the licence, if there was one; and claiming possession. To my mind this licence was not revocable by the mother at will. It was certainly not revocable as against the daughter-in-law, who was still living in the house with her baby, deserted by the son. Looking simply at what is reasonable, it seems to me that the mother could not turn the daughter-in-law and child out, at all events when the daughter-in-law was ready to pay the £7 a week'.

In all these cases of contracts or family arrangements, I ask the question: In the case of an unforeseen turn of events, is the Court justified in asking itself: What is the fair and just solution of the problem? or, is this altogether too vague and uncertain? Does it leave too much to the discretion of the Judge?

5 Looking for help

1 Negotiations and subsequent conduct

Over the years there has been much controversy on the extent to which the Court can go beyond the letter of the contract — so as to ascertain the meaning. The common lawyers held that no evidence could be adduced to add to, vary, or contradict a written document. So they looked at the words used by the parties and interpreted them in their grammatical meaning without recourse to outside aids at all. That was natural enough when the parties could not give evidence themselves. But once it is realised that words are imperfect instruments to express the meaning or intent of the parties, there is a strong case for bringing in extrinsic aids — so as to clear up uncertainties or ambiguities in the written word. Two aids have come much under discussion. One is the correspondence and negotiations leading up to a contract. The other is the subsequent conduct of the parties after they have made the contract. On both heads I have often expressed the view that these aids are admissible. But the current opinion of the House of Lords is that neither of these aids is admissible. Negotiations are excluded by *Prenn v Simmonds*[1]. Subsequent conduct is excluded by *Wickman Tools v Schuler*[2]. Those rulings are entirely acceptable when the words used in the contract are clear: but not so acceptable when the meaning is not clear. So ways are emerging in which the effect of those cases is being discounted. One way that has been successfully pursued is to ask for the contract

1. [1971] 1 WLR 1381.
2. [1974] AC 235.

54

to be rectified on the ground that the written contract did not represent the real intention of the parties. By that means the negotiations can be given in evidence and, once in evidence, do influence the result. In many a case the Courts have decided in favour of the party who seeks rectification – but have done it on the ground of construction – saying that there is no need in the circumstances to decide on rectification: but, in truth, being influenced on construction by the evidence given about the negotiations. That is, I fancy, what happened in the leading case of *Shipley v Bradford Corporation*[1].

Another way which has recently emerged is the doctrine of the 'factual matrix' as explained by Lord Wilberforce in *Reardon Smith v Hansen*[2] when he said:

'What the Court must do is to place itself in thought in the same factual matrix in which the parties were'.

In order to ascertain the factual matrix I ask: What better material is there than to look at the correspondence which discloses the circumstances in which the parties contracted?

So far as subsequent conduct is concerned the Court always looks at the happenings, after the contract, leading up to the breach that is alleged. It is difficult for any Judge to put this evidence out of his mind when construing the contract. If the words are not clear, he will be unwilling to treat conduct as a breach, when the parties themselves did not consider it to be so.

I put this question: How far is it permissible to use extrinsic aids in the construction of the written words?

2 A master of words

So you see that in construing any document you have first to consider the meaning of the words. If they cover the situation that has arisen – in a just and reasonable way – then you must apply them as they stand. But if, taken

1. [1936] 1 Ch 375.
2. [1976] 1 WLR 989.

literally, they lead to a result which is unjust or unreasonable, then you must think again. You must use all your skill – as a craftsman in words – to avoid that unjust or unreasonable result. There are many tools at hand for you to use. The most useful is the one by which you point out to the Judge that that word or phrase is capable of more than one meaning. It can be given a broad meaning or a narrow meaning. Then invite the Judge to take the one which leads to a just and reasonable result. You will find that in many cases he will respond favourably. Every Judge will seek to arrive at a just and reasonable result if he can do so consistently with the law. If that tool fails – so that, on any view, the actual meaning of the word or phrase itself is against you – is against right and justice – then you must try the next tool. This is to urge the Judge to read something into the document which is not expressed in it. You will suggest that this or that is implicit in the statute; or must have been intended by the testator; or that both parties to the contract must be taken to have intended it. You will have many a Judge resistant to this argument. He will say: 'I cannot write into the statute something which Parliament has not written. That would be a naked usurpation of the legislative power'. Or he will say: 'I cannot tell what the testator intended except by looking at the words of his will. Anything else is speculation'. Or he will say: 'I cannot write any such implication into the contract: because I cannot mend any man's contract. I cannot make a contract for the parties'. At the end of his judgment, he will say: 'Much as I regret it, the language is too strong for me to overcome'. His conscience is clear because he feels he is obeying the law. But I would ask: Is not this too narrow a view? A Judge should not be a servant of the words used. He should not be a mere mechanic in the power-house of semantics. He should be the man in charge of it.

The time is not yet here, but I hope it is coming when Judges will realise that the people who draft statutes, wills or contracts cannot envisage all the things that the future may bring; that words are a most imperfect instrument to express the mind of man, and that the better role of a Judge is to be a master of words, and to mould them to fit the purpose in hand — by way of implication, presumed intention or what you will — so as to do therein 'what to justice shall appertain'. Such was the task entrusted by our Sovereign to the Justices on the opening of every Assize. Such is the task which they would do well to undertake today.

Part two

Misuse of ministerial powers

Introduction

The power structure today is very different from what it was in the 19th century. In those days the Government concerned itself with keeping the peace; with defence; and with foreign affairs. It left industry to the manufacturers, the merchants and the traders. It left welfare to the charitable bodies. It did no planning for anything or anybody. The philosophy of the time was *laissez-faire* or, in English, individualist or libertarian.

In the present century the Government has concerned itself with every aspect of life. We have the Welfare State and the Planned State. The Government departments have been given much power in many directions. They set up tribunals and inquiries. They exercise unfettered discretion. They regulate housing, employment, planning, social security, and a host of other activities. The philosophy of the day is socialism or collectivism.

But whatever philosophy predominates, there is always a danger to the ordinary man. It lies in the fact that all power is capable of misuse or abuse. The great problem before the Courts in the 20th century has been: In an age of increasing power, how is the law to cope with the abuse or misuse of it?

It was nearly 30 years ago that I said at the end of my little book *Freedom under the Law:*

'Our procedure for securing our personal freedom is efficient, but our procedure for preventing the abuse of power is not. Just as the pick and shovel is no longer suitable for the winning of coal, so also the procedure of mandamus, certiorari, and actions on the case are not suitable for the winning of freedom in the new age . . . . We have in our time to deal with changes which are of equal constitutional significance to those which took place 300 years ago. Let us prove ourselves equal to the challenge'.

In these pages now I hope to show how the challenge has been met. I will take one by one the law as it stood 30 years ago: and the law as it stands today. It is a fascinating story. I will show that previous decisions have been departed from; that long-accepted propositions have been overthrown; that 'ouster' clauses have themselves been ousted; and that literal interpretation has gone by the board. All in support of the rule of law. All done so as to curb the abuse of power by the executive authorities.

1 Deciding wrongly

1 When Tribunals fall into error

Thirty years ago departmental tribunals were proliferating. Governments were appointing them by the score. The Ministers regarded them as part of the machinery of administration. The Judges had no control over a Tribunal so long as it kept within its jurisdiction. A Tribunal might go completely wrong in law. It might go utterly wrong in fact. The error, however grave, could not be questioned. This was a rule which went back for over 100 years. It had been explicitly stated in 1841 and repeatedly affirmed afterwards. The only way in which the decision of a Tribunal could be questioned was by showing that it had gone outside its jurisdiction altogether. That could rarely be done. It was always said: 'If the Tribunal had jurisdiction to decide the case rightly: so also it had jurisdiction to decide it wrongly'.

This distinction — between within and without jurisdiction — has given much trouble ever since. It depends on what you mean by 'jurisdiction'. In one sense no tribunal ever has jurisdiction to decide a case wrongly on a point of law. When Parliament sets up a Tribunal, it does so in the belief that it will decide cases in accordance with law and not contrary to it. So much so that it may be said that it is a condition of the grant of jurisdiction that it should decide according to law.

2 The *Northumberland* case

The first breach in the old law came in 1951. It is one of the most important cases of our time. So forgive me if I dwell upon it for a while. It was the *Northumberland Compensation Appeal Tribunal* case[1]. It was all about a clerk and his claim for compensation. On the setting up of the National Health Service, the clerk Mr. Shaw had been made redundant. As a result, he became entitled to compensation to be determined by a compensation tribunal. The members of the Tribunal gave him far too little. They went wrong in construing the very complicated regulations about compensation. They had made an error of law. But at that time everyone thought that the High Court could not correct the error. Eight years earlier there had been a decision in the Court of Appeal directly in point. It was the reserved judgment of a strong Court presided over by Lord Greene MR (*Racecourse Betting Control Board v Secretary of State for Air*[2]). He was one of the most accomplished and distinguished intellects of our time — with a First in Greats at Oxford and a Fellow of All Souls. Could the Court of Appeal eight years later over-rule him? especially as Lord Justice Goddard, of sound common-sense, was sitting beside him and agreed with him.

Yet the Courts in the *Northumberland* case did manage to depart from that *Racecourse* case. By this time Lord Goddard had become Lord Chief Justice of England. The *Northumberland* case came before him sitting at first instance. He got over it somehow. In passing I would tell you that it is always easier to overcome a decision when you have been a party to it yourself. You can correct your own mistakes. So Lord Goddard got over the *Racecourse* case. The *Northumberland* case then came to us in the Court of Appeal. I looked into my books at home. I have always kept at home a complete set of the Law Reports, the English Reports, and many others. Then we gave judgment. I first stated the question:

'The question in this case is whether the Court of King's Bench can intervene to correct the decision of a statutory tribunal which is erroneous in point of law. No one has ever

1. [1952] 1 KB 338.
2. [1944] Ch 114.

doubted that the Court of King's Bench can intervene to prevent a statutory tribunal from exceeding the jurisdiction which Parliament has conferred on it; but it is quite another thing to say that the King's Bench can intervene when a tribunal makes a mistake of law. A tribunal may often decide a point of law wrongly whilst keeping well within its jurisdiction. If it does so, can the King's Bench intervene?'

Then after some pages I gave the answer which I based on my researches:

'The Court of King's Bench has from very early times exercised control over the orders of statutory tribunals, just as it has done over the orders of justices. The earliest instances that I have found are the orders of the Commissioners of Sewers, who were set up by statute in 1532 to see to the repairs of sea walls and so forth. The Court of King's Bench used on certiorari to quash the orders of the commissioners for errors on the face of them, such as when they failed to set out the facts necessary to show that they had jurisdiction in the matter, or when they contained some error in point of law. It is recorded that on one celebrated occasion the commissioners refused to obey a certiorari issued out of the King's Bench, and for this the whole body of them were "laid by the heels" . . . . Since that time it has never been doubted that certiorari will lie to any statutory tribunal. It was suggested before us on behalf of the Crown that, in the case of these statutory tribunals, the Court of King's Bench only interfered by certiorari to keep them within their jurisdiction, and not to correct their errors of law. There are, however, many cases in the books where certiorari was used to correct errors of law on the face of the record. A striking instance was where the Commissioners of Sewers imposed an excessive fine, and it was quashed by the Court of King's Bench on the ground that in law their fines ought to be reasonable'.

We were of course placed in some difficulty by the previous decision of Lord Greene in the *Racecourse* case but we overcame it by a little subtlety. I said:

65

'I look upon that decision as merely a decision as to the scope of the remedy of setting aside on motion. It is not a decision on substantive law. It does not take away or diminish the inherent jurisdiction of the Court of King's Bench to interfere by certiorari'.

So I came to the conclusion:

'We have here a simple case of error of law by a tribunal, an error which they frankly acknowledge. It is an error which deprives Mr. Shaw of the compensation to which he is by law entitled. So long as the erroneous decision stands, the compensating authority dare not pay Mr. Shaw the money to which he was entitled lest the auditor should surcharge them. It would be quite intolerable if in such case there were no means of correcting the error. The authorities to which I have referred amply show that the King's Bench can correct it by certiorari'.

So the *Northumberland* case was decided. There was no appeal to the House of Lords. So it became of authority. It transformed the law about statutory tribunals. It was in terms limited to errors of law 'on the face of the record'; but, as there was no binding decision as to what constituted the 'record', it was possible to extend it to include not only the order of the Tribunal itself – when it was a 'speaking order' – but in addition all the documents properly before the Tribunal and considered by them. As case after case arose, the Court always admitted every document which showed that the Tribunal had gone wrong in law.

3 What is an 'error of law'?

As you will have observed, the decision in the *Northumberland* case was restricted to 'error of law'. If this phrase had been narrowly construed, it would have been unduly limiting. But it has never been narrowly construed. Speaking from experience. I find that when a tribunal has gone wrong, the High Court is usually able to find that it has made an 'error of law'. Thus in 1959 when I was in the Lords an 'error of law' was given a wide interpretation. It was in *Baldwin and Francis Ltd v Patents Appeal Tribunal*[1] :

'Is that an error of law? I have no doubt that it is: and it is an error of such a kind as to entitle the Queen's Bench to interfere. There are many cases in the books which show that if a tribunal bases its decision on extraneous considerations which it ought not to have taken into account, or fails to take into account a vital consideration which it ought to have taken into account, then its decision may be quashed on certiorari and a mandamus issued for it to hear the case afresh. The cases on mandamus are clear enough: and if mandamus will go to a tribunal for such a cause, then it must follow that certiorari will go also: for when a mandamus is issued to the tribunal, it must hear and determine the case afresh, and it cannot well do this if its previous order is still standing. The previous order must either be quashed on certiorari or ignored: and it is better for it to be quashed.
. . . .

'In some of those cases it has been said that the tribunal, in falling into an error of this particular kind, has exceeded its jurisdiction. No tribunal, it is said, has any jurisdiction to be influenced by extraneous considerations or to disregard vital matters. This is good sense and enables the court of Queen's Bench to receive evidence to prove the error. But an *excess* of jurisdiction in this sense is very different from *want* of jurisdiction altogether which is, of course, "determinable at the commencement, not at the conclusion of the inquiry". Whereas an excess of jurisdiction is determinable in the course of or at the end of the inquiry. But allowing that a tribunal which falls into an error of this particular kind does exceed its jurisdiction, as I am prepared to do, nevertheless I am quite clear that at the same time it falls into an error of law too: for the simple reason that it has "not determined according to law". And the decision in the *Northumberland* case itself shows that, even though no evidence is given,

1. [1959] AC 663.

nevertheless if such an error appears from the documents properly before the court, or by legitimate inference therefrom, then certiorari may be granted to quash the decision: and the certiorari can properly be said to be for error of law on the face of the proceedings. It may be excess of jurisdiction as well, but it is certainly error of law'.

2 Clauses ousting the Courts

1 An *obiter dictum*

So far so good. But there were some big obstacles yet to be cleared. These were set up by Parliament in order to stop the High Court interfering with tribunals. They were called 'ouster' clauses. These were clauses saying that the decisions of some particular tribunals were 'not to be removed by certiorari' or were to be 'final and conclusive' or words to that effect. If these clauses were given literal effect, it meant that those tribunals were to be a law unto themselves. Their decisions were not to be reviewed by the Courts of Law. No matter how wrong in law or otherwise, the Courts were not to interfere with them. How were such clauses to be overcome?

I threw out a suggestion by way of an *obiter dictum* in *Taylor v National Assistance Board*[1] :

'The remedy is not excluded by the fact that the determination of the Board is by Statute made "final": Parliament only gives the impress of finality to the decisions of the board on the condition that they are reached in accordance with the law; and the Queen's Courts can issue a declaration to see that that condition is fulfilled'.

That dictum was destined to have important consequences. Expanded a little it meant that Parliament only conferred jurisdiction on a Tribunal or Board on condition that it made its determination in accordance with law. If it went wrong in

1. [1957] P 101 at 111.

law, it went outside the jurisdiction conferred on it. Its decision was therefore void. It had jurisdiction to decide rightly but no jurisdiction to decide wrongly.

2 A decision made 'final'

A few weeks later the point arose for actual decision. It was a decision of a Medical Appeal Tribunal[1]. I happened to know a good deal about these tribunals as I had been the nominated Judge for Pension Appeals. It was the policy of Parliament that medical questions should be decided by medical men and that their decision should be 'final'. The Statute expressly provided that the decision of a Tribunal was to be a 'final'. A workman lost the sight of one eye in an accident at work. Nineteen years later he lost the sight of the other eye, owing to an accident at work. The Medical Appeal Tribunal assessed his disablement as a 'one-eye' case whereas they should have assessed it as a 'two-eye' case. The workman applied ex parte for certiorari to quash the error of law on the face of the record. It came before Lord Goddard CJ in the Divisional Court. Now Lord Goddard was a great Judge, but he had one fault. He was too quick. He jumped too soon. And his colleagues sometimes were not bold enough to say 'Stop'. Here he simply said, 'Application dismissed' and gave no reason. No doubt he thought that a decision on disablement should be left to the medical men. The workman then applied to the Court of Appeal. Now I was by this time presiding. I had sitting beside me Lord Justice Parker, afterwards Lord Chief Justice. He was at this very time in the midst of the Committee on Administrative Tribunals and Inquiries. So he knew all about tribunals. He was a modest and quiet man — quite the reverse of Lord Goddard — but of great ability. He saw at once that this point about 'final' was of the first importance. We gave leave to appeal. When the appeal came on for hearing, Rodger Winn appeared for the Ministry. He had done outstanding

1. *R v Medical Appeal Tribunal, ex parte Gilmore* [1957] 1 QB 574.

work during the War in seeking out the enemy U-boats. He was the Treasury Devil, afterwards Lord Justice Winn. He was always concise and to the point. In this *Medical Appeal Tribunal* case, he threw his hand in. He admitted that the Tribunal were wrong in law and that their decision should be quashed. We might have left it there and said little or nothing on the point of principle. But Lord Justice Parker asked him: 'Do you agree that this case is breaking new ground?' He replied: 'It is ground which has already been lightly forked over'. So we ourselves dug up the new ground. I applied my dictum in *Taylor*'s case and said:

'The Act of 1946 provides that "any decision of a claim or question . . . shall be final". Do those words preclude the Court of Queen's Bench from issuing a certiorari to bring up the decision?

'This is a question which we did not discuss in *R v Northumberland Compensation Appeal Tribunal, ex parte Shaw*, because it did not there arise. It does arise here, and on looking again into the old books I find it very well settled that the remedy by certiorari is never to be taken away by any statute except by the most clear and explicit words. The word "final" is not enough. That only means "without appeal". It does not mean "without recourse to certiorari". It makes the decision final on the facts, but not final on the law. Notwithstanding that the decision is by a statute made "final", certiorari can still issue for excess of jurisdiction or for error of law on the face of the record'.

That passage has often since been quoted and applied.

Then I turned to the other type of 'ouster' clause, the 'no certiorari' clause. I explained that, notwithstanding that clause, the Courts had always intervened if the Tribunal exceeded its jurisdiction:

'In contrast to the word "final" I would like to say a word about the old statutes which used in express words to take away the remedy by certiorari by saying that the decision of the tribunal "shall not be removed by certiorari". Those

71

statutes were passed chiefly between 1680 and 1848, in the days when the courts used certiorari too freely and quashed decisions for technical defects of form. In stopping this abuse the statutes proved very beneficial, but the court never allowed those statutes to be used as a cover for wrongdoing by tribunals. If tribunals were to be at liberty to exceed their jurisdiction without any check by the courts, the rule of law would be at an end. Despite express words taking away certiorari, therefore, it was held that certiorari would still lie if some of the members of the tribunal were disqualified from acting: see *R v Cheltenham Commissioners* where Lord Denman CJ said: "The statute cannot affect our right and duty to see justice executed". So, also, if the tribunal exceeded its jurisdiction: see *Ex parte Bradlaugh;* or if its decision was obtained by fraud: see *R v Gillyard,* the courts would still grant certiorari'.

3 The *Anisminic* case

So far so good. But those who frame 'ouster' clauses were not to be outdone. They invented a new 'ouster' clause which they thought would be foolproof – or shall I say, proof against any interference by the Courts. It came up for consideration in the great *Anisminic v Foreign Compensation Commission* case[1]. The statute which set up the Foreign Compensation Tribunal went further than any other to exclude the Courts. It said:

'The determination by the Tribunal of any application made to them under this Act shall not be called in question in any Court of Law'.

The Anisminic Company claimed that, on the true construction of the Order, they were entitled to participate in a compensation fund. The Compensation Tribunal rejected the Company's claim. The Company then brought an action in the Courts claiming a declaration that the claim was good.

1. [1969] 2 AC 147.

The Compensation Tribunal pleaded that, by reason of the Statute, the High Court had no jurisdiction to entertain the proceedings.

The Compensation Tribunal tried to get rid of the action by taking a short cut. They applied to the Court to have the question of jurisdiction determined as a preliminary point of law. They said that, even assuming that the Compensation Tribunal came to the wrong determination on the construction of the Order, there was no jurisdiction in the High Court. This application came before a Court in which I was sitting with Lords Justices Harman and Diplock. It was in 1964. I remember well the argument. Mr. Roger Parker, QC, a most forceful advocate, appeared for the Anisminic Company. He analysed the facts and the Order with great skill. He persuaded two of us that there might be a way of overcoming this 'ouster' clause. We held that the action should go for trial on all points. Lord Justice Diplock dissented. He thought that the Statute was a complete bar. It was a good thing that we did let the case go for trial: because it revolutionised the law on the subject.

At the trial the Judge had to look into the nature of error. This was done by Browne J in a judgment which was a masterpiece. He was reversed by the Court of Appeal, but restored by the House of Lords. His judgment was given immortality by being printed in full in the House of Lords Reports.

It is not my purpose now to analyse the speeches in the House of Lords. The only thing that is clear is that the House held (by 3 to 2) that the Compensation Tribunal made an error of law in misconstruing the Order: and that this error was of such a serious nature that the Compensation Tribunal went outside its jurisdiction — so far outside that its determination was a nullity.

This left open the very difficult question: How do you decide whether an error of law is so serious as to produce a nullity? or is a mere error of law which does not produce that result? No ordinary mortal can be expected to answer that question with any hope of being right. If you count the heads of all who heard the *Anisminic* case, four holders of high

73

judicial office held that the error of law took the Tribunal outside its jurisdiction so far as to produce a nullity (Lords Reid, Pearce and Wilberforce, and Browne J): four equally eminent held that it was an error of law within its jurisdiction and could not be challenged in the Courts (Lord Morris of Borth-y-Gest, Lords Justices Sellers, Diplock and Russell). One Law Lord held that the Tribunal made no error of law at all. He was Lord Pearson — one of the best Judges ever. He had no equal on a matter of this kind.

So we are left with a question which no one can expect to answer rightly. Is it not then time to go back to the starting point? And to ask: Were the Courts right in the beginning to draw the distinction between within and without jurisdiction?

4 Error of law goes to jurisdiction

This brings me to the latest case. In it I ventured to suggest that whenever a tribunal goes wrong in law, it goes outside the jurisdiction conferred on it and its decision is void, because Parliament only conferred jurisdiction on the tribunal on condition that it decided in accordance with the law. The case is *Pearlman v Governors of Harrow School* decided on 14 July 1978[1]. It arose out of the leasehold Reform Act 1967. This Act gave the leaseholder a right to buy the freehold, but only if the rateable value of his house was below £1500. Mr. Pearlman had installed at his own expense a new central heating system. He claimed that his rateable value should be reduced on this account. This depended on a few words in Schedule 8 of the Housing Act 1974. Was it an improvement 'amounting to a structural alteration'? The determination of this question was left to the county court but the Act said that 'any such determination shall be final and conclusive'. Two householders each installed a new central heating system. The two cases were quite indistinguishable on the facts. One county court Judge held that it was a 'structural alteration'. Another held it was not. There was an 'ouster' clause in the Statute which

1. [1978] 3 WLR 736.

was quite as wide as the 'ouster' clause in the *Anisminic* case. It was section 107 of the County Courts Act 1959. It said:

'No judgment or order of any judge of County Courts, nor any proceedings brought before him or pending in his Court, shall be removed by appeal, motion, certiorari or otherwise into any other Court whatever'.

As to this clause I said that:

'It does not exclude the power of the High Court to issue certiorari for absence of jurisdiction. It has been held that certiorari will issue to a county court judge if he acts without jurisdiction in the matter – see *Regina v Hurst* [1960] 2 Queen's Bench 133. If he makes a wrong finding on a matter on which his jurisdiction depends, he makes a jurisdictional error: and certiorari will lie to quash his decision – see *Anisminic v Foreign Compensation Commission* [1969] 2 Appeal Cases at page 208 by Lord Wilberforce. But the distinction between an error which entails absence of jurisdiction – and an error made within the jurisdiction – is very fine. So fine indeed that it is rapidly being eroded. Take this very case. When the judge held that the installation of a full central heating system was not a "structural alteration or addition" we all think – all three of us – that he went wrong in point of law. He misconstrued those words. That error can be described on the one hand as an error which went to his jurisdiction. In this way:- If he had held that it was a "structural alteration or addition" he would have had jurisdiction to go on and determine the various matters set out in paragraphs (b) (c) and (d) of the Schedule. By holding that it was not a "structural alteration or addition" he deprived himself of jurisdiction to determine those matters. On the other hand, his error can equally well be described as an error made by him within his jurisdiction. It can plausibly be said that he had jurisdiction to inquire into the meaning of the words "structural alteration or addition"; and that his wrong interpretation of them was only an error within his jurisdiction, and not an error taking him outside it.

'That illustration could be repeated in nearly all these cases.

So fine is the distinction that in truth the High Court has a choice before it whether to interfere with an inferior court on a point of law. If it chooses to interfere, it can formulate its decision in the words: "The Court below had no jurisdiction to decide this point wrongly as it did". If it does not choose to interfere, it can say: "The Court had jurisdiction to decide it wrongly, and did so". Softly be it stated, but that is the reason for the difference between the decision of the Court of Appeal in *Anisminic* and the House of Lords.

'I would suggest that this distinction should now be discarded. The High Court has, and should have, jurisdiction to control the proceedings of inferior courts and tribunals by way of judicial review. When they go wrong in law, the High Court should have power to put them right. Not only in the instant case to do justice to the complainant. But also so as to secure that all courts and tribunals, when faced with the same point of law, should decide it in the same way. It is intolerable that a citizen's rights in point of law should depend on which judge tries his case, or in what court it is heard. The way to get things right is to hold thus: No court or tribunal has any jurisdiction to make an error of law on which the decision of the case depends. If it makes such an error, it goes outside its jurisdiction and certiorari will lie to correct it. In this case the finding – that the installation of a central heating system was not a "structural alteration" – was an error on which the jurisdiction of the county court depended: and, because of that error, the county court judge was quite wrong to dismiss the application outright. He ought to have found that the installation was an "improvement" within section 8, paragraph 2 (2) (a), and gone on to determine the other matters referred to in section 8, paragraph 2 (2) (b) (c) and (d).

'On these grounds I am of opinion that certiorari lies to quash the determination of the county court judge, even though it was made by statute "final and conclusive" '.

If this be correct, then it does appear that, notwithstanding any 'ouster' clause which Parliament may insert into the Act setting up a tribunal, the Courts can by means of certiorari, set aside any determination of the Tribunal which is shown to be erroneous in point of law: on the ground that it is an error which goes outside the jurisdiction of the Tribunal: and the determination is therefore void.

5 Void or voidable

But if it is void, what is to happen? Unless and until someone applies to quash it, the determination of the Tribunal will appear to be good. As Lord Radcliffe once said: 'It bears no brand of invalidity on its forehead'. Much work may have been done in pursuance of the void order. Many persons may have acted on it in the belief that it is good. In such circumstances the Court has a discretion whether to quash the order by certiorari or declare it bad; and if it does quash it, to make such consequential orders as it may think fit to do justice between the parties. Under the new Rules of the Supreme Court for Judicial Review, this includes an award of damages.

I confess that at one time I used to say that such a decision was not void but only voidable. But I have seen the error of my ways. It was in *Firman v Ellis*[1] , a very complicated case. So I will only quote the passage where I changed my mind:

'I think that the order of July 11, 1973, was a nullity and void ab initio for two reasons: (i) it was made under a fundamental mistake in that the registrar was told and believed that the Smiths agreed to it, when they had not: and (ii) it was made contrary to the rules of natural justice, because no notice of appointment had been given to the Smiths' solicitor. Such failures make the order a nullity and void ab initio: see *Anisminic Ltd v Foreign Compensation Commission* [1969] 2 AC 147, 171 by Lord Reid, and at p. 195 by Lord Pearce. It is true, of course, that the Smiths might have waived their right to complain of it. They might have entered an unconditional appearance. But they did not

1. [1978] 3 WLR 1.

waive it. They entered a conditional appearance and got it set aside. On being set aside, it is thereupon shown to have been a nullity from the beginning and void. So, after some vacillation, I would adopt the meanings of "void" and "voidable" given by Professor Wade in his *Administrative Law* 4th ed. (1977), pp. 300, 450. Seeing that it was a nullity, it follows that in point of law no action had been "commenced" against the Smiths'.

3 Declarations

1 The case of the *Dock Labour Board*

Thirty years ago it was assumed by many that the Courts could not interfere with tribunals except by certiorari. But in 1953 that belief was shown to be wrong. Recourse was had to the new method of declaration and injunction or rather it was refurbishing an existing method. It was in *Barnard v National Dock Labour Board*[1]. A docker had been suspended from work by a Tribunal without pay. He alleged that the suspension was made without jurisdiction and he wanted to be reinstated and have his back pay. It was said that the Courts had no power to interfere. Mr. Paull argued it. He was always a most formidable opponent. This is how I came to answer it. I will set it out at large because our decision was afterwards approved and applied by the House of Lords in *Vine v National Dock Labour Board*[2]:

'Finally, Mr. Paull said (and it was his principal argument) that these courts have no right to interfere with the decisions of statutory tribunals except by the historical method of certiorari. He drew an alarming picture of what might happen if once the court intervened by way of declaration and injunction. It meant, he said, that anyone who was dissatisfied with the decision of a tribunal could start an action in the courts for a declaration that it was bad, and thus, by a side-wind, one could get an appeal to the courts in cases where Parliament intended that there should be none. I think that there is much force in Mr. Paull's contention; so much so

1. [1953] 2 QB 18.
2. [1957] AC 488.

that I am sure that in the vast majority of cases the courts will not seek to interfere with the decisions of statutory tribunals; but that there is power to do so, not only by certiorari, but also by way of declaration, I do not doubt. I know of no limit to the power of the court to grant a declaration except such limit as it may in its discretion impose upon itself; and the court should not, I think, tie its hands in this matter of statutory tribunals. It is axiomatic that when a statutory tribunal sits to administer justice, it must act in accordance with the law. Parliament clearly so intended. If the tribunal does not observe the law, what is to be done? The remedy by certiorari is hedged round by limitations and may not be available. Why then should not the court intervene by declaration and injunction? If it cannot so intervene, it would mean that the tribunal could disregard the law, which is a thing no one can do in this country.

'The authorities show clearly that the courts can intervene.
. . . .

'In the course of the argument, Mr. Paull was compelled to admit that if the men had no remedy by way of declaration they had no remedy at all. He agreed that the men in this case could not have obtained redress by certiorari for the simple reason that they did not know the facts. In certiorari there is no discovery, whereas in an action for a declaration it can be had. The men only discovered the true position shortly before the trial, two and a half years after the suspension. That shows that but for these proceedings the truth would never have been known. The port manager could have gone on indefinitely assuming a jurisdiction which did not belong to him, and the men would be subjected to penal orders which were null and void, and they would have had no redress. I should be sorry to think that these courts were powerless to put right such a situation.

'. . . . I hasten to say that it was not the fault of the official, who is a man well spoken of by all. It was the fault of the system. The lightermen felt that they had not been treated justly, and they sought redress in the Queen's courts. Yet it is said by the board that the Queen's courts have no power to interfere. Let us take the argument into account by all means, but let us also remember that if the men cannot get redress here, they can get it nowhere else. I think that they are entitled to redress, and I agree with my Lord that we should declare that the suspension was unlawful'.

2 *Pyx Granite*

The amplitude of the power was emphatically reaffirmed a few years later. It was in the *Pyx Granite Co Ltd v Ministry of Housing & Local Government* case[1]. The Statute made provision for a determination by the Minister which was expressly made 'final'. The Pyx Company did not go to the Minister. Instead they sought a declaration in the High Court. The Minister said that the Court had no jurisdiction to entertain a claim for a declaration. By this time I was in the Lords and came back to the Court of Appeal to hear the case. This is a good thing for a Law Lord to do − so as to be more in touch with contemporary problems. In this *Pyx* case I said: 'I take it to be settled law that the jurisdiction of the High Court to grant a declaration is not to be taken away except by clear words'. In the House of Lords Lord Simonds gave it his approval saying[2]:

'But I agree with Lord Denning and Morris LJ in thinking that this circuity is not necessary. It is a principle not by any means to be whittled down that the subject's recourse to Her Majesty's courts for the determination of his rights is not to be excluded except by clear words. That is, as McNair J called it in *Francis v Yiewsley and West Drayton Urban District Council,* a "fundamental rule" from which I would not for my part sanction any departure. It must be asked, then, what is there in the Act of 1947 which bars such recourse. The answer is that there is nothing except the fact that the Act provides him with another remedy. Is it, then,

1. [1958] 1 QB 554.
2. [1960] AC 260 at 286.

an alternative or an exclusive remedy? There is nothing in the Act to suggest that, while a new remedy, perhaps cheap and expeditious, is given, the old and, as we like to call it, the inalienable remedy of Her Majesty's subjects to seek redress in her courts is taken away'.

It has been suggested that there is a limitation in the power of the High Court to make a declaration — that it cannot make a declaration as to whether a tribunal came to a correct determination in point of law. I took a different view in *Punton v Ministry of Pensions*[1]. I hope I was right. It can be said that no tribunal has any jurisdiction to decide a point of law wrongly. Its decision is void and a nullity. And the High Court can so declare.

1. [1963] 1 WLR 1176.

4 Other points on tribunals

1 Appeals from Tribunals

It is not my purpose here to go into the vast improvements made by the Tribunals and Inquiries Act 1958. I would only say that I took some part in it. I made my maiden speech in the House of Lords upon the Report of Lord Franks' Committee[1]. It was on 27 November 1957. I was so nervous that I learnt it by heart. I did not read it. To read a speech is contrary to the tradition of the House. It is in Hansard[2]:

'My Lords, it has been my lot as a Judge to review the decisions of many tribunals, and may I say how welcome it is that this important Report should be accepted by all Parties in the State, because it contains and re-affirms a constitutional principle of first importance – namely, that these tribunals are not part of the administrative machinery of government under the control of departments; they are part of the judicial system of the land under the rule of law. This Report shows how that principle should be put into practice. These tribunals should, whenever appropriate, give reasons for their decisions, and their decisions should be subject to appeal to the courts on points of law. Many cases have come before the courts to show the need for action on these matters. The courts have exercised a jurisdiction in the past to control tribunals, but they have been fettered by antiquated rules. It is said that they can interfere if the tribunals go outside their jurisdiction altogether but that they

1. Cmnd. 218.
2. 206 HL Official Report (5th Series) 27 November 1957, col. 544.

cannot interfere if the tribunals exercise their jurisdiction badly.

'. . . . there is need to affirm most strongly the recommendation of the Committee that there should be an appeal to the courts on any point of law.

'. . . . a liberal interpretation should be given as to what constitutes a point of law'.

I am glad to say the Committee's Report was implemented in full. I spoke at every step in the House. Many tribunals now are bound to give their decisions in writing and their decisions are subject to appeal on points of law.

2 Natural justice

I have spent much time on error of law by a tribunal, but very little time on want of natural justice, or bias and the like. The reason is because these have given rise to no controversy. It is beyond doubt that, if a tribunal fails to observe the rules of natural justice, or is biased — its decision is a nullity and void; and it can be quashed on certiorari; or declared void by a declaration to that effect. Sufficient to illustrate this is *Kanda v Government of Malaya*[1] . Inspector Kanda was dismissed by the Government of Malaya on the basis of a report which he had not seen. He brought an action for a declaration claiming that his dismissal was void, inoperative and of no effect. He succeeded in the Privy Council. This so encouraged him that he afterwards was called to the Bar by Lincoln's Inn and returned to Malaya and practised there with good success. In that case I said:

'In the opinion of their Lordships, however, the proper approach is somewhat different. The rule against bias is one thing. The right to be heard is another. Those two rules are the essential characteristics of what is often called natural justice. They are the twin pillars supporting it. The Romans put them in the two maxims: *Nemo judex in causa sua*, and

1. [1962] AC 322.

Audi alteram partem. They have recently been put in the two words, Impartiality and Fairness. But they are separate concepts and are governed by separate considerations. In the present case inspector Kanda complained of a breach of the second. He said that his constitutional right had been infringed. He had been dismissed without being given a reasonable opportunity of being heard.

'If the right to be heard is to be a real right which is worth anything, it must carry with it a right in the accused man to know the case which is made against him. He must know what evidence has been given and what statements have been made affecting him: and then he must be given a fair opportunity to correct or contradict them. This appears in all the cases from the celebrated judgment of Lord Loreburn LC in *Board of Education v Rice* down to the decision of their Lordships' Board in *Ceylon University v Fernando*. It follows, of course, that the judge or whoever has to adjudicate must not hear evidence or receive representations from one side behind the back of the other. The court will not inquire whether the evidence or representations did work to his prejudice. Sufficient that they might do so. The court will not go into the likelihood of prejudice. The risk of it is enough. No one who has lost a case will believe he has been fairly treated if the other side has had access to the judge without his knowing.

'Applying these principles, their Lordships are of opinion that inspector Kanda was not in this case given a reasonable opportunity of being heard.

'. . . . Their Lordships do not think it was correct to let the adjudicating officer have the report of the board of inquiry unless the accused also had it so as to be able to correct or contradict the statements in it to his prejudice.

'Since their Lordships have already reached the conclusion that the dismissal was void on the ground that the Commissioner of Police had no authority to effect it, it is unnecessary for their Lordships to consider whether the setting aside of the proceedings would result also in avoiding the dismissal or merely in rendering it wrongful. Their Lordships notice that, before Rigby J, it was suggested that the only remedy was by certiorari. But their Lordships agree with him that the remedy by declaration is available also'.

3 Bias

I ought also to speak of the disqualification of a person from sitting. If a disqualified person takes part in a decision, it is a nullity and void. The point came up for decision in *Metropolitan Properties Co (FGC) Ltd v Lannon*[1]. Mr. Lannon was the Chairman of a Rent Assessment Committee. He was a solicitor. One day the Freshwater Company made an application to his Committee. He sat on it. But it was discovered that his father had a case pending against that Company. On that ground he was disqualified. I said:

'A man may be disqualified from sitting in a judicial capacity on one of two grounds. First, a "direct pecuniary interest" in the subject-matter. Second, "bias" in favour of one side or against the other.

'So far as "pecuniary interest" is concerned, I agree with the Divisional Court that there is no evidence that Mr. John Lannon had any direct pecuniary interest in the suit.

. . . .

'So far as bias is concerned, it was acknowledged that there was no actual bias on the part of Mr. Lannon, and no want of good faith. But it was said that there was, albeit unconscious, a real likelihood of bias. This is a matter on which the law is not altogether clear: but I start with the oft-repeated saying of Lord Hewart CJ in *R v Sussex Justices, ex parte McCarthy:* "It is not merely of some importance, but is of fundamental importance that justice should not only be done, but should manifestly and undoubtedly be seen to be done".

'In *R v Barnsley Licensing Justices, ex parte Barnsley and District Licensed Victuallers' Association,* Devlin J appears to have limited that principle considerably, but I would stand

1. [1969] 1 QB 577.

by it. It brings home this point: in considering whether there was a real likelihood of bias, the court does not look at the mind of the justice himself or at the mind of the chairman of the tribunal, or whoever it may be, who sits in a judicial capacity. It does not look to see if there was a real likelihood that he would, or did, in fact favour one side at the expense of the other. The court looks at the impression which would be given to other people. Even if he was as impartial as could be, nevertheless if right-minded persons would think that, in the circumstances, there was a real likelihood of bias on his part, then he should not sit. And if he does sit, his decision cannot stand: Nevertheless there must appear to be a real likelihood of bias. Surmise or conjecture is not enough. There must be circumstances from which a reasonable man would think it likely or probable that the justice, or chairman, as the case may be, would, or did, favour one side unfairly at the expense of the other. The court will not inquire whether he did, in fact, favour one side unfairly. Suffice it that reasonable people might think he did. The reason is plain enough. Justice must be rooted in confidence: and confidence is destroyed when right-minded people go away thinking: "The judge was biased".

'Applying these principles, I ask myself: Ought Mr. John Lannon to have sat? I think not. If he was himself a tenant in difference with his landlord about the rent of his flat, he clearly ought not to sit on a case against the selfsame landlord, also about the rent of a flat, albeit another flat. In this case he was not a tenant, but the son of a tenant. But that makes no difference'.

5 Administrative decisions

1 'Judicial' v 'Administrative'

Thirty years ago everyone in the law drew a distinction between 'judicial' and 'administrative'. If a public authority was acting judicially, its conduct was subject to control by the Courts by means of certiorari and mandamus. But if it was acting administratively, its decisions were virtually exempt from any control by the Courts. Certiorari and mandamus did not lie: and no one thought of asking for a Declaration. The distinction had been repeatedly taken during the War and immediately after it. The Courts were most reluctant to interfere with the discretion of the Ministers — in fighting the war — and repairing the ravages done by it. Thus in the *Stevenage* case[1] when the Minister made an order designating Stevenage as a new town, the House of Lords declined to entertain the objections made by the local landowners. The House rested their decision on the ground that the Minister was not acting judicially. He had no judicial duty or quasi-judicial duty imposed on him.

The distinction remained in everybody's minds until 1958 when it was held that it did not apply to the remedy by declaration. It was in the *Pyx Granite* case[2]. The Minister had granted a planning permission subject to conditions. The applicant contended that the conditions were invalid and sought a declaration. Mr. Squibb, a most learned and

1. [1948] AC 87.
2. [1958] 1 QB 554.

88

scholarly member of the Bar, argued that the remedy of declaration was not available:

'Mr. Squibb also said that if the conditions are invalid, the only remedy is by certiorari, and not by declaration, thus implicitly admitting that there ought to be a remedy, but that the company had pursued the wrong form of it.

. . . .

'It is one of the defects of certiorari that it so often involves an inquiry into the distinction between judicial acts and administrative acts which no one has been able satisfactorily to define. No such difficulty arises with the remedy by declaration, which is wide enough to meet this deficiency. It applies to administrative acts as well as judicial acts whenever their validity is challenged because of a denial of justice, or for other good reason. It is clearly available to enable the court to declare whether conditions imposed by a licensing authority are valid, no matter whether that authority is acting judicially or administratively'.

2 The *Padfield* case

Eight years later the distinction – between 'judicial' and 'administrative' – came up for discussion in regard to the prerogative writs of certiorari and mandamus. It was in the famous *Padfield* case[1]. Some farmers in the south-east of England asked the Minister to appoint a Committee to investigate price differentials in the milk industry. He refused. He said that he had an unfettered discretion whether to appoint a Committee or not. The farmers applied to the Divisional Court over which Lord Parker CJ presided. They sought the prerogative writ of mandamus. Lord Parker granted it. It was in February 1966. I remember that he regarded the case as of the first importance. He told me so. It came to the Court of Appeal in July 1966. I supported Lord Parker. But I was in the minority. But as my view was upheld later in the House of Lords I would like to set out

1. [1968] AC 997.

what I then said. We were faced with the usual argument that the Minister's decision was administrative and not judicial. This is how I dealt with it:

'It is plain to me that by these provisions Parliament has provided machinery by which complaints of farmers can be investigated by a committee which is independent of the board and by which those complaints, if justified, can be remedied. No other machinery is provided. This case raises the important question: How far can the Minister reject the complaint out of hand? Is the Minister at liberty in his unfettered discretion to withhold the matter from the committee of investigation and thus refuse the farmers a hearing by the committee? And by refusing a hearing, refuse a remedy? Mr. Kemp, who appeared for the Milk Marketing Board, contended that the Minister need not consider the complaint at all. He could throw it into the waste paper basket without looking at it. The Solicitor General did not support this argument. It is clearly untenable. The Minister is under a duty to consider every complaint so as to see whether it should be referred to the committee of investigation. I can well see that he may quite properly reject some of the complaints without more ado. They may be frivolous or wrong-headed: or they may be repetitive of old complaints already disposed of. But there are others which he cannot properly reject. In my opinion every genuine complaint which is worthy of investigation by the committee of investigation should be referred to that committee. The Minister is not at liberty to refuse it on grounds which are arbitrary or capricious. Nor because he has a personal antipathy to the complainant or does not like his political views. Nor on any other irrelevant ground.

'It is said that the decision of the Minister is administrative and not judicial. But that does not mean that he can do as he likes, regardless of right or wrong. Nor does it mean that the courts are powerless to correct him. Good administration requires that complaints should be investigated and that grievances should be remedied. When Parliament has set up machinery for that very purpose, it is not for the Minister to brush it on one side. He should not refuse to have a complaint investigated without good reason.

'But it is said that the Minister is not bound to give any reason at all. And that, if he gives no reason, his refusal cannot be questioned. So why does it matter if he gives bad reasons? I do not agree. This is the only remedy available to a person aggrieved. Save, of course, for questions in the House which Parliament itself did not consider suitable. Else why did it set up a committee of investigation? If the Minister is to deny the complainant a hearing – and a remedy – he should at least have good reasons for his refusal: and, if asked, he should give them. If he does not do so, the court may infer that he has no good reason. If it appears to the court that the Minister has been, or must have been, influenced by extraneous considerations which ought not to have influenced him – or, conversely, has failed, or must have failed, to take into account considerations which ought to have influenced him – the court has power to interfere. It can issue a mandamus to compel him to consider the complaint properly'.

Later on in 1968 my judgment and that of Lord Parker CJ were upheld in the House of Lords. Mandamus was issued commanding the Minister to consider the complaint of the farmers according to law.

3 *Re HK*

Meanwhile, however, Lord Parker CJ had taken the opportunity again of disapproving the distinction between 'judicial' and 'administrative'. It was in another important case decided by the Divisional Court in December 1976. It is called *Re HK*[1]. An immigration officer had refused entry to a boy on the ground that he was over 16. The boy said he was only 15 and sought to quash the immigration officer's decision. Lord Parker CJ held that:

'Good administration and an honest or bona fide decision

1. [1967] 2 QB 617.

must, as it seems to me, require not merely impartiality, nor merely bringing one's mind to bear on the problem, but acting fairly; and to the limited extent that the circumstances of any particular case allow, and within the legislative framework under which the administrator is working, only to that limited extent do the so-called rules of natural justice apply, which in a case such as this is merely a duty to act fairly. I appreciate that in saying that it may be said that one is going further than is permitted on the decided cases because heretofore at any rate the decisions of the courts do seem to have drawn a strict line in these matters according to whether there is or is not a duty to act judicially or quasi-judicially. It has sometimes been said that if there is no duty to act judicially or quasi-judicially there is no power in the court whatever to interfere'.

As a result of those cases the distinction between 'judicial' and 'administrative' has been eliminated at any rate to this extent: that an 'administrative' decision is not exempt from review simply because it is administrative. Thus in the case of aliens, after referring to some earlier cases, I said in *Schmidt v Secretary of State for Home Affairs*[1] :

'Some of the judgments in those cases were based on the fact that the Home Secretary was exercising an administrative power and not doing a judicial act. But that distinction is no longer valid. The speeches in *Ridge v Baldwin* [1964] AC 40 show that an administrative body may, in a proper case, be bound to give a person who is affected by their decision an opportunity of making representations. It all depends on whether he has some right or interest, or, I would add, some legitimate expectation, of which it would not be fair to deprive him without hearing what he has to say'.

4 The duty to act fairly

Nevertheless, despite those rulings, there have been occasions when many an administrative body has tried to gain exemption from judicial review. It usually submits that the

1. [1969] 2 Ch 149.

rules of natural justice do not apply to it. Thus Crockfords, a wellknown gaming club, applied to the Gaming Board for a licence to employ two men as croupiers. Mr. Quintin Hogg, surely the most able advocate of all, appeared for Crockfords. It was during the time that he was a plain Queen's Counsel, having renounced his peerage. They complained that the Board had not acted fairly. The Board submitted that they were not bound to observe the rules of natural justice. It is reported in *R v Gaming Board, ex parte Benaim*[1]. This is what I said:

'If Mr. Hogg went too far on his side, I think Mr. Kidwell went too far on the other. He submitted that the Gaming Board are free to grant or refuse a certificate as they please. They are not bound, he says, to obey the rules of natural justice any more than any other executive body, such as, I suppose, the Board of Trade, which grants industrial development certificates, or the Television Authority, which awards television programme contracts. I cannot accept this view. I think the Gaming Board are bound to observe the rules of natural justice. The question is: What are those rules?

'It is not possible to lay down rigid rules as to when the principles of natural justice are to apply: nor as to their scope and extent. Everything depends on the subject-matter. At one time it was said that the principles only apply to judicial proceedings and not to administrative proceedings. That heresy was scotched in *Ridge v Baldwin* [1964] AC 40. At another time it was said that the principles do not apply to the grant or revocation of licences. That too is wrong.

'So let us sheer away from those distinctions and consider the task of this Gaming Board and what they should do. The best guidance is, I think, to be found by reference to the cases of immigrants. They have no right to come in, but they have a right to be heard. The principle in that regard was well laid down by Lord Parker CJ in *Re HK (an infant)*:
".... even if an immigration officer is not in a judicial or quasi-judicial capacity, he must at any rate give the

1. [1970] 2 QB 417.

immigrant an opportunity of satisfying him of the matters in the subsection, and for that purpose let the immigrant know what his immediate impression is so that the immigrant can disabuse him. That is not, as I see it, a question of acting or being required to act judicially, but of being required to act fairly".

'Those words seem to me to apply to the Gaming Board. The statute says in terms that in determining whether to grant a certificate, the board "shall have regard only" to the matters specified. It follows, I think, that the board have a duty to act fairly. They must give the applicant an opportunity of satisfying them of the matters specified in the subsection. They must let him know what their impressions are so that they can disabuse them. But I do not think that they need quote chapter and verse against him as if they were dismissing him from an office; or depriving him of his property. After all, they are not charging him with doing anything wrong. They are simply inquiring as to his capability and diligence and are having regard to his character, reputation and financial standing. They are there to protect the public interest, to see that persons running the gaming clubs are fit to be trusted.

'Seeing the evils that have led to this legislation, the board can and should investigate the credentials of those who make application to them. They can and should receive information from the police in this country or abroad who know something of them. They can, and should, receive information from any other reliable source. Much of it will be confidential. But that does not mean that the applicants are not to be given a chance of answering it. They must be given the chance, subject to this qualification: I do not think they need tell the applicant the source of their information, if that would put their informant in peril or otherwise be contrary to the public interest'.

5 Inquiries into a company's affairs

A year or two later a similar attempt was made to gain

exemption from judicial review. The Minister had appointed inspectors to investigate the affairs of a company, the Pergamon Press Ltd, which was run by Mr. Robert Maxwell. The case is *Re Pergamon Press Ltd*[1]. On behalf of the directors it was claimed 'that the inspectors should conduct the inquiry much as if it were a judicial inquiry in a Court of Law in which Mr. Maxwell and his colleagues were being charged with an offence'. This is how this claim was answered:

'It seems to me that this claim on their part went too far. This inquiry was not a court of law. It was an investigation in the public interest, in which all should surely co-operate, as they promised to do. But if the directors went too far on their side, I am afraid that Mr. Fay, for the inspectors, went too far on the other. He did it very tactfully, but he did suggest that in point of law the inspectors were not bound by the rules of natural justice. He said that in all the cases where natural justice had been applied hitherto, the tribunal was under a duty to come to a determination or decision of some kind or other. He submitted that when there was no determination or decision but only an investigation or inquiry, the rules of natural justice did not apply.

'I cannot accept Mr. Fay's submission. It is true, of course, that the inspectors are not a court of law. Their proceedings are not judicial proceedings. They are not even quasi-judicial, for they decide nothing; they determine nothing. They only investigate and report. They sit in private and are not entitled to admit the public to their meetings. They do not even decide whether there is a prima facie case.

'But this should not lead us to minimise the significance of their task. They have to make a report which may have wide repercussions. They may, if they think fit, make findings of fact which are very damaging to those whom they name. They may accuse some; they may condemn others; they may ruin reputations or careers. Their report may lead to judicial proceedings. It may expose persons to criminal prosecutions or to civil actions. It may bring about the winding up of the

1. [1971] Ch 388.

company, and be used itself as material for the winding up. Even before the inspectors make their report, they may inform the Board of Trade of facts which tend to show that an offence has been committed: see section 41 of the Act of 1967. When they do make their report, the Board are bound to send a copy of it to the company; and the Board may, in their discretion, publish it, if they think fit, to the public at large.

'Seeing that their work and their report may lead to such consequences, I am clearly of the opinion that the inspectors must act fairly. This is a duty which rests on them, as on many other bodies, even though they are not judicial, nor quasi-judicial, but only administrative. The inspectors can obtain information in any way they think best, but before they condemn or criticise a man, they must give him a fair opportunity for correcting or contradicting what is said against him. They need not quote chapter and verse. An outline of the charge will usually suffice.

'That is what the inspectors here propose to do, but the directors of the company want more. They want to see the transcripts of the witnesses who speak adversely of them, and to see any documents which may be used against them. They, or some of them, even claim to cross-examine the witnesses.

'In all this the directors go too far. This investigation is ordered in the public interest. It should not be impeded by measures of this kind'.

6 Clauses giving unfettered discretion

1 'If it appears to the Minister'

But here again in these administrative matters we have to deal with 'ouster' clauses. Very often Parliament uses words which seem to put it entirely in the Minister's discretion whether or not to take an administrative decision. It uses such words as 'if it appears to the Minister' or 'if the Minister is satisfied' and so forth. Time and again a Minister has claimed that those words exempt his decision from judicial review. Thus in *Employment Secretary v ASLEF (No. 2)* the Secretary of State was empowered to order a ballot of the workmen if it appeared that industrial action was imminent[1]. I said:

' "If it appears to the Secretary of State"? This, in my opinion, does not mean that the Minister's decision is put beyond challenge. The scope available to the challenger depends very much on the subject-matter with which the Minister is dealing. In this case I would think that, if the Minister does not act in good faith, or if he acts on extraneous considerations which ought not to influence him, or if he plainly misdirects himself in fact or in law, it may well be that a court would interfere; but when he honestly takes a view of the facts or the law which could reasonably be entertained, then his decision is not to be set aside simply because thereafter someone thinks that his view was wrong. After all, this is an emergency procedure. It has to be set in motion quickly, when there is no time for minute analysis of facts or of law. The whole process would be made of no

1. [1972] 2 QB 455 at 492-3.

97

effect if the Minister's decision was afterwards to be conned over word by word, letter by letter, to see if he has in any way misdirected himself. That cannot be right'.

Then there was a case in which the Home Secretary claimed to revoke a television licence for which Mr. Congreve – a solicitor in a City firm – had paid the licence fee of £12 in advance. He claimed to revoke the licence by a section in an Act of Parliament which gave him a power to revoke it. The Judge at first instance held that the Home Secretary could do it. But the Court of Appeal held that he could not. The case is *Congreve v Home Office*[1] . I said:

'But now the question comes: can the Minister revoke the overlapping licence which was issued so lawfully? He claims that he can revoke it by virtue of the discretion given him by section 1 (4) of the Act. But I think not. The licensee has paid £12 for the 12 months. If the licence is to be revoked – and his money forfeited – the Minister would have to give good reasons to justify it. Of course, if the licensee had done anything wrong – if he had given a cheque for £12 which was dishonoured, or if he had broken the conditions of the licence – the Minister could revoke it. But when the licensee has done nothing wrong at all, I do not think the Minister can lawfully revoke the licence, at any rate, not without offering him his money back, and not even then except for good cause. If he should revoke it without giving reasons, or for no good reason, the courts can set aside his revocation and restore the licence. It would be a misuse of the power conferred on him by Parliament: and these courts have the authority – and, I would add, the duty – to correct a misuse of power by a Minister or his department, no matter how much he may resent it or warn us of the consequences if we do. *Padfield v Minister of Agriculture, Fisheries and Food* [1968] AC 997 is proof of what I say. It shows that when a Minister is given a discretion – and exercises it for reasons which are bad in law – the courts can interfere so as to get him back on to the right road.

1. [1976] QB 629.

. . . .

'The conduct of the Minister, or the conduct of his department, has been found by the Parliamentary Commissioner to
be maladministration. I go further. I say it was unlawful. His
trump card was a snare and a delusion. He had no right whatever to refuse to issue an overlapping licence, or, if issued, to
revoke it. His original demand, "Pay £6 or your licence will
be revoked", was clearly unlawful — in the sense that it was a
misuse of power — especially as there was no offer to refund
the £12, or any part of it. . . . The licence is granted for 12
months and cannot be revoked simply to enable the Minister
to raise more money. Want of money is no reason for
revoking a licence. The real reason, of course, in this case was
that the department did not like people taking out overlapping licences so as to save money. But there was nothing
in the Regulations to stop it. It was perfectly lawful: and the
department's dislike of it cannot afford a good reason for
revoking them'.

2 'If the Minister is satisfied'

A similar point arose in a case where the Secretary for
Education ordered a local education authority to turn its
grammar schools into comprehensive schools. The Statute
enabled him to do it if he were 'satisfied' that the local
authority was acting 'unreasonably'. The case is *Education
Secretary v Tameside BC*[1] . I reviewed the history of such a
phrase in the following passage:

'So far as "satisfied" is concerned, it is suggested — and was
suggested by the chief officers of the local authority on June
21, 1976 — that once the Secretary of State said that he was
"satisfied" his decision could not be challenged in the courts
unless it was shown to have been made in bad faith. We were
referred by Mr. Bingham to *Liversidge v Anderson* [1942]
AC 206, where Lord Atkin drew attention to cases where the

1. [1977] AC 1014.

Defence Regulations required the Secretary of State to be "satisfied" of something or other. Lord Atkin said, at p. 233: "In all these cases it is plain that unlimited discretion is given to the Secretary of State, assuming as everyone does that he acts in good faith". . . . Those statements were made, however, in relation to regulations in wartime or immediately after the war when the decisions of the executive had to be implemented speedily and without question. Those statements do not apply today. Much depends on the matter about which the Secretary of State has to be satisfied. If he is to be satisfied on a matter of opinion, that is one thing. But if he has to be satisfied that someone has been guilty of some discreditable or unworthy or unreasonable conduct, that is another. To my mind, if a statute gives a minister power to take drastic action if he is "satisfied" that a local authority has acted or is proposing to act improperly or unreasonably, then the minister should obey all the elementary rules of fairness before he finds that the local authority is guilty or before he takes drastic action overruling them. He should give the party affected notice of the charge of impropriety or unreasonableness and a fair opportunity of dealing with it. I am glad to see that the Secretary of State did so in this case. He had before him the written proposals of the new council and he met their leaders. In addition, however, the minister must direct himself properly in law. He must call his own attention to the matters he is bound to consider. He must exclude from his consideration matters which are irrelevant to that which he has to consider and the decision to which he comes must be one which is reasonable in this sense: that it is, or can be, supported with good reasons or at any rate is a decision which a reasonable person might reasonably reach. Such is, I think, plain from *Padfield v Minister of Agriculture, Fisheries and Food* [1968] AC 997 which is a landmark in our administrative law and which we had in mind in *Secretary of State for Employment v ASLEF (No. 2)* [1972] 2 QB 455, 493, 510. So much for the requirements if the minister is to be "satisfied".

100

. . . .

'In the circumstances, it seems to me that the minister's directions were not validly made in accordance with the Act of Parliament'.

The decision of the Court of Appeal was upheld in the House of Lords when Lord Wilberforce expressly approved what was said in the *ASLEF* case.

7 Prerogative power

1 Freddie Laker's 'Skytrain'

Those 'ouster' clauses were inserted by Parliament into Statutes. But there was a more ominous claim by a Minister yet to be made. It was a claim that he had a prerogative power which could not be examined in the Courts. Freddie Laker had an exciting project for putting 'Skytrain' into the air. It was blocked by the Secretary of State who said he could stop it by virtue of his prerogative. The Courts rejected his claim. 'Skytrain' took off. It revolutionised air-travel. The case is reported in *Laker Airways v Department of Trade*[1]. This is how I dealt with the claim:

'The Attorney-General contended that the power of the Secretary of State "to withdraw" the designation was a prerogative power which could not be examined in the courts. It was a power arising under a treaty which, he said, was outside the cognizance of the courts. The Attorney-General recognised that by withdrawing the designation, the Secretary of State would put a stop to Skytrain, but he said that he could do it all the same. No matter that Laker Airways had expended £6 million to £7 million on the faith of the designation, the Secretary of State could withdraw it without paying a penny compensation.

. . . .

'Much of the modern thinking on the prerogative power of the executive stems from John Locke's treatise on the *True End of Civil Government*, which I have read again with much

1. [1977] QB 643.

102

profit, especially chapter 14, "Of Prerogative". It was the source from which Sir William Blackstone drew in his *Commentaries;* and on which Viscount Radcliffe based his opinion in *Burmah Oil Co Ltd v Lord Advocate.* The prerogative is a discretionary power exercisable by the executive government for the public good, in certain spheres of governmental activity for which the law has made no provision, such as the war prerogative (of requisitioning property for the defence of the realm), or the treaty prerogative (of making treaties with foreign powers). The law does not interfere with the proper exercise of the discretion by the executive in those situations: but it can set limits by defining the bounds of the activity: and it can intervene if the discretion is exercised improperly or mistakenly. That is a fundamental principle of our constitution. It derives from two of the most respected of our authorities. In 1611 when the King, as the executive government, sought to govern by making proclamations, Sir Edward Coke declared that: "the King hath no prerogative, but that which the law of the land allows him": see the *Proclamations' Case* (1611) 12 Co Rep 74, 76. In 1765 Sir William Blackstone added his authority, *Commentaries,* vol I, p. 252:

"For prerogative consisting (as Mr Locke has well defined it) in the discretionary power of acting for the public good, where the positive laws are silent, if that discretionary power be abused to the public detriment, such prerogative is exerted in an unconstitutional manner".

'Quite recently the House of Lords set a limit to the war prerogative when it declared that, even in time of war, the property of a British subject cannot be requisitioned or demolished without making compensation to the owner of it. It has also circumscribed the treaty prerogative by holding that it cannot be used to violate the legal rights of a British subject, except on being liable for any damage he suffered.

'Seeing that the prerogative is a discretionary power to be exercised for the public good, it follows that its exercise can be examined by the courts just as any other discretionary power which is vested in the executive. At several times in

our history, the executive have claimed that a discretion given by the prerogative is unfettered: just as they have claimed that a discretion given by statute or by regulation is unfettered. On some occasions the judges have upheld these claims of the executive – notably in the *Ship Money* case, *R v Hampden* (1637) 3 State Tr 826 and in one or two cases during the Second World War, and soon after it – but the judges have not done so of late. The two outstanding cases are *Padfield v Minister of Agriculture, Fisheries and Food* [1968] AC 997, and *Secretary of State for Education and Science v Tameside Metropolitan Borough Council* [1977] AC 1014, where the House of Lords have shown that when discretionary powers are entrusted to the executive by statute, the courts can examine the exercise of those powers to see that they are used properly, and not improperly or mistakenly. By "mistakenly" I mean under the influence of a misdirection in fact or in law. Likewise it seems to me that when discretionary powers are entrusted to the executive by the prerogative – in pursuance of the treaty-making power – the courts can examine the exercise of them so as to see that they are not used improperly or mistakenly.
. . . .

'We have considered this case at some length because of its constitutional importance. It is a serious matter for the courts to declare that a minister of the Crown has exceeded his powers. So serious that we think hard before doing it. But there comes a point when it has to be done. These courts have the authority – and I would add, the duty – in a proper case, when called upon to inquire into the exercise of a discretionary power by a minister or his department. If it is found that the power has been exercised improperly or mistakenly so as to impinge unjustly on the legitimate rights or interests of the subject, then these courts must so declare. They stand, as ever, between the executive and the subject, alert, as Lord Atkin said in a famous passage – "alert to see that any coercive action is justified in law": see *Liversidge v Anderson* [1942] AC 206, 244. To which I would add, alert to see that a discretionary power is not exceeded or misused. In this case the judge has upheld this principle. He has declared that the minister did exceed his powers. I agree with him. I would dismiss the appeal'.

8 The ultra vires clause

1 The _Ashbridge_ case

Yet there is one more 'ouster' clause to be considered. I have
left it till last because there is much controversy about it.
There are two decisions of the House of Lords which are said
to be conflicting about it.

In cases under the Housing Acts, there is a proviso that a
person aggrieved by an Order may question its validity within
six weeks, but unless he does so within that time, the Order
'shall not be questioned in any legal proceedings whatever'. It
is specifically provided also, that even within the six weeks,
he can only question its validity 'on the ground that it is not
within the powers of this Act or that any requirement of
this Act has not been complied with'. In _Smith v East Elloe
RDC_[1] the majority of the Law Lords gave it a narrow literal
meaning, so that, even within six weeks, the Court could only
quash the order if it went beyond what was authorised by
the Statute. But nine years later, by a remarkable turn of
events, that narrow literal meaning was rejected. The one
who did it – strange to relate – was the Minister himself;
through his mouthpiece – the Treasury Devil. The case was
Ashbridge Investments Ltd v Minister of Housing[2]. I
remember it well because three months earlier we had had
occasion closely to consider the section and knew of the
difficulty. So I was grateful when, in the _Ashbridge_ case,
counsel for the Minister accepted this view. It was a question
whether on the evidence a building was a 'house' and whether

1. [1956] AC 736.
2. [1965] 1 WLR 1320.

106

it was 'fit for human habitation'. This is how I stated the principle:

'Seeing that that decision is entrusted to the Minister, we have to consider the power of the court to interfere with his decision. It is given in Schedule 4, para. 2. The court can only interfere on the ground that the Minister has gone outside the powers of the Act or that any requirement of the Act has not been complied with. Under this section it seems to me that the court can interfere with the Minister's decision if he has acted on no evidence; or if he has come to a conclusion to which on the evidence he could not reasonably come; or if he has given a wrong interpretation to the words of the statute; or if he has taken into consideration matters which he ought not to have taken into account, or vice versa; or has otherwise gone wrong in law. It is identical with the position when the court has power to interfere with the decision of a lower tribunal which has erred in point of law.

'We have to apply this to the modern procedure whereby the inspector makes his report and the Minister gives his letter of decision, and they are made available to the parties. It seems to me that the court should look at the material which the inspector and the Minister had before them, just as it looks at the material before an inferior court, and see whether on that material the Minister has gone wrong in law'.

Since that case, we have had many cases in which counsel for the Minister has accepted that as correct. It has never been challenged. What is the justification for it? It seems to me that, when the Act conferred powers on the Minister or other authority, it did so in the belief – and on the condition – that the Minister would exercise them in accordance with the law, and exercise a sound discretion in accordance with the requirements of natural justice. If the Minister broke this condition – by going wrong in law, or by acting on irrelevant considerations, or by doing something contrary to natural justice – then he was going outside his powers. Like the cases I have discussed concerning statutory tribunals, he was given jurisdiction on condition that he exercised it in accordance

107

with the law. If he went wrong in law, he was doing something he had no jurisdiction to do. This is in accordance with some words of Lord Pearce in the *Anisminic* case[1] which I quoted in *R v Southampton Justices*[2] :

'Lack of jurisdiction may arise in various ways. . . . While engaged on a proper inquiry, the tribunal may depart from the rules of natural justice; or it may ask itself the wrong questions; or it may take into account matters which it was not directed to take into account. Thereby it would step outside its jurisdiction'.

2 Unguarded statements

Now I have to make a confession. I made some unguarded statements in a recent case on this subject. My only excuse is that it was *ex tempore.* The judgment was not reserved. The case was *R v Secretary of State for the Environment, ex parte Ostler*[3]. It was a case where the Minister made a compulsory purchase order for a piece of land at Boston. The order was made in 1974. The land was acquired. Much work was done on it. Afterwards the landowner alleged that there was a want of natural justice, and that there was a want of good faith. Looking at it with hindsight it seems to me that if the landowner had come within the six weeks and had proved that allegation, he ought to have succeeded. No doubt the Minister's decision was an administrative decision, but that gives no exemption from judicial review. If the decision was reached contrary to natural justice or in bad faith, it was beyond the power of the Minister: because his power was only conferred on him on condition that he reached his decision in good faith in accordance with natural justice. So it would be a nullity and void just as the order in the *Anisminic* case. So I would wish that the decision in *Ostler*'s case had rested on this last paragraph:

1. [1969] 2 AC 147 at 195.
2. [1976] QB 11 at 21.
3. [1977] QB 122.

'Looking at it broadly, it seems to me that the policy underlying the statute is that when a compulsory purchase order
has been made, then if it has been wrongly obtained or made,
a person aggrieved should have a remedy. But he must come
promptly. He must come within six weeks. If he does so, the
court can and will entertain his complaint. But if the six
weeks expire without any application being made, the court
cannot entertain it afterwards. The reason is because, as soon
as that time has elapsed, the authority will take steps to
acquire property, demolish it and so forth. The public interest
demands that they should be safe in doing so. Take this very
case. The inquiry was held in 1973. The orders made early in
1974. Much work has already been done under them. It
would be contrary to the public interest that the demolition
should be held up or delayed by further evidence or
inquiries'.

Part three

Locus standi

Introduction

Now I come to a matter of moment. When there is an abuse
or misuse of power, who can bring a case before the Court?
Can any member of the public come? Or must he have some
private right of his own?

During the 19th century the Courts were reluctant to let
anyone come unless he had a particular grievance of his own.
He had usually to show that he had some legal right of his
own that had been infringed or some property of his own
that had been injuriously affected. It was not enough that he
was one of the public who was complaining in company with
hundreds or thousands of others. But during the 20th
century the position has been much altered. In most cases
now the ordinary individual can come to the Courts. He will
be heard if he has a 'sufficient interest' in the matter in hand.
But that test of a 'sufficient interest' is very elusive. It has yet
to be worked out by the Courts. In this part I will seek to
trace its development.

1 Modern extensions

1 'Person aggrieved'

In many statutes it is enacted that, in case of non-compliance, a 'person aggrieved' may complain to the Courts or to a tribunal. During the 19th century those words were construed very restrictively. It was said that a man was not a 'person aggrieved' unless he himself had suffered particular loss in that he had been injuriously affected in his money or property rights. He was not 'aggrieved' simply because he had a grievance. That was laid down in 1880 by a distinguished Judge, Lord Justice James, in the *Sidebotham case*[1]. But a case came before Lord Justice Parker and myself in 1957 when we departed from that old test. It is a case which is only reported in the Local Government Reports – *R v Thames Magistrates' Court*[2]. It was about a pitch in a street market in Bermondsey. The magistrates had awarded the pitch to a seller of jellied eels. But a newspaper seller thought that he ought to have had the pitch. He had no legal right to the pitch. But we held that he had a *locus standi* and quashed the order of the magistrates. This was followed a few years later by the case of a ratepayer who said that the valuation list of the whole area had not been properly prepared. He was not able to show that his own property was rated wrongly. His only complaint was that the whole list was wrong. In this

1. (1880) 14 Ch D 458 at 465.
2. (1957) 5 LGR 129.

case, *R v Paddington Valuation Officer, ex parte Peachey Property Corpn Ltd*[1] , I said:

'The question is whether the Peachey Property Corporation are "persons aggrieved" so as to be entitled to ask for certiorari or mandamus. Mr. Blain contended that they are not persons aggrieved because, even if they succeeded in increasing all the gross values of other people in the Paddington area, it would not make a pennyworth of difference to them . . . . But I do not think grievances are to be measured in pounds, shillings and pence. If a ratepayer or other person finds his name included in a valuation list which is invalid, he is entitled to come to the court and apply to have it quashed. He is not to be put off by the plea that he has suffered no damage, any more than the voters were in *Ashby v White*. The court would not listen, of course, to a mere busybody who was interfering in things which did not concern him. But it will listen to anyone whose interests are affected by what has been done . . . . So here it will listen to any ratepayer who complains that the list is invalid'.

This was afterwards approved by the House of Lords in *Arsenal Football Club v Ende*[2] .

2 The Prerogative Orders

The common law Courts had three great writs by which they restrained the abuse or misuse of power. We must still call them by their old names in Norman-French — certiorari, mandamus and prohibition. But at the outset I must point out that in general these remedies can only be used against public authorities exercising statutory powers. For instance if a government department or a local authority or any other public authority does wrong in not fulfilling its statutory duties, any individual with a sufficient interest can come to the Courts and ask for the wrong to be put right. But these remedies are not available against non-public authorities

1. [1966] 1 QB 380 at 400—1.
2. [1977] 2 WLR 974.

exercising non-statutory duties. They are not available, therefore, against the big industrial concerns, or the great trade unions.

So far as *locus standi* is concerned, the Courts of common law, when granting certiorari, mandamus, or prohibition, have always kept their options open. They have held that it is in the discretion of the Court whom it shall hear: and whether to grant such a remedy or not. The tendency in the past was to limit them to persons who had a particular grievance of their own over and above the rest of the public. But in recent years there has been a remarkable series of cases in which private persons have come to the Court and have been heard. There is now a much wider concept of *locus standi* when complaint is made against a public authority. It extends to anyone who is not a mere busybody but is coming to the Court on behalf of the public at large.

2 The *Blackburn* cases

1 A matter of constitutional significance

The principal figure in this movement is Mr. Raymond
Blackburn. He was at one time a Member of Parliament. He
is a fluent speaker. He is always concise and to the point. He
has come before the Court of Appeal on many occasions.
Always in person. Always on some matter of public concern.
Nearly always his intervention has proved most useful.

In one case he raised a matter of great constitutional
significance. It is *Blackburn v Attorney-General*[1]. When the
Government was about to join the Common Market, he
brought an action in the Courts challenging the Government's
right to do it. He sought a declaration that, by signing the
Treaty of Rome, Her Majesty's Government would be
surrendering in part the sovereignty of the Crown in
Parliament; and that it had no right to do so. The Court
heard that argument and rejected it. But on the question of
locus standi to claim a declaration, I said:

'A point was raised as to whether Mr. Blackburn has any
standing to come before the Court. That is not a matter on
which we need rule today. He says that he feels strongly and
that it is a matter in which many people in this country are
concerned. I would not myself rule him out on the ground
that he has no standing. But I do rule him out on the ground

1. [1971] 1 WLR 1037.

118

that these Courts will not impugn the treaty-making power of Her Majesty'.

And, as a result, the law was enforced.

2 The gaming clubs of London

Another case concerned gaming houses. Mr. Blackburn had made a diligent inquiry on his own as to what went on in the big gambling clubs of London. He discovered that they were openly breaking the law. He took it up with the Metropolitan Police. He found out that the police were failing to prosecute because of a 'policy decision' which had been issued to them. Mr. Blackburn applied to the Court for a mandamus to compel the Commissioner of Police to do his duty. Mr. Blackburn came just as a private citizen. He had no greater interest than any other member of the public. He came just to ask that the law be enforced. It was submitted that he had no *locus standi*. But we did hear him. And, as a result, the policy decision was revoked. The law was enforced. It is reported as *R v Commissioner of Police of the Metropolis, ex parte Blackburn*[1]. It is so important – not only on *locus standi*, but also on police powers – that I venture to quote from it:

'In 1966 Mr. Blackburn was concerned about the way in which the big London clubs were being run. He went to see a representative of the Commissioner of the Police of the Metropolis and told him that illegal gaming was taking place in virtually all London casinos. He was given to understand, he says, that action would be taken. But nothing appeared to be done . . . .

'The policy decision was a confidential instruction issued to senior officers of the Metropolitan Police . . . . It was dated April 22, 1966, and was in effect an instruction to take no proceedings against clubs for breach of the gaming laws unless there were complaints of cheating or they had become haunts of criminals . . . .

'The result of the policy decision was that thenceforward,

1. [1968] 2 QB 118.

119

in this great metropolis, the big gaming clubs were allowed to carry on without any interference by the police. We were told that in one or two cases observations had previously been started: but after this policy decision they were discontinued. No prosecutions were instituted in the metropolis against these clubs. That is what Mr. Blackburn complains of. He says that the policy decision was erroneous and that it was the duty of the commissioner to prosecute. To this I now turn . . . .

'I hold it to be the duty of the Commissioner of Police of the Metropolis, as it is of every chief constable, to enforce the law of the land. He must take steps so to post his men that crimes may be detected; and that honest citizens may go about their affairs in peace. He must decide whether or no suspected persons are to be prosecuted; and, if need be, bring the prosecution or see that it is brought. But in all these things he is not the servant of anyone, save of the law itself. No Minister of the Crown can tell him that he must, or must not, keep observation on this place or that; or that he must, or must not, prosecute this man or that one. Nor can any police authority tell him so. The responsibility for law enforcement lies on him. He is answerable to the law and to the law alone . . . .

'A question may be raised as to the machinery by which he could be compelled to do his duty. On principle, it seems to me that once a duty exists, there should be a means of enforcing it. This duty can be enforced, I think, either by action at the suit of the Attorney-General or by the prerogative writ of mandamus. I am mindful of the cases cited by Mr. Worsley which he said limited the scope of mandamus. But I would reply that mandamus is a very wide remedy which has always been available against public officers to see that they do their public duty . . . . No doubt the party who applies for mandamus must show that he has sufficient interest to be protected and that there is no other equally convenient remedy. But once this is shown, the remedy of mandamus is available, in case of need, even against the Commissioner of Police of the Metropolis.

120

'Can Mr. Blackburn invoke the remedy of mandamus here? It is I think an open question whether Mr. Blackburn has a sufficient interest to be protected. No doubt any person who was adversely affected by the action of the commissioner in making a mistaken policy decision would have such an interest. The difficulty is to see how Mr. Blackburn himself has been affected. But without deciding that question, I turn to see whether it is shown that the Commissioner of Police of the Metropolis has failed in his duty . . . .

'. . . . On December 30, 1967, the commissioner issued a statement in which he said: "It is the intention of the Metropolitan Police to enforce the law as it has been interpreted". That implicitly revoked the policy decision of April 22, 1966; and the commissioner by his counsel gave an undertaking to the court that that policy decision would be officially revoked. We were also told that immediate steps are being taken to consider the "goings-on" in the big London clubs with a view to prosecution if there is anything unlawful. That is all that Mr. Blackburn or anyone else can reasonably expect.

This case has shown a deplorable state of affairs. The law has not been enforced as it should. The lawyers themselves are at least partly responsible. The niceties of drafting and the refinements of interpretation have led to uncertainties in the law itself. This has discouraged the pllice from keeping observation and taking action. But it does not, I think, exempt them also from their share of the responsibility. The proprietors of gaming houses have taken advantage of the situation. By one device after another they have kept ahead of the law. As soon as one device has been held unlawful, they have started another. But the day of reckoning is at hand. No longer will we tolerate these devices. The law must be sensibly interpreted so as to give effect to the intentions of Parliament; and the police must see that it is enforced. The rule of law must prevail'.

That last paragraph was put to good use by a cartoonist. He portrayed a man with a sandwich-board on which was written: 'The day of reckoning is at hand'. The sandwich-man

121

had been knocked down by the proprietor of a gambling club. Underneath was the caption with the stricken sandwich-man saying: 'Dear Friend, I repeat — I am *not* Lord Denning'. The High Court journalists presented me with the original of this cartoon.

That case had important consequences. The Home Secretary (Mr. James Callaghan) invited me to see him to discuss the reform of the law by introducing a licensing system. It was reformed — to the good of all. It is the best illustration I can give in support of this proposition:

Every responsible citizen has an interest in seeing that the law in enforced: and that is sufficient interest in itself to warrant his applying for certiorari or mandamus to see that it is enforced.

3 Pornography in Soho

This principle was accepted as correct in another important case brought by Mr. Blackburn. This time he discovered that the laws against pornography were not being enforced. It led to a complete overhaul of the Obscene Publications Squad of the Metropolitan Police and in due course to the prosecution of several senior officers for corruption. This time Mr. Blackburn again came in person. He had no interest except that his children might see the publications — just as anyone else's children. We heard him and were ready to grant a mandamus against the Commissioner of Police — except that, as it happened, we were told that the Commissioner had recently taken the position in hand. It was a new Commissioner, Sir Robert Mark. He was a police officer of such outstanding qualities that we were confident that he would clear it up. And he did so. This case, *R v Police Commissioner, ex parte Blackburn*[1], is such an important illustration of the principle that again I would quote from it:

'Nearly five years ago Mr. Blackburn came before us saying that the Commissioner of Police was not doing his duty

1. [1973] QB 241.

"Dear friend, I repeat – I am not Lord Denning."

in regard to gambling clubs: see *R v Commissioner of Police of the Metropolis, ex parte Blackburn* [1968] 2 QB 118. He comes again today: but this time it is in regard to obscene publications. He comes with his wife out of concern, he says, for their five children. He draws our attention to the shops in Soho which sell "hard" pornography (that is, publications which are extremely obscene) .... Mr. Blackburn condemned the evil in a telling phrase. Pornography, he said, is powerful propaganda for promiscuity. So it is for perversions. To those who come under its influence, it is altogether bad. We have been shown examples of it. The court below declined to look at them. We felt it our duty to do so, distasteful as it is. They are disgusting in the extreme. Prominent are the pictures. As examples of the art of coloured photography, they would earn the highest praise. As examples of the sordid side of life, they are deplorable .... Mr. Blackburn's principal point was a legal one. He said that there was no legal justification for the police referring all cases to the director (Director of Public Prosecutions). It causes delay. They can and should act at once without his advice. I have therefore looked into the law: and I find that Mr. Blackburn has a point worthy of serious consideration. ....

'In *R v Commissioner of Police of the Metropolis, ex parte Blackburn,* we made it clear that, in the carrying out of their duty of enforcing the law, the police have a discretion with which the courts will not interfere. There might, however, be extreme cases in which he was not carrying out his duty. And then we would. I do not think this is a case for our interference. In the past the commissioner has done what he could under the existing system and with the available manpower. The new commissioner is doing more. He is increasing the number of the Obscene Publications Squad to 18 and he is reforming it and its administration. No more can reasonably be expected.

'The plain fact is, however, that the efforts of the police have hitherto been largely ineffective. Mr. Blackburn amply demonstrated it by going out from this court and buying these pornographic magazines — hard and soft — at shops all over the place. I do not accede to the suggestion that the police turn a blind eye to pornography or that shops get a "tip-off" before the police arrive. The cause of the ineffectiveness lies with the system and the framework in which the police have to operate . . . . If the people of this country want pornography to be stamped out, the legislature must amend the Obscene Publications Act 1959 so as to make it strike unmistakably at pornography: and it must define the powers and duties of the police so as to enable them to take effective measures for the purpose. The police may well say to Parliament: "Give us the tools and we will finish the job". But, without efficient tools, they cannot be expected to stamp it out. Mr. Blackburn has served a useful purpose in drawing the matter to our attention: but I do not think it is a case for mandamus'.

Lord Justice Phillimore was very suspicious of what was going on: and his suspicions, as things turned out, were amply justified. He said:

'It seems obvious, from the evidence before us, that the police searches have been far less effective than the activities of Mr. Blackburn. It is not for a member of this court to tell the commissioner how to go about his duties, but I wonder how long it is before the identity of every member of the squad is well known in Soho. I suspect that if one of the squad is seen in that area, particularly coming out of one of these shops, any "hard porn" on the premises is likely to be removed with some rapidity in order to anticipate the probable search. In my judgment the evidence put before us amply justifies the view of Lawton LJ that the whole subject merits inquiry, and indeed Mr. Blackburn has done a public service in bringing the whole situation into the open'.

4 Censorship by the GLC

There is one further case in which Mr. Raymond Blackburn again came in person. He found that pornographic films were

125

being exhibited in London: and the Greater London Council were doing nothing to stop them. He applied for a writ of prohibition and he succeeded. In the course of it, I sought to summarise the law in regard to those cases where an ordinary citizen comes and says that a government department, or a person or body set up by statute, is not doing its duty. The case was *R v GLC, ex parte Blackburn*[1] . I said:

'It was suggested that Mr. Blackburn has no sufficient interest to bring these proceedings against the GLC. It is a point which was taken against him by the Commissioner of Police: see *R v Commissioner of Police of the Metropolis, ex parte Blackburn* . . . and against the late Mr. McWhirter of courageous memory by the Independent Broadcasting Authority . . . . On this point, I would ask: Who then can bring proceedings when a public authority is guilty of a misuse of power? Mr. Blackburn is a citizen of London. His wife is a ratepayer. He has children who may be harmed by the exhibition of pornographic films. If he has no sufficient interest, no other citizen has. I think he comes within the principle which I stated in *McWhirter's* case [1973] QB 629, 649, which I would recast today so as to read:
"I regard it as a matter of high constitutional principle that if there is good ground for supposing that a government department or a public authority is transgressing the law, or is about to transgress it, in a way which offends or injures thousands of Her Majesty's subjects, then any one of those offended or injured can draw it to the attention of the courts of law and seek to have the law enforced, and the courts in their discretion can grant whatever remedy is appropriate".
'The applications by Mr. Blackburn and Mr. McWhirter did much good. They show how desirable such a principle is. One remedy which is always open, by leave of the court, is to apply for a prerogative writ, such as certiorari, mandamus or prohibition. These provide a discretionary remedy and the discretion of the court extends to permitting an application to be made by any member of the public . . . . ; though it will

1. [1976] 1 WLR 550.

refuse it to a mere busybody who is interfering in things which do not concern him . . . . Another remedy open likewise is by asking for a declaration . . . . Also by injunction . . . .
. . . .

'In my opinion, therefore, Mr. Blackburn has made out his case. He has shown that the GLC have been exercising their censorship powers in a manner which is unlawful: because they have been applying a test which is bad in law. If they continue with their present wrong test and in consequence give their consent to films which are grossly indecent, they may be said to be aiding and abetting a criminal offence. In these circumstances this court can and should issue an order of prohibition to stop them'.

Now here I must ask all of you to note that those were all cases where an ordinary citizen sought one of the prerogative remedies — of certiorari, mandamus, or prohibition. These are available against government departments or any person or body set up by statutory authority affecting the rights of individuals. And I have shown, I hope, that any responsible citizen has a sufficient interest — such as to entitle him to be heard — if he complains that the law is not being enforced as it should.

3 Declaration and injunction

1 The courageous Ross McWhirter

The *Blackburn cases* extended *locus standi* for the prerogative writs, but not for the remedies by declaration or injunction. On principle one would think that if an ordinary citizen had *locus standi* for one set of remedies he ought to have *locus standi* for the others. But the law did not develop that way. This is for historical reasons. The common law Courts knew nothing of declarations or injunctions. Those remedies were the preserve of the Court of Chancery. If an ordinary citizen sought to assert a public right, that is, a right which he enjoyed equally with everyone else; or to enforce a public duty, that is, a duty owed to the public at large; then the Court of Chancery held that his only remedy was to apply to the Attorney-General for his consent to bring a 'relator' action. If the Attorney-General consented, the action proceeded as an action by the Attorney-General himself 'on the relation of' that person: but if the Attorney-General did not consent, that person could do nothing. The Court of Appeal ventured to challenge this in an important case brought by another remarkable person – who was concerned for the public good – Mr. Ross McWhirter. He was one of twin brothers who produced the Guinness Book of Records. He came before us in person on three or four occasions but only one was reported. He took a stand against evil. In particular, against terrorism. He was always courageous in support of the rule of law. He died in support of it. On coming home from work one day, he was shot dead by gunmen on his own doorstep.

Now Mr. Ross McWhirter came to us one afternoon at 3 pm and told us that the television people were going to show a film that evening about an actor called Andy Warhol. He showed us reports by newspaper reporters who had seen it. They said it was outrageous – 'a shocker, the worst ever'. On that information we granted an injunction to stop it being shown. As it happened, we saw it later. It was in fact quite harmless. So far from shocking us, we thought it was dreary and dull. But for present purposes, the important point is whether we were right to hear him or not. The Attorney-General came and told us we ought not to do so unless he (the Attorney-General) agreed to it. By a majority we held that we could hear him, even though the Attorney-General did not consent. This is what I said in *Attorney-General v Independent Broadcasting Authority*[1] :

'When Mr. McWhirter came on Tuesday, January 16, 1973, he represented to us that it was a matter of great urgency. The Independent Broadcasting Authority were proposing, he said, that very evening, to broadcast a television film which did not comply with the statutory requirements laid down by Parliament. He produced evidence, in the shape of newspaper reports, which showed that it contained matter which offended against decency and was likely to be offensive to public feeling. He said that he had put that evidence before the Attorney-General's office, but the Attorney-General had declined to take action ex officio. So he had himself come to the courts to seek an injunction. He claimed that he had a sufficient interest. He was himself the owner of a television set; he had paid his licence fee. When he switched it on, he was entitled to expect that the programme would comply with the statutory requirements. There were thousands like him sitting at home watching. All were entitled to have their privacy respected.

. . . .

'The first point is whether Mr. McWhirter had any *locus standi*

1. [1973] QB 629.

to come to the court at all . . . .This is a point of constitutional significance. We live in an age when Parliament has placed statutory duties on government departments and public authorities — for the benefit of the public — but has provided no remedy for the breach of them. If a government department or a public authority transgresses the law laid down by Parliament, or threatens to trangress it, can a member of the public come to the court and draw the matter to its attention? He may himself be injuriously affected by the breach. So may thousands of others like him. Is each and every one of them debarred from access to the courts? . . . .
. . . .

'In such a situation I am of opinion — and I state it as a matter of principle — that the citizen who is aggrieved has a *locus standi* to come to the courts. He can at least seek a declaration. That is the view expressed in a resourceful book to which Mr. Roger Parker referred us, *Zamir, The Declaratory Judgment* (1962), p. 275. It is based on the celebrated case of *Dyson v Attorney-General* [1911] 1 KB 410; [1912] 1 Ch 158 to which I have just referred. In 1910 the Commissioners of Inland Revenue sent out a questionnaire which they required eight millions of people to answer. It was illegal. It was contrary to an Act of Parliament. A private individual, Mr. Dyson, objected to it. He came to the courts and sought a declaration. At that time he could not sue the Commissioners of Inland Revenue themselves. So he sued the Attorney-General as representing them. The Attorney-General regarded his action as frivolous and vexatious. He sought to strike it out . . . . It is plain that he would never have given leave to Mr. Dyson to bring the action. This court refused to strike the action out. It declared that the questionnaire was illegal and that Mr. Dyson was under no obligation to comply with it.
. . . .

'In the light of all this I am of opinion that, in the last resort, if the Attorney-General refuses leave in a proper case, or improperly or unreasonably delays in giving leave, or his machinery works too slowly, then a member of the public who has a sufficient interest can himself apply to the court itself. He can apply for a declaration and, in a proper case, for an injunction, joining the Attorney-General, if need be, as defendant. In these days when government departments and public authorities have such great powers and influence, this is a most important safeguard for the ordinary citizens of this country: so that they can see that those great powers and influence are exercised in accordance with law. I would not restrict the circumstances in which an individual may be held to have a sufficient interest. Take the recent cases when Mr. Raymond Blackburn applied to the court on the ground that the Commissioner of Police was not doing his duty in regard to gaming or pornography. Mr. Blackburn had a sufficient interest, even though it was shared with thousands of others. I doubt whether the Attorney-General would have given him leave to use his name: see *R v Commissioner of Police for the Metropolis, ex parte Blackburn* [1968] 2 QB 118, 137, 139. But we heard Mr. Blackburn in his own name. His intervention was both timely and useful.

'. . . . As Mr. McWhirter's case presented to us, it was of a highly exceptional character. There was evidence from which it could be inferred that the Independent Broadcasting Authority had not done their duty: that the Attorney-General had refused to take action himself ex officio: and that there was no time to do all the things necessary for a relator action. It was a case of the last resort: and I hold that we were entitled to hear him as we did. I have said so much because I regard it as a matter of high constitutional principle that if there is good ground for supposing that a government department or a public authority is transgressing the law, or is about to transgress it, in a way which offends or injures thousands of Her Majesty's subjects, then in the last resort any one of those offended or injured can draw it to the attention of the courts of law and seek to have the law enforced. But this, I would emphasise, is only in the last resort when there is no other remedy reasonably available to secure that the law is obeyed.

'It was suggested that the person aggrieved should approach

131

the Minister so that he should give a notice under section 18 (3) of the Television Act 1964, or should approach his Member of Parliament so that he could ask a question in the House. But those do not seem to me to be remedies that are reasonably available. They are not so accessible. They are not so speedy or effective. They are not so independent as the courts of law'.

2 The high constitutional principle

Now I regret to say that this high constitutional principle did not find favour with the House of Lords. They disapproved it in the *Gouriet* case[1]. But, as I understand it, this was only on a very narrow ground. It was because of the remedy which Mr. McWhirter was seeking. If he had been in a position to bring one of the prerogative writs such as certiorari, mandamus or prohibition, we could, as I understand it, have heard him. Undoubtedly the Independent Television Authority was a statutory authority against whom any of the prerogative writs could lie. It seems to me a strange state of the law that Mr. McWhirter should have sufficient interest to bring certiorari, mandamus or prohibition: but not sufficient interest to bring a claim for a declaration or injunction. This anomaly has, however, been removed by the new Rules of Court to which I now turn. So the high constitutional principle is, I hope, restored in its entirety.

1. [1978] AC 435.

4 The remedy of judicial review

In January 1978 the new Rules of Court were brought into force. Order 53 introduced a comprehensive system of judicial review. By Rules 1(1) and 1(2) it enables an application to cover, under one umbrella, all the remedies of certiorari, mandamus and prohibition and also a declaration and injunction. In respect of all these remedies, it lays down one simple test of *locus standi* in Order 53, Rule 3(5). It is this: the applicant must have 'a sufficient interest in the matter to which the application relates'. What is the test of 'sufficient interest'? The Rules Committee have not attempted a definition; but I would suggest that it is legitimate to adopt the test laid down in the *Blackburn* and *McWhirter* cases. The Court will not listen to a busybody who is interfering in things which do not concern him, but it will listen to an ordinary citizen who comes asking that the law should be declared and enforced, even though he is only one of a hundred, or one of a thousand, or one of a million who are affected by it. As a result, therefore, of the new procedure, it can I hope be said that we have in England an *actio popularis* by which an ordinary citizen can enforce the law for the benefit of all — as against public authorities in respect of their statutory duties.

5 Private rights

This discourse would not have been complete unless I drew attention to another way in which an ordinary citizen can enforce the public law. It is when he has a private right. This was emphasised in the recent case of *Ex parte Island Records*[1]. A pop group played and sang a hit song live in a theatre. A recording company made a record of it. A person in the audience had a tiny machine in his pocket. He recorded on tape the exciting performance by the pop group; then from the tape he made cassettes or gramophone records and sold them on the black market. The performers had no copyright in their performance. Nor had the recording company. The man in the audience was guilty of a criminal offence contrary to the Musical Performers' Acts. The question was whether the performers or recording company could get an injunction to restrain the criminal offence. The Court of Appeal held that they could. I said:

'The result of *Gouriet's* case[2] may be summarised thus: when a statute creates a criminal offence — prescribing a penalty for the breach of it but not giving any civil remedy — the general rule is that no private individual can bring an action to enforce the criminal law, either by way of an injunction or by damages. It must be left to the Attorney-General to bring an action, either of his own motion or at the instance of a member of the public who "relates" the facts to him.

1. [1978] 3 WLR 23.
2. [1978] AC 435.

134

'But there is an exception to this rule in any case where the criminal act is not only an offence against the public at large, but also causes or threatens to cause special damage to a private individual. If a private individual can show that he has a private right which is being interfered with by the criminal act — thus causing or threatening to cause him special damage over and above the generality of the public — then he can come to the court as a private individual and ask that his private right be protected . . . . The court can, in those circumstances, grant an injunction to restrain the offender from continuing or repeating his criminal act . . . .

'The exception depends, however, on the private individual having a private right which he is entitled to have protected . . . .

'The question, therefore, becomes this: has the plaintiff a particular right which he is entitled to have protected? To this the answer which runs through all the cases is this: A man who is carrying on a lawful trade or calling has a right to be protected from any unlawful interference with it . . . . It is a right which is in the nature of a right of property. Such as a right to have the access to your premises kept clear without being obstructed by nuisance or smells . . . . : or a right to run a ferry for profit across the river Mersey without being injured by rail traffic contrary to the penal statute . . . . : or a right to prevent spurious notes being circulated to the damage of the plaintiff's interests . . . . : or a right to prevent passing off . . . . : or a right to have your servants come unhindered to work, even though it is only made unlawful by a penal statute . . . . : or a right to have your contractual relations maintained inviolate without interference by others, unless there is just cause or excuse . . . . : or a right in a workman to have his pay slip properly vouched, even though it is only made unlawful by a penal statute . . . . In all these cases the unlawful interference may be a tort, such as fraud or passing-off; or it may be a crime, such as a public nuisance; or a breach of a statute which imposes only criminal penalties: but whatever be the nature of the unlawful interference, the party concerned is entitled to come himself to the courts of law and ask to be protected from the unlawful interference. It is no answer for the defendant to say: "It is a crime: and so you cannot sue me". It would be a sorry state of the law if a man could excuse himself by such a plea — and thus cause special damage with impunity. For the fact must be faced: the criminal law is a broken reed in some of these cases. At any rate in this particular case. The police have not the men or the means to investigate the offence or to track down the offenders or to prosecute them. Nor have they the will. Nor has the Attorney-General. He has, we are told, refused his consent to a relator action — presumably because no public rights are involved. So perforce if the law is to be obeyed — and justice be done — the courts must allow a private individual himself to bring an action against the offender — in those cases where his private rights and interests are specially affected by the breach.

This principle is capable of extension so as to apply not only to rights of property or rights in the nature of it, but to other rights or interests, such as the right of a man to his good name and reputation . . . and his right to the lawful transmission of his mail . . .'.

6 The *Gouriet* case

1 The story is told

Lastly, I come to the *Gouriet* case[1]. It was quite by chance that I sat on that case. On Friday evening, 14 January 1977, I was just about to leave the Courts to walk over Waterloo Bridge. It was 5.30. My train was 6.10. I looked into the clerk's room to say I was going. My clerk told me: 'There is an urgent application to be made tomorrow morning. But there is no need for you to come up for it. There are two Lords Justices in London who can take it'. I asked what it was about. He told me in a sentence: 'The Judge in chambers has just refused an injunction against the Post Office Union. The losers want to appeal'. I said: 'I think I ought to come up and sit on it myself'. So I did. I walked across the bridge, went home by train the 60 miles to Whitchurch, and back by the first train on Saturday morning. It is a very rare thing for a Court now to sit on Saturday mornings though all Courts used to sit regularly on Saturdays before the First War.

On the Saturday morning, I sat with Lords Justices Lawton and Ormrod. Mr. George Newman, a young and able counsel, made the application. It was opposed by Mr. Ian Hunter, equally young and equally able. In outline this was the time-table:

On Thursday evening, 13 January, the General Secretary of the Union, Mr. Tom Jackson during the 9 o'clock television news of the BBC said that the Union of Post Office

1. [1978] AC 435.

workers were going to stop all transmission of mail to South Africa from Sunday for one week. The interviewer put to him that this was unlawful. Mr. Jackson said: 'The laws have never been tested in the Courts. They date from Queen Anne and are more appropriate for dealing with highwaymen and footpads'.

On the next day at 12.45 pm Mr. Gouriet's lawyer went to the Attorney-General's chambers in the Law Courts and asked for his consent to bring an action to stop the proposed breach of the law. Three hours later, at 3.32 pm, the Attorney-General refused his consent. Within 20 minutes, at 3.50 pm, Mr. Newman applied to the Judge's chambers for an injunction. The hearing took nearly one and a half hours. At 5.15 pm the Judge said: 'I am sorry, but without the consent of the Attorney-General I can do nothing. The Courts are powerless to enforce the law'.

The applicants came at once to my clerk's room. That took five minutes along a long corridor. They asked him if the Court of Appeal could sit early on Saturday morning. He said he would try to arrange it. And did so.

We sat at 10.30 am on the Saturday. The argument took the morning. We granted an injunction to stop any inter-ference with communications with South Africa. I said[1] :

'. . . . It seems to me there is impending a breach of the law directed, encouraged or procured by the executive of this Union of Post Office Workers. That is plain. There is nothing that was urged to the contrary.

'What is to be done about it? Are the courts to stand idly by? Is the Attorney-General the final arbiter as to whether the law should be enforced or not? It is a matter of great constitutional principle . . . .

. . . .

'. . . . All we are asked to do is to make an order on the union saying that it must obey the Act of Parliament. Surely no objection could be taken by anyone in the land to an order in that form'.

1. [1977] 2 WLR 310 at 317.

Our order was effective. The trade union, to its credit, obeyed it. So there was no trouble. The mails went through to South Africa. The breach of the law was averted.

But there were some people who wished to defy our order. The 'Socialist Worker' attacked us. They looked up the shareholdings of the judges. They discovered that my wife had shares in a Company which traded in South Africa — a thing she did not know herself. Yet they used it so as to undermine the confidence of their readers in judicial integrity. They said:

'. . . His wife owns 450 shares in Plesseys, the firm whose arms connection with South Africa were exposed this week. . . No wonder the Lords Justices are so concerned with businessmen who have business dealings with South Africa . . . . These three wealthy bigots, who have never been elected by anyone, have assumed the right to dictate to elected union executives, and even the elected government.
We should defy the law . . . we must re-impose the ban on Grunwick mail, whatever the Courts say'.

Fortunately there were good post-office workers who were not influenced by that calumny. A copy of a leaflet in like terms was sent to me by an ordinary postman, with this letter:

'. . . Enclosed was one of several circulated in our dining halls at the above office this day. Not many, if any, are in agreement with Tom Jackson. I myself feel quite sure that enclosed is sheer contempt of Court . . .'.

No doubt it was contempt of Court: but no one prosecuted the 'Socialist Worker'.

So our order was effective at the time. But the Trade Union appealed to the House of Lords. They held that we had no power to make that order: that the proceedings were misconceived and should have been struck out.

We must, of course, loyally accept the decision of the House of Lords. But I cannot help asking: What would have happened if we had sat idly by and done nothing? or rather, had done what we ought to have done — told Mr. Newman, 'We are not going to listen to you. You have no *locus standi*'. There is no doubt that the Union of Post Office Workers would have gone on with their declared intent. They would have banned all communications with South Africa — for one whole week. That would have caused great inconvenience and loss to many innocent people.

There was also the likelihood of more serious consequences. This would have been regarded by the Union as a precedent which they could follow safely in future cases. There had been a previous case in 1973 when they boycotted the mail to France. At that time there was a Conservative Attorney-General in office — and no action was taken. In the present case a Labour Attorney-General was in office — and did nothing. Such occasions might soon create a precedent. That is the situation about which I made this forecast when I came to give a considered judgment on Wednesday, 27 January:

'What then does it all come to? If the contention of the Attorney-General is correct, it means he is the final arbiter as to whether the law should be enforced or not. If he does not act himself — or refuses to give his consent to his name being used — then the law will not be enforced. If one Attorney-General after another does this, if each in his turn declines to take action against those who break the law — then the law becomes a dead letter. It may be that each Attorney-General would have good reason of his own for not intervening. He may fear the repercussions if he lends the weight of his authority to proceedings against the infringers. But as one like situation follows another — as it does here — it means that a powerful trade union will feel that it can repeat its performance with impunity. It will be above the law. That cannot be.

. . . .

'. . . . To every subject in this land, no matter how powerful, I would use Thomas Fuller's words over 300 years ago: "Be you never so high, the law is above you".

. . . .

140

'. . . . When the Attorney-General comes, as he does here, and tells us that he has a prerogative – a prerogative by which he alone is the one who can say whether the criminal law should be enforced in these courts or not – then I say he has no such prerogative. He has no prerogative to suspend or dispense with the laws of England. If he does not give his consent, then any citizen of the land – any one of the public at large who is adversely affected – can come to this court and ask that the law be enforced. Let no one say that in this we are prejudiced. We have but one prejudice. That is to uphold the law. And that we will do, whatever befall. Nothing shall deter us from doing our duty'.

2 The decision of the House of Lords

Alas, I was too bold. Not only too bold, but altogether wrong. The House of Lords have so declared. They accompanied their decision with a rebuke to the Court of Appeal. Lord Diplock said that our judgment was besmirched with 'some confusion and an unaccustomed degree of rhetoric'[1] and Lord Edmund-Davies said that some of our expressions were 'regrettable'.[2]

But two of their Lordships did suggest that the Attorney-General ought not simply to have refused his consent. He ought to have publicly declared that the law should be obeyed. Lord Wilberforce said[3]:

'The sections (of the Post Office Acts) are perfectly clear as to their meaning without the need for judicial interpretation.

'This being so it is surprising and, I would say, regrettable that, after Mr. Jackson's expressed and broadcast doubts as to their applicability, opportunity was not taken for an authoritative statement that they represent the law and that the law must be obeyed. If such a course had been taken, much of the difficulty which faced the Court of Appeal could have been avoided'.

1. [1978] AC 435 at 496.
2. Ibid. at 506.
3. Ibid. at 475.

And Lord Dilhorne said[1]:

'. . . . If, when he gave his decision on the Friday, the Attorney-General had made a statement that if Mr. Jackson or anyone solicited or endeavoured to procure any officer of the Post Office to detain or delay a postal packet, a criminal offence would be committed, that should have sufficed to dispel Mr. Jackson's doubts and any doubts which had arisen in the minds of members of the Union in consequence of Mr. Jackson's statements on television'.

Those statements show that, in the opinion of the Law Lords, the Attorney-General on the Friday evening should have himself declared the law, and presumably gone on television to tell the trade union that they would be breaking the law. Would such a statement have had any influence on the trade union? No one can say. We do not know whether the Attorney-General considered making a public statement such as the Law Lords suggested. He may have considered it and thought it inappropriate or, what is more likely, it never occurred to him. At any rate, he did not do it: and not having done it, the law would certainly have been broken – all communications with South Africa would have been stopped – unless the Court of Appeal had intervened.

So the great constitutional issue has been settled – by the decision of the House of Lords. There is no possibility of the law being changed by any Government.

So I can only ask this question of the students of our constitution: Were we right or wrong to grant that injunction on that Saturday morning?

3 The effect of the *Gouriet* case

Despite my disappointment the effect of the *Gouriet* case may not be so great as might be supposed. In many cases the plaintiff may be able to assert that a private right of his is being infringed. It may be a private right which he shares in

1. Ibid. at 485.

common with many others. As Lord Wilberforce himself explained in the *Gouriet* case[1] in referring to *Dyson v Attorney-General*[2]:

'A right is none the less a right, or a wrong any the less a wrong, because millions of people have a similar right or may suffer a similar wrong'.

If the case had been brought — not by Mr. Gouriet — but by a firm which communicated daily by telephone, telex or mail to South Africa, such a firm would have *locus standi* because of its private right. It might have failed against the trade union because of the statutory immunity conferred on trade unions: but it might have succeeded against its officers on the ground that it was not done in contemplation or furtherance of a trade dispute. Lord Dilhorne thought there was no trade dispute.

In other cases the defendant may be a public authority which is not fulfilling its statutory duties, and then any person with a 'sufficient interest' can apply under the new Rules of Court for a judicial review, in which he can ask not only for certiorari, mandamus or prohibition, but also a declaration or injunction. If the *Blackburn* cases are correct, they show that a member of the public may have a sufficient interest (even though it is one which he shares with many others) in having the law enforced. The House in the *Gouriet* case did not express any views on the correctness of the *Blackburn* cases[3].

I ask the question therefore — it is one of much importance: Was the Court of Appeal right in hearing Mr. Blackburn? or ought they to have refused him as having no sufficient interest? and said nothing on the points which he raised.

1. Ibid. at 483.
2. [1912] 1 Ch 158.
3. [1978] AC 435 at 495.

Conclusion

In administrative law the question of *locus standi* is the most vexed question of all. I must confess that whenever an ordinary citizen comes to the Court of Appeal and complains that this or that government department — or this or that local authority — or this or that trade union — is abusing or misusing its power — I always like to hear what he has to say. For I remember what Mr. T. P. Curran of the Middle Temple said in the year 1790:

'It is ever the fate of the indolent to find their rights become a prey to the active. The condition upon which God hath given liberty to man is eternal vigilance'.

The ordinary citizen who comes to the Court in this way is usually the vigilant one. Sometimes he is a mere busybody interfering with things which do not concern him. Then let him be turned down. But when he has a point which affects the rights and liberties of all the citizens, then I would hope that he would be heard: for there is no other person or body to whom he can appeal. But I am afraid that not everyone agrees with me.

Part four

Abuse of 'group' powers

Introduction

In the 19th century the individual was predominant in our affairs. In the 20th century it is the group. The industrial scene is dominated by groups — of employers on the one hand — and of employees on the other hand. The nationalised undertakings and large companies control the destinies of thousands and spend millions of money. The associations of workmen — organised officially and unofficially — exert enormous powers over working men and women and have great impact on the daily lives of the people.

Like the powers of government, these powers of the groups are capable of misuse or abuse. Likewise too, the question is: Has the law any means of restraining the abuse or misuse of them?

Many of these groups are described by lawyers as 'voluntary associations'. But that gives no clue to their identity. To know who they are, I will give you some illustrations. The political parties — Labour, Conservative and Liberal — are all voluntary associations. The Trade Unions and the Employers' Associations are all voluntary associations. The professional bodies like the Inns of Court are all voluntary associations. So are the bodies who govern sport, such as the Jockey Club. That catalogue of voluntary associations speaks for itself. They wield tremendous power over every man and woman in the land. They can give or take away his or her right to work. They can put him or her on the dole. They can call strikes or order lockouts. By so doing they can inflict widespread damage — and pain and suffering beyond measure — on thousands and thousands of innocent victims. All in pursuit of their own sectional interests – the interests of their particular group – of their own voluntary association.

The question at once arises: If these groups of people abuse or misuse their powers, can the courts of law do anything to restrain them? It is the most important question affecting society today. None of the old machinery of certiorari, mandamus or prohibition is available against these groups because they are not public authorities. If there is to be machinery, it has to be newly designed and newly made.

The subject must be divided into two chapters. First, those cases where the committee or officers of the associations use their powers unjustly or unfairly against one of their own members. Secondly, where they use their powers so as to inflict damage or suffering on persons who are not members of the group, that is, on non-members or on the public at large.

1 Powers against own members

1 Look at the rules

Thirty years ago there was virtually no means of control available. The Courts had tied their own hands by a fiction of their own devising. They held – contrary to the fact – that these voluntary associations were the product of a contract between the individual members. Each member, it was said, had agreed with the other members to abide by the Rules of the Association; and by those Rules he was bound. No matter how unreasonable they were – no matter how unfair to him – they were binding on him, just as any contract which a man makes is binding. So whenever a member was unfairly treated by the group – or expelled unjustly from the group – then, so long as the Rules permitted it, he had no remedy. Whenever a difference arose between a voluntary association and its members, the Courts said: 'Let us look at the Rules'. Then they got into a pretty pickle. Usually because of the obscurity of the Rules. In point of drafting, the Rules of these Associations are the worst ever. Time and time again they have given the lawyers 'toil, tears and sweat'. We had a lot of tears over the Rules of the Actors' 'Equity' Association[1]. We had a lot of toil and sweat over the Rules of the Labour Party – *Lewis v Heffer*[2]. I trust, however, that they will be construed in the spirit I expressed in *British Equity v Goring*[3]:

'They should be construed, not literally according to the very

1. [1977] ICR 393, [1978] ICR 791.
2. [1978] 1 WLR 1061.
3. [1977] ICR 393 at 396.

letter, but according to the spirit, the purpose, the intend-
ment, which lies behind them, so as to ensure – especially in
a matter affecting the constitution – that they should be
interpreted fairly, having regard to the many interests which
its constitutional code is designed to serve'.

During the last 30 years, the Courts have done much to
protect the individual member against injustice by the
association itself. They have condemned Rules that are in
unreasonable restraint of trade and held them to be invalid.
They have overthrown the decisions of domestic tribunals
which were unjust. They have interfered with the discretion
of committees when exercised unfairly. They have, in
accordance with their long tradition, upheld the weak and
put down the 'oppressor's wrong'.

2 Domestic Tribunals must observe the law

The Courts got off to a slow start. It was in 1951 that I was
first concerned: and I was sorry about the outcome. It was in
Abbott v Sullivan[1]. Mr. Abbott was a cornporter in the
London docks. He went to work whilst six of his gang stayed
away. The Trade Union committee fined him 10s and
ordered him to pay the day's money to the six complainants.
He felt this was unjust. So in the street outside he hit the
convener of the committee. He hit him on the nose. The
convener called the committee together immediately. They
struck Mr. Abbott's name off the register of cornporters.
That meant that he could no longer be employed in the
London docks. He brought an action for damages against the
Union and against the committee and the convener. He
failed. The majority of the Court held that he could get no
damages. I took a different view; and in the hope that some
day some Court may agree with me, I would repeat it here:

'. . . . The jurisdiction of a domestic tribunal such as the
Cornporters' Committee must in the last resort be based

1. [1952] 1 KB 189.

upon contract, express or implied. Outside the regular courts of this country no set of men can sit in judgment on their fellows except so far as Parliament authorises it or the parties agree to it. Sometimes the jurisdiction of a domestic tribunal is contained in a written set of rules to which the parties subscribe, as in the case of the Jockey Club. In other cases it is contained in no written code, but in the custom and practice of a profession, as in the case of the Inns of Court, in which case the consent is not express but is to be inferred from the very fact of joining the profession. So in the case of the cornporters, everyone who applies for admission, and is accepted by the Cornporters' Committee, must be taken to agree to the jurisdiction of the committee as by custom established. These bodies, however, which exercise a mono-poly in an important sphere of human activity, with the power of depriving a man of his livelihood, must act in accordance with the elementary rules of justice. They must not condemn a man without giving him an opportunity to be heard in his own defence: and any agreement or practice to the contrary would be invalid.

'So much is so well established that I need not cite authorities in support of it. The question in this case is: what are the bounds of the jurisdiction of the Cornporters' Committee? They clearly have jurisdiction to deal with breaches of the cornporters' working rules, but have they jurisdiction to deal with a cornporter for a common assault in the street? No evidence was given of any customary jurisdiction in that behalf. Indeed, the evidence was to the contrary . . . . In the circumstances I think the accused man should be convicted by a court of law before he can be removed . . . .

'. . . . Now I come to the question, Is Mr. Abbott entitled to damages for the ultra vires action of the committee? The judge thought not. He said he could not see any legal peg on which to hang an award of damages. I should be sorry to think that, if a wrong has been done, the plaintiff is to go without a remedy simply because no one can find a peg to hang it on. We should then be going back to the days when a man's rights depended on whether he could fit them into a prescribed form of action; whereas in these days the principle to be applied is that where there is a right there should be a remedy. It has been said by high authority that it is an actionable wrong for any man intentionally to injure another without just cause or excuse . . . . If this is correct, there can be no doubt that the conduct of the Cornporters' Committee and Mr. Platt was an actionable wrong; for they intended to deprive the plaintiff of his livelihood and they succeeded in doing so; and they had no just cause or excuse for their action, because they should have known it was ultra vires. But I do not think that this wide proposition has yet been accepted into our law'.

3 The case of the *Showmen's Guild*

Although that view was not acceptable to the majority of the Court, nevertheless three months later — in a Court differently constituted — we took a decisive step forward. We brought domestic tribunals under the control of the Courts. It was in *Lee v The Showmen's Guild*[1]. Frank Lee ran a roundabout called Noah's Ark. He had a recognised pitch at the Bradford Summer Fair. Another showman, William Shaw, claimed the pitch. The Trade Union committee decided in favour of Shaw. They found that Lee has been guilty of 'unfair competition' and fined him £100. Lee brought an action against the Trade Union - the Showmen's Guild — claiming that the committee's decision was invalid. The Court upheld Lee's claim. I said:

'Although the jurisdiction of a domestic tribunal is founded on contract, express or implied, nevertheless the parties are not free to make any contract they like. There are important limitations imposed by public policy. The tribunal must, for instance, observe the principles of natural justice. They must give the man notice of the charge and a reasonable opportunity of meeting it. Any stipulation to the contrary would be invalid. They cannot stipulate for a power to

1. [1952] 2 QB 329.

condemn a man unheard . . . . Another limitation arises out of the well-known principle that parties cannot by contract oust the ordinary courts from their jurisdiction . . . . They can, of course, agree to leave questions of law, as well as questions of fact, to the decision of the domestic tribunal. They can, indeed, make the tribunal the final arbiter on questions of fact, but they cannot make it the final arbiter on questions of law. They cannot prevent its decisions being examined by the courts. If parties should seek, by agreement, to take the law out of the hands of the courts and put it into the hands of a private tribunal, without any recourse at all to the courts in case of error of law, then the agreement is to that extent contrary to public policy and void . . . .

'The question in this case is: to what extent will the courts examine the decisions of domestic tribunals on points of law? This is a new question which is not to be solved by turning to the club cases. In the case of social clubs, the rules usually empower the committee to expel a member who, in their opinion, has been guilty of conduct detrimental to the club; and this is a matter of opinion and nothing else. The courts have no wish to sit on appeal from their decisions on such a matter any more than from the decisions of a family conference. They have, nothing to do with social rights or social duties. On any expulsion they will see that there is fair play. They will see that the man has notice of the charge and a reasonable opportunity of being heard. They will see that the committee observe the procedure laid down by the rules; but they will not otherwise interfere . . . .

'It is very different with domestic tribunals which sit in judgment on the members of a trade or profession. They wield powers as great as, if not greater than, any exercised by the courts of law. They can deprive a man of his livelihood. They can ban him from the trade in which he has spent his life and which is the only trade he knows. They are usually empowered to do this for any breach of their rules, which, be it noted, are rules which they impose and which he has no real opportunity of accepting or rejecting. In theory their powers are based on contract. The man is supposed to have contracted to give·them these great powers; but in practice he has no choice in the matter. If he is to engage in the trade, he has to submit to the rules promulgated by the committee. Is such a tribunal to be treated by these courts on the same footing as a social club? I say no. A man's right to work is just as important to him as, if not more important than, his rights of property. These courts intervene every day to protect rights of property. They must also intervene to protect the right to work.

'But the question still remains: to what extent will the courts intervene? They will, I think, always be prepared to examine the decision to see that the tribunal has observed the law. This includes the correct interpretation of the rules . . . . The courts have never allowed a master to dismiss a servant except in accordance with the terms of the contract between them. So also they cannot permit a domestic tribunal to deprive a member of his livelihood or to injure him in it, unless the contract, on its true construction, gives the tribunal power to do so. I repeat "on its true construction", because I desire to emphasise that the true construction of the contract is to be decided by the courts and by no one else. Sir Frank Soskice argued that it was for the committee of the guild to construe the rules, and that, so long as they put an honest construction on them, their construction was binding on the members, even though it was a wrong construction.

'I cannot agree with that contention. The rules are the contract between the members. The committee cannot extend their jurisdiction by giving a wrong interpretation to the contract, no matter how honest they may be. They have only such jurisdiction as the contract on its true interpretation confers on them, not what they think it confers. The scope of their jurisdiction is a matter for the courts, and not for the parties, let alone for one of them'.

4 Damages for wrongful expulsion

Notice that that decision did not give a member any right to sue his trade union for damages. There was a long-standing authority — dating back to 1915 — saying that he could not. This was most unjust. It was afterwards put right, not by the Court of Appeal, but by the House of Lords. It is a case of the first importance in which the legal position of trade unions came under close consideration. The case is *Bonsor v Musicians' Union*[1]. The Musicians' Union operated a 'closed shop'. Mr. Bonsor was a member but he got into arrear with his subscription. For that reason the secretary of the Union expelled him, without referring it to the committee. Mr. Bonsor brought an action against the Union, claiming that his expulsion was invalid and also claiming damages. We all held that his expulsion was invalid, but the majority of the Court felt bound by the 1915 authority to say that he could not recover damages. I dissented. Nearly two years later the House of Lords reversed that decision and awarded Mr. Bonsor damages[2]. It was too late to do him any good because he had died during the time it took for the case to get to the Lords. Seeing that the House of Lords upheld my dissenting judgment, I may perhaps be excused for setting out the telling facts and the reasoning:

'This case well illustrates the great powers wielded by trade unions at the present day. This union, the Musicians' Union, has the power to dictate both to employers and to workmen. It has in this case excluded the plaintiff from the occupation as a musician in which he has spent his life, and which is the only occupation he knows; and all because he fell into arrears with his subscriptions. It is, indeed, a grievous punishment to inflict upon him. He was reduced at one time to accepting employment to remove rust from a Brighton pier. At the time of the trial he was only getting £6 a week in an engineering works, whereas previously, earning his livelihood as a musician, he was earning well over £10 a week. This exclusion has lasted for four years, and his loss of earnings must be very considerable, to say nothing of the worry and trouble to which he has been put. And the exclusion was unlawful. It was done unlawfully by the secretary of the

1. [1954] Ch 479.
2. [1956] AC 104.

155

Brighton branch, who had no right to do it. When the plaintiff tried to get reinstated, the secretary showed him no sympathy, but insisted on payment of all fines and arrears forthwith. It was only £4, but the plaintiff simply could not find the money at once, and the secretary would not let him pay out of his first week's wages. So he was excluded from his profession. The judge says that "the blame must be laid fairly and squarely upon the shoulders of the secretary, whose behaviour does him no credit". We have already held that this exclusion was a breach of contract. Yet it is said that we cannot award the plaintiff damages for the injury done to him. If this be so, then it is a grievous thing; for I know of no other case where the law allows a party to break a contract with impunity. A man's right to work is just as important to him, indeed more important, than his right of property. If he is unlawfully deprived of his right to work, the courts should intervene to protect him. They have always protected him against wrongful dismissal by his employer. They should also protect him against wrongful exclusion by his union.

. . . .

'Let me first show, however, that a trade union is a legal entity. And I start by observing that as simple matter of fact, not law, a trade union has a personality of its own distinct from its members. Professor Dicey pointed that out long ago. He said: "When a body of twenty, or two thousand, or two hundred thousand men, bind themselves together to act in a particular way for some common purpose, they create a body, which by no fiction of law, but by the very nature of things, differs from the individuals of whom it is constituted" . . . . And Professor Maitland expressed his wholehearted concurrence with unrivalled clarity and felicity . . . . He quotes the incident in the House of Commons in 1904 when the Prime Minister, Mr. Balfour, spoke of trade unions as corporations. Sir Robert Reid (afterwards Lord Loreburn) interrupted him with "The trade unions are not corporations". "I know that", retorted Mr. Balfour, "I am talking English, not law". I take it to be clear, therefore, that a trade union is an entity in fact. The question is whether it is also an entity in law.

. . . .

'But once it is held that a trade union is a legal entity, the nature of the contract by every in-coming member becomes clear. It is a contract between him and the union, not a contract between him and his fellow members; and it is a contract whereby he, for his part, agrees to abide by the rules of the union, and the union, for its part, impliedly agrees that he shall not be excluded by the union or its officers except in accordance with the rules. This view is supported by the statement in Mr. Citrine's book, *Trade Union Law* (1950), p. 175, when he says that the rules "constitute the contract existing between the members and the union, upon the exact terms of which will depend the objects and powers of the union and the rights and liabilities of both contracting parties".

'Once the contract of membership is held to be a contract between the member and the union, then it follows in point of law that if a member is wrongfully excluded by the union or its officers in breach of the contract, he has a remedy in damages against the union. The position of the trade union is then indistinguishable from the position of a proprietary club which has been held liable in damages for wrongful exclusion.

. . . .

'In conclusion, I would say that Parliament has legalized trade unions and has given them large immunities from the ordinary process of the law. It has exempted them from any liability for tort, and also from liability for certain contracts; but it has never exempted them from liability for wrongful exclusion of a member. Nowadays exclusion from membership means exclusion from his livelihood. No one in this country should be unlawfully excluded from his livelihood without having redress for the damage thereby done to him'.

5 Refusal to admit to membership

That decision did a great deal for a man who was already a

member and had been wrongfully expelled from a trade union. But there remained a very important question. Suppose that a union refused to *admit* a man as a member. This might operate very hardly on him. He might not be able to get work at his trade unless he was a member: because every shop in his town was a 'closed shop'. Could he complain about his non-admission? This point was considered in *Faramus v Film Artistes' Association*[1]. Mr. Faramus was a man of excellent character. He was aged 40. He had been a member of the Film Artistes' Association for eight years. Someone in the Union then got a grudge against him and discovered that, 20 years before, when Faramus was a young man in Jersey (during the German occupation), he had been sentenced to six months for getting unemployment pay for his wife. Thereupon the officers of the Union said that he was not, and never had been, a member of the Union, because they had a Rule that 'no one who had been convicted of a criminal offence shall be eligible for or retain membership'. Mr. Faramus said that Rule was unreasonable and invalid. He claimed a declaration that he was still a member. The Judge so held and I agreed with him. The Trade Union appealed to the Court of Appeal. To my dismay I found all the Judges, save me, in favour of the Trade Union. Nevertheless, I suggest that what I said may still be of use – except that I went too far in saying that a Rule may be invalidated simply because it is unreasonable. It is only invalid if it is in unreasonable restraint of trade. I said:

'The trade union appeal to this court. The rule, they say, is certain. It is at once both imperative and comprehensive. It has no geographical limits. No one is eligible who has been convicted in a court of law anywhere in the world. And this, of course, includes the Channel Islands. It has no time limit either. No one is eligible who has been convicted at any time in the distant past, even if it was 20 years ago. And it does not matter that he has lived an exemplary life ever since. Nay, more. The rule knows no degree of crime. It cares

1. [1963] 2 QB 527, [1964] AC 925.

158

nothing how serious or trivial the conviction. (Save, of course, motoring cases not punishable by imprisonment.) The man who, as a boy, was convicted of riding a bicycle without a rear lamp is disqualified equally with the pickpocket with 50 convictions. Finally, and most serious of all, the trade union say they have no discretion to relax the rule. It is absolute. Even if all the members of one accord wished to let the plaintiff stay in the union, it could not be done. For he is, by this conviction, completely barred from membership. He is not a member, they say; never has been and never can be'.

Then I turned to the unreasonableness of the Rule:

'In case I am wrong about the construction of the rule and it means what the trade union contend, then I must say that, in my opinion, it is in unreasonable restraint of trade. This trade union is a "closed shop". No one can enter this trade unless he is a member. Insisting as it does on a monopoly, it is in my opinion unreasonable that it should shut out absolutely from membership – or expel automatically without a hearing – anyone who has had a conviction recorded against him anywhere, no matter how long ago, how trivial, and how irrelevant it may be. He may under this rule, as they construe it, be debarred from entering this trade by reason of a conviction which may be just as irrelevant to membership as the colour of his hair. It might be different if the committee had a discretion to admit him just as everyone else: but they have none. He is out.

'What is the law when a trade union makes a rule which is in unreasonable restraint of trade? Beyond all doubt the rule is bad, unless it is saved by some statutory privilege. The common law has had to deal with the rules of trade associations for centuries. The trade union is only the modern equivalent of the medieval guild of craftsmen. A trade union has by statute the power and duty to make rules for its members and to impose fines and forfeitures on them. The old guild had by its charter power to make by-laws for its members and to inflict fines and penalties on them. There is no difference in principle between them. Many of the old cases are concerned with by-laws which excluded a craftsman from his trade. Always it was held that the by-laws "must ever be subject to the general law of the realm as subordinate to it". . . . They were held to be bad. if they were repugnant to the general law. In particular if they were in unreasonable restraint of trade. Just as in the case of contracts, so also in the case of trade associations, an unreasonable restraint of trade was held to be contrary to public policy and, therefore, void. . . . So now with trade unions their rules are bad if they are in unreasonable restraint of trade unless they are saved by some statutory privilege'.

When the case reached the House of Lords, they agreed with me that the Rule was in unreasonable restraint of trade, but they held that it had been validated by statute. That was certainly the view of Lord Pearce. He said:

'Since there is here a "closed shop" which can only be entered through membership of this union, the court would, in my opinion, intervene on the ground of restraint of trade, were it not for section 3 of the Trade Union Act 1871. But now it cannot'.

So it was owing to the statute that Mr. Faramus failed. It was the statute which enabled the Trade Union to make that Rule and to enforce it. But when there is no such statute, the court is, I suggest, strong enough to intervene when voluntary associations have an unreasonable Rule and exclude a person by virtue of it.

6 Refusing a woman because of her sex

This was followed in *Nagle v Feilden*[1]. A lady, who trained horses, applied to the Jockey Club for a licence. They refused her because she was a woman. They relied on a Rule giving them power at their discretion to grant or refuse licences. On her behalf it was argued that this did not justify her exclusion. I said:

1. [1966] 2 QB 633.

'. . . . If we were here considering a social club, it would be necessary for the plaintiff to show a contract. If a man applies to join a social club and is black-balled, he has no cause of action: because the members have made no contract with him. They can do as they like. They can admit or refuse him, as they please. But we are not considering a social club. We are considering an association which exercises a virtual monopoly in an important field of human activity. By refusing or withdrawing a licence, the stewards can put a man out of business. This is a great power. If it is abused, can the courts give redress? That is the question.

'It was urged before us that the members of a trading or professional association were like a social club. They had, it was said, an unrestricted power to admit, or refuse to admit, any person whom they chose: and that this was established by a case in 1825 concerning the Inns of Court. In *R v The Benchers of Lincoln's Inn,* Bayley J said: "They make their own rules as to the admission of members; and even if they act capriciously upon the subject this court can give no remedy in such a case, because in fact there has been no violation of any right".

'I venture to question this statement, notwithstanding the eminence of the judge from whom it fell. The common law of England has for centuries recognised that a man has a right to work at his trade or profession without being unjustly excluded from it. He is not to be shut out from it at the whim of those having the governance of it. If they make a rule which enables them to reject his application arbitrarily or capriciously, not reasonably, that rule is bad. It is against public policy. The courts will not give effect to it . . . .

'We cannot, of course, decide the matter today. All I say is that there is sufficient foundation for the principle for the case to go to trial. We live in days when many trading or professional associations operate "closed shops". No person can work at his trade or profession except by their permission. They can deprive him of his livelihood. When a man is wrongly rejected or ousted by one of these associations, has he no remedy? I think he may well have,

161

even though he can show no contract. The courts have power to grant him a declaration that his rejection and ouster was invalid and an injunction requiring the association to rectify their error. He may not be able to get damages unless he can show a contract or a tort. But he may get a declaration and injunction . . . . All through the centuries courts have given themselves jurisdiction by means of fictions; but we are mature enough, I hope, to do away with them. The true ground of jurisdiction in all these cases is a man's right to work. I have said before, and I repeat it now, that a man's right to work at his trade or profession is just as important to him as, perhaps more important than, his rights of property. Just as the courts will intervene to protect his rights of property, they will also intervene to protect his right to work.

. . . .

'In this case the plaintiff alleges that the stewards of the Jockey Club make a practice of refusing any woman trainer who applies for a licence. She is refused because she is a woman, and for no other reason. The practice is so uniform that it amounts to an unwritten rule. The only way she can get round it is to get her head lad to apply. The licence is granted to him, not to her.

'It seems to me that this unwritten rule may well be said to be arbitrary and capricious. It is not as if the training of horses could be regarded as an unsuitable occupation for a woman, like that of a jockey or speedway-rider. It is an occupation in which women can and do engage in most successfully. It may not be a "vocation" within the Sex Disqualification (Removal) Act 1919, but still it is an occupation which women can do as well as men: and there would seem to be no reason why they should be excluded from it'.

7 A challenge by Boots

The next problem arose, not with the Rules of the Associations themselves − but with rules of conduct, with a small 'r' — as to the way in which members should behave. They laid down rules of conduct which they required their members to obey: and in default they could expel him or suspend him or give him a money penalty. In such cases the question arose: Could the Courts interfere with the rules of conduct laid down by the association? This was answered in *Dickson v Pharmaceutical Society*[1]. The Pharmaceutical Society wanted their members to do what chemists have done for years — to do dispensing and also sell traditional articles like photographic material. But not to sell other materials. And they made a new rule to enforce it. Boots wanted to sell new materials. They challenged the new rule. Every Court up to the House of Lords held that it was invalid. I said:

'If a pharmacist or company chemist should object to the proposed new rule, there is a remedy open to him. He can ignore the rule, sell what goods he likes, fight the issue before the statutory committee and if need be appeal to the High Court . . . .

'But do not think that is the only remedy. In my opinion, if a professional body lays down a rule of conduct for its members, which is regarded as binding on them, then the courts of law have jurisdiction to inquire into the validity of the rule. As with the old guilds, so also with modern professional bodies. Their rules are only valid if they come within the powers granted to them by their charter. Suppose this society were to make a rule that they would not admit a woman to membership, so that no woman could ever become a registered pharmacist. I have no doubt that the court would intervene and declare the rule to be invalid and compel the society to admit her: see *Nagle v Feilden*. Take trading activities. Some professions have a rule prohibiting a member from carrying on a trade. That may be reasonable in the case of a profession like the legal profession. But it would be quite unreasonable in the case of the pharmaceutical profession. Suppose this society were to make a rule that no pharmacist

1. [1967] Ch 708.

should sell any goods other than pharmaceutical goods. Such a rule would put nearly every pharmacist out of business, because no pharmacist can make a living except by selling other goods. Such a rule would be unreasonable and bad. Any member affected could bring an action for a declaration that it was invalid and an injunction to restrain the society from seeking to enforce it. He would not have to wait until he was brought before the statutory committee. He could bring his action at once so as to know where he stood . . . . Not only a member but a party interested could bring it, such as a company chemist . . .; for the company is just as much affected as a member . . . .

'So also with this proposed new rule under which the council [of the Pharmaceutical Society] seeks to forbid the selling of non-traditional goods. The persons affected are entitled to know where they stand. In opening a new chemist's shop or extending their existing lines, they are entitled to know what goods they can sell. They should not be left in uncertainty. The courts can grant a declaration that the proposed rule is valid or is not valid; and, if invalid, it can grant an injunction to prevent the council carrying it into effect.

. . . .

'I expect that most people, when they go for their medicines, would prefer to go to an old-time chemist's shop with its green and red carboys in the window: but that is no longer possible. The chemist has to go into trade in order to live. And once he goes into trade, it is for him to decide what goods he shall sell. His colleagues cannot say to him: "You must trade in these goods and not in those". That would be too great an interference with his freedom'.

8 Unfair exclusion from membership

Following on those cases there came another problem. It was this: If the committee of an association exercised a discretion given them by the Rules, could the Courts interfere with that discretion if it was exercised unfairly? It could be said – and was said – that discretion was an administrative matter, not judicial, and that the Courts could not interfere. This was answered by two cases in the same year, 1971. The first was *Edwards v SOGAT*[1] . Mr. Edwards was employed by a printing firm. It was a 'closed shop'. The Union admitted him as a 'temporary member'. He made arrangements with the Union by which his weekly contributions to the Union would be paid by his employers direct to the Union. Owing to the Union's own mistake, the employers were not notified and the contributions were not paid. So he was – without any fault on his part – in arrear with his subscription. Thereupon the Union said he was not a member at all. They relied on one of the Rules which said: 'Temporary membership shall terminate automatically if the member becomes over six weeks in arrear'. He applied for re-admission but the Committee refused. They said it was a matter for their discretion. The consequences were disastrous for Mr. Edwards. The other men said they would not work with him as he was not a member. They would go on strike unless he was dismissed. So his employers dismissed him. He claimed damages from the Union. The Rule was held bad: and the discretion was held to have been unfairly exercised. I said:

'. . . . I do not think this trade union, or any other trade union, can give itself by its rules an unfettered discretion to expel a man or to withdraw his membership. The reason lies in the man's right to work. This is now fully recognised by law. It is a right which is of especial importance when a trade union operates a "closed shop" or "100 per cent. membership": for that means that no man can become employed or remain in employment with a firm unless he is a member of the union. If his union card is withdrawn, he has to leave the employment. He is deprived of his livelihood. The courts of this country will not allow so great a power to be exercised arbitrarily or capriciously or with unfair discrimination, neither in the making of rules, nor in the enforcement of

1. [1971] Ch 354.

them. The law has means at its disposal. A trade union exists to protect the right of each one of its members to earn his living and to take advantage of all that goes with it. It is the very purpose of its being. If the union should assume to make a rule which destroys that right or puts it in jeopardy — or is a gratuitous and oppressive interference with it — then the union exceeds its powers. The rule is ultra vires and invalid. Thus if the union should make a rule purporting to give itself uncontrolled discretion to expel a member without hearing him, that rule would be bad. No union can stipulate for a power to expel a man unheard . . . . And the union cannot get round it by calling him a "temporary member". A temporary member is just as much a member of the union as a full member. He pays his dues just the same: and he is entitled to equal protection by the law. The union has no right to expel a temporary member arbitrarily any more than it has a right so to expel a full member. To call him a "temporary member" is only a covert way of claiming to exclude him at their discretion: and, as such, it cannot be allowed.

. . . .

'The union excluded him by virtue of a rule commonly called the "automatic forfeiture" rule. It is rule 18 (4) (h), which says: "Temporary membership shall terminate automatically if the member becomes over six weeks in arrear".

'That rule is so positive in its language that I see no way of limiting it, not by way of construction, nor by way of an implied term. Why then does it not apply to this case? I think it is for this simple reason: this rule, like the other, is invalid. It is an unwarranted encroachment on a man's right to work. Just think. A man may fall into arrears without any real fault of his own. It may be due to oversight on his part, or because he is away sick, or on holiday. It may be due, as here, to the union's own fault in not forwarding the "check-off" slip. But, whatever the cause, this rule, if valid, would put it into the power of the union, as soon as a man was six weeks in arrears, either to enforce his exclusion, or to waive it, or to readmit him. They could be as arbitrary or capricious as they pleased. They could discriminate in favour of some and against others as they liked (as indeed Mr. Edwards thought happened to him). They could turn him out of his work without any good or sufficient cause. Such cannot be permitted. It is ultra vires. No union can stipulate for automatic exclusion of a man without giving him the opportunity of being heard . . . .

'Next, I would consider Mr. Edwards' application for readmission. Once he was excluded, the union treated his readmission as a matter for their discretion. He applied twice and each time he was refused. Such a refusal may sometimes be justified, as when the trade is oversupplied with labour. But it will not be justified if it is exercised in an arbitrary or capricious manner or with unfair discrimination . . . . In this case, seeing that Mr. Edwards was wrongfully excluded in the first place, it was doubly wrong to refuse him readmission'.

9 Unfair exclusion of shop steward

This issue of discretion arose again the same year. It was in *Breen v AEU*[1] . Mr. Breen was elected by his fellow workers as a shop steward. The District Committee refused to approve his appointment. There was a Rule which said: 'Shop stewards elected by members are subject to approval by the District Committee and shall not function until such approval is given'. It turned out that the District Committee were under a complete misapprehension in refusing to approve his appointment. He had been accused of misappropriation but the accusation was completely unfounded. He brought an action challenging their decision. On the facts he failed – owing to their bona fides – but on the law there was, I believe, substantial agreement. At any rate, it is a matter of such importance that I hope it will be acceptable. This is what I said:

'The judge held that it was not open to the courts to review the decision of the district committee: because they were not

1. [1971] 2 QB 175.

exercising a judicial or quasi-judicial function. It was entirely a matter for discretion whether Mr. Breen was approved or not. It could be vitiated if it was made in bad faith, but not otherwise. And he declined to find bad faith.

'In so holding, the judge was echoing views which were current some years ago. But there have been important developments in the last 22 years which have transformed the situation. It may truly now be said that we have a developed system of administrative law. These developments have been most marked in the review of decisions of statutory bodies: but they apply also to domestic bodies.

. . . .

'Does all this apply also to a domestic body? I think it does, at any rate when it is a body set up by one of the powerful associations which we see nowadays. Instances are readily to be found in the books, notably the Stock Exchange, the Jockey Club, the Football Association, and innumerable trade unions. All these delegate power to committees. These committees are domestic bodies which control the destinies of thousands. They have quite as much power as the statutory bodies of which I have been speaking. They can make or mar a man by their decisions. Not only by expelling him from membership, but also by refusing to admit him as a member: or, it may be, by a refusal to grant a licence or to give their approval. Often their rules are framed so as to give them a discretion. They then claim that it is an "unfettered" discretion with which the courts have no right to interfere. They go too far. They claim too much. The Minister made the same claim in the *Padfield* case, and was roundly rebuked by the House of Lords for his impudence. So should we treat this claim by trade unions. They are not above the law, but subject to it. Their rules are said to be a contract between the members and the Union. So be it. If they are a contract, then it is an implied term that the discretion should be exercised fairly. But the rules are in reality more than a contract. They are a legislative code laid down by the council of the union to be obeyed by the members. This code should be subject to control by the courts just as much as a code laid down by

Parliament itself. If the rules set up a domestic body and give it a discretion, it is to be implied that that body must exercise its discretion fairly. Even though its functions are not judicial or quasi-judicial, but only administrative, still it must act fairly. Should it not do so, the courts can review its decision, just as it can review the decision of a statutory body. The courts cannot grant the prerogative writs such as certiorari and mandamus against domestic bodies, but they can grant declarations and injunctions which are the modern machinery for enforcing administrative law.

'Then comes the problem: ought such a body, statutory or domestic, to give reasons for its decision or to give the person concerned a chance of being heard? Not always, but sometimes. It all depends on what is fair in the circumstances. If a man seeks a privilege to which he has no particular claim — such as an appointment to some post or other — then he can be turned away without a word. He need not be heard. No explanation need be given . . . . But if he is a man whose property is at stake, or who is being deprived of his livelihood, then reasons should be given why he is being turned down, and he should be given a chance to be heard. I go further. If he is a man who has some right or interest, or some legitimate expectation, of which it would not be fair to deprive him without a hearing, or reasons given, then these should be afforded him, according as the case may demand. The giving of reasons is one of the fundamentals of good administration . . . .

'So here we have Mr. Breen. He was elected by his fellow workers to be their shop steward. He was their chosen representative. He was the man whom they wished to have to put forward their views to the management, and to negotiate for them. He was the one whom they wished to tell the union about their needs. As such he was a key figure. The Royal Commission on Trade Union and Employers' Associations [(1968) Cmnd. 3623] under Lord Donovan paid tribute to men such as he [p. 29, para. 110]:
"Shop stewards are rarely agitators pushing workers towards unconstitutional action . . . . quite commonly they are

169

supporters of order exercising a restraining influence on their members in conditions which promote disorder".

'Seeing that he had been elected to this office by a democratic process, he had, I think, a legitimate expectation that he would be approved by the district committee, unless there were good reasons against him. If they had something against him, they ought to tell him and to give him a chance of answering it before turning him down. It seems to me intolerable that they should be able to veto his appointment in their unfettered discretion. This district committee sit in Southampton some miles away from Fawley. None of them, so far as I know, worked in the oil refinery. Who are they to say nay to him and his fellow workers without good reason and without hearing what he has to say?'

I pause to ask: Are those principles acceptable? Can the Courts hold a Rule bad on the ground that it is unreasonable? Can they interfere with the discretion of the officers or committee of a voluntary association on the ground that it was exercised unfairly?

10 A lawyer for the defence

There remains the final question: If a man is brought up before a domestic tribunal, is he entitled to have a lawyer to defend him? Some Associations have a Rule denying legal representation; others say nothing about it. This was the point in the last case of this series – *Enderby Town Football Club v Football Association*[1] . A football club had been fined £500 and censured by a local Association because it had not kept its accounts properly. It appealed to the Football Association and wanted to be represented by solicitors and counsel. The Football Association had a Rule which said: 'Any person summoned must attend personally and not be legally represented'. I said:

'The case thus raises this important point: Is a party who is charged before a domestic tribunal entitled *as of right* to be

1. [1971] 1 Ch 591.

170

legally represented? Much depends on what the rules say about it. When the rules say nothing, then the party has no absolute right to be legally represented. It is a matter for the *discretion* of the tribunal. They are masters of their own procedure: and, if they, in the proper exercise of their discretion, decline to allow legal representation, the courts will not interfere. Such was held in the old days in a case about magistrates.... It is the position today in the tribunals under the Tribunals and Inquiries Act 1921. I think the same should apply to domestic tribunals, and for this reason: In many cases it may be a good thing for the proceedings of a domestic tribunal to be conducted informally without legal representation. Justice can often be done in them better by a good layman than by a bad lawyer. This is especially so in activities like football and other sports, where no points of law are likely to arise, and it is all part of the proper regulation of the game. But I would emphasise that the discretion must be properly exercised. The tribunal must not fetter its discretion by rigid bonds. A domestic tribunal is not at liberty to lay down an absolute rule: "We will *never* allow anyone to have a lawyer to appear for him". The tribunal must be ready, in a proper case, to allow it. That applies to anyone in authority who is entrusted with a discretion. He must not fetter his discretion by making an absolute rule from which he will never depart . . . .

'. . . . Here there is a rule which says that legal representation is not allowed. The question is whether the rule is valid.

'A preliminary point arises here: Has the court any power to go behind the wording of the rule and consider its validity? On this point Sir Elwyn Jones made an important concession. He agreed that if the rule was contrary to natural justice, it would be invalid. I think this concession was rightly made and I desire to emphasise it. The rules of a body like this are often said to be a contract. So they are in legal theory. But it is a fiction – a fiction created by the lawyers so as to give the courts jurisdiction. This is no new thing. There are many precedents for it from the time of John Doe onwards. Putting the fiction aside, the truth is that the rules are nothing more nor less than a legislative code — a set of regulations laid down by the governing body to be observed by all who are, or become, members of the association. Such regulations, though said to be a contract, are subject to the control of the courts. If they are in unreasonable restraint of trade, they are invalid . . . . If they seek to oust the jurisdiction of the court, they are invalid . . . . If they unreasonably shut out a man from his right to work, they are invalid . . . . If they lay down a procedure which is contrary to the principles of natural justice, they are invalid . . . . All these are cases where the judges have decided, avowedly or not, according to what is best for the public good. I know that over 300 years ago Hobart CJ said that "Public policy is an unruly horse". It has often been repeated since. So unruly is the horse, it is said [per Burrough J in *Richardson v Mellish* (1824) 2 Bing 229, 252], that no judge should ever try to mount it lest it run away with him. I disagree. With a good man in the saddle, the unruly horse can be kept in control. It can jump over obstacles. It can leap the fences put up by fictions and come down on the side of justice, as indeed was done in *Nagle v Feilden* [1966] 2 QB 633. It can hold a rule to be invalid even though it is contained in a contract.

. . . .

'Seeing that the courts can inquire into the validity of the rule, I turn to the next question: Is it lawful for a body to stipulate in its rules that its domestic tribunal shall not permit legal representation? Such a stipulation is, I think, clearly valid so long as it is construed as directory and not imperative: for that leaves it open to the tribunal to permit legal representation in an exceptional case when the justice of the case so requires. But I have some doubt whether it is legitimate to make a rule which is so imperative in its terms as to exclude legal representation altogether, without giving the tribunal any discretion to admit it, even when the justice of the case requires it. Suppose a case should arise when both the parties and the tribunal felt that it was essential in the interests of justice that the parties should be legally represented, and that the tribunal should have the assistance of a lawyer. Would not the tribunal be able to allow it, or, at any rate, to allow the rule to be waived? I do not find it necessary to express any opinion on this point. I will know how to decide it when it arises . . . .'

My quip about public policy brought me a birthday card from students at the University of Toronto. It shows a horse and rider leaping over a fence, 'Obstruction to Justice'. The horse has a streamer on his tail, 'Public Policy'. The rider is a Judge, in joyous mood and full control, with wig and gown flying. Inside it says: 'Happy Birthday. We hope you're not saddle sore'.

"We hope you're not saddle sore . . . ."

11 Statutory protection

By the Trade Union and Labour Relations Act 1974 a worker is given special statutory protection. If he is excluded or expelled from membership 'by way of arbitrary or unreasonable discrimination' he can apply to an industrial tribunal, and get redress. Whilst this is a valuable protection, the Statute expressly preserves the common law rights of a person who has been refused admission to a trade union or been expelled from it. So the common law, as I have described it, is still of much significance.

2 Powers against other persons

Introduction

Now I come to the other part of this discourse. It is concerned with the powers of groups of people, industrial companies or working men, when those powers are directed — not against their own members — but against third persons or against the public at large. Here I have a sorry tale to tell. If these groups abuse or misuse their powers, the Courts are often unable to do anything about it. So long, that is, as the groups do not break the letter of the law. A dominating group of companies, subsidiaries of a big holding company, can form a cartel and gain a monopoly in essential supplies — using it to force up prices — yet the law does not forbid it unless in some way the Restrictive Practices Act can be prayed in aid. They can cut prices, ruin small traders and put them into bankruptcy. Yet the Courts can do nothing to protect the little man. They can buy up the services of experts or get information of know-how. No one can say them nay — all because the common law has no doctrine of 'unfair competition' or of 'abuse of dominant position'. The European Economic Community has, however, enacted those doctrines in the Treaty of Rome. It is now part of our law. In so far as our industrial companies cross the Channel and go into Europe, they have now to comply with Article 85 of the Treaty which prohibits all 'concerted practices' which have as their object or effect the 'distortion of competition'. They have to comply with Article 86 which declares that any 'abuse of a dominant position within the Common Market'

175

shall be prohibited as incompatible with the Common Market.

If I turn now from industrial companies to working men, their groups, in the shape of trade unions, can exercise immense powers over those who do not belong to their particular group. They can stop a man from working at his trade. They can insist on a 'closed shop' so that no non-member can work there. They can compel the employer to dismiss any man if he is not a member: and the employer has no option but to comply. They can demand high wages — sometimes more than the business can afford — and use industrial action to enforce their demand.

All this is legal because the common law says that any group of persons can combine together to further their own interests — no matter how unreasonably — so long as they are seeking their own advantage and are not doing it out of spite to injure others. Only too often, the action of these groups injures the public at large more than anyone else. If industrial companies abuse their dominant position, they force up prices. The public have to pay too much for their goods — unless the Price Commission intervenes. If trade unions call a strike or a work-to-rule, it inflicts great hardship and suffering on innocent travellers or bystanders; and there is no one to protect them. Not even the Attorney-General. He cannot, even if he would, for there is no law against it.

When I say that the common law can do nothing to prevent abuse, I must add this proviso — provided that the groups use no unlawful means and pursue no unlawful end. For the common law did forge some weapons with which to counter the abuse of power. None of these powers exercised by industrial companies or working men are permissible if the groups concerned use unlawful means to attain a lawful end; or use lawful means to attain an unlawful end. And the Courts have gradually widened the concept of 'unlawful means' and 'unlawful end' so as to prohibit some of the abuses. To this I will return in later pages. But these efforts of the common law have been set at naught in large measure by the intervention of Parliament. Many of the means or the ends which the common law would have regarded as unlawful have been rendered lawful by statute. Especially in the field of trade disputes. To this too I will return.

1 Inducing breach of contract

The principal kind of 'unlawful means' which has come before the Courts is 'knowingly inducing a breach of contract'. Over 125 years ago this was held to be unlawful. Mr. Lumley engaged Miss Wagner to sing at the Opera House at Covent Garden for three months with a term that she should not sing elsewhere during that time. Mr. Gye knew of her engagement, but nevertheless persuaded her to give up her contract with Mr. Lumley. To us it seems a plain case but in those days it provoked much argument. Mr. Gye's conduct was held to be unlawful, despite a most learned dissent by a very good Judge, Coleridge J – *Lumley v Gye*[1]. That is the seedling which was planted in 1853. It has grown steadily ever since. It has been of much consequence in industrial disputes. Often enough when officers of a trade union call men out on strike, they bring about breaches of contract in many directions. They induce the strikers to break their contracts of employment with their employers. This prevents or hinders the employers from performing their contracts with their customers, and the customers with their customers – and so on. The law (which says that it is unlawful to induce a breach of contract) would have made most strikes illegal unless Parliament had intervened to make them lawful. I will deal later with those statutes. But meanwhile I will trace the law on this subject – through the cases in which (at the time they were decided) Parliament had not intervened. It may still be of use in cases where Parliament has not intervened. In the recent case about cricket – *Greig v Insole*[2] – Slade J referred to them all.

1. (1853) 2 E & B 216.
2. [1978] 1 WLR 302.

2 Turning a blind eye

The first way in which the law about 'inducing a breach of contract' was extended was by stretching the 'knowingly' part of it. It was held to be unlawful to induce a breach, not only when you knew the terms of the contract (as Mr. Gye did) but also when you guessed that there might be a contract and turned a blind eye to it. It was so held in *Emerald Construction Co Ltd v Lowthian*[1]. Higgs & Hill, the main contractors, were erecting a great power station. They employed some of the bricklayers as 'labour only' sub-contractors — or on the 'lump', as it is called — by which these bricklayers were not employed as servants but as sub-contractors, and were not bound to join a trade union. This annoyed the trade union a great deal. They tried to get Higgs & Hill to give up these 'labour only' contracts. Their local officers threatened to call all the Union men off the site. They picketed the site. They staged a half-day token strike. An injunction was sought. I said:

'Such being the facts, how stands the law? This "labour only" subcontract was disliked intensely by this trade union and its officers. But nevertheless it was a perfectly lawful contract. The parties to it had a right to have their contractual relations preserved inviolate without unlawful interference by others . . . . If the officers of the trade union, knowing of the contract, deliberately sought to procure a breach of it, they would do wrong . . . . Even if they did not know of the actual terms of the contract, but had the means of knowledge — which they deliberately disregarded — that would be enough. Like the man who turns a blind eye. So here, if the officers deliberately sought to get this contract terminated, heedless of its terms, regardless whether it was terminated by breach or not, they would do wrong. For it is unlawful for a third person to procure a breach of contract knowingly, or recklessly, indifferent whether it is a breach or not. Some would go further and hold that it is unlawful for a third person deliberately and directly to interfere with the

1. [1966] 1 WLR 691.

execution of a contract, even though he does not cause any breach . . . . It is unnecessary to pursue this today. Suffice it that if the intention of the defendants was to get this contract terminated at all events, breach or no breach, they were prima facie in the wrong.

'The evidence at present before us points in this direction. The object of the defendant officers was plain. It was to get Higgs & Hill Ltd. to terminate this "labour only" sub-contract; and the evidence suggests that they did not care how it was terminated, so long as it was terminated . . . .

'The Trade Disputes Acts, 1906 and 1965, do not avail the defendants, for although this may have been a "trade dispute", nevertheless this "labour only" subcontract is not, as it appears to me at present, a "contract of employment" within section 3 of the Trade Disputes Act 1906, or section 1 of the Trade Disputes Act 1965. The words "contract of employment" in this context seem to me prima facie to denote a contract between employer and workman; and not a contract between an employer and a subcontractor, even though he be a subcontractor for labour only.

'Should, therefore, we issue an interlocutory injunction? I think we should . . . . There is a prima facie case that the conduct of the defendants in seeking to terminate this contract is unlawful. This conduct is doing grave harm to the plaintiffs and is putting their contract in jeopardy. If an injunction is not granted, irreparable damage may be done to the plaintiffs; whereas, if it is granted, the defendants will suffer little or no damage'.

3 Hindering or preventing performance

The second way in which the law about 'inducing a breach of contract' was extended was by stretching the 'breach' part. It was held to be unlawful, not only to induce a breach of contract, but also to hinder or prevent the performance of it. A good example was in the case of the Imperial Hotel at Torquay. The hotel got all its supplies of oil from the Esso Company; but there was clause in the contract which excused

Esso if they were hindered or prevented from delivering the oil by labour disputes. The Imperial Hotel employed no members of the Transport Union. But the Union thought that the manager was opposed to them. The Union gave 'blacking' instructions. They 'blacked' any oil destined for the Imperial Hotel. They put pickets outside the hotel – knowing that the drivers of oil tankers would not cross the picket lines. This was held to be unlawful. It is reported in *Torquay Hotel Co Ltd v Cousins*[1]. I said:

'The Imperial Hotel had a contract with Esso under which the Imperial Hotel agreed to buy their total requirements of fuel-oil from Esso for one year, the quantity being estimated at 120,000 gallons, to be delivered by road tank wagon at a minimum of 3,000 gallons a time . . . . But there was a *force majeure* or *exception clause* . . . .

'It is plain that, if delivery was hindered or prevented by labour disputes, as, for instance, because their drivers would not cross the picket line, Esso could rely on that exception clause as a defence to any claim by Imperial. They would not be liable in damages. And I am prepared to assume that Esso would not be guilty of a breach of contract. But I do not think that would exempt the trade union officials from liability if they unlawfully hindered or prevented Esso from making deliveries. The principle of *Lumley v Gye* (1853) 2 E & B 216 extends not only to inducing breach of contract, but also to preventing the performance of it . . . . So here I think the trade union officials cannot take advantage of the force majeure or exception clause in the Esso contract. If they unlawfully prevented or hindered Esso from making deliveries, as ordered by Imperial, they would be liable in damage to Imperial, notwithstanding the exception clause'.

4 A strike notice of proper length

If that extension had been carried to its full extent, it would have done much to stop the abuse of power. At one time I

1. [1969] 2 Ch 106.

suggested it might be stretched so as to cover all interference with the performance of a contract, direct or indirect – see *Daily Mirror Newspapers v Gardner*[1] . But that was found to be going too far.

Many strikes interfere with the performance of a contract: but they are not on that account to be considered unlawful. This was shown by another important case about that time. It is *Morgan v Fry*[2] . 650 workmen in London docks belonged to the Transport Union. 30 of them formed a breakaway union. Mr. Fry, a senior official of the Transport Union, thought this was most undesirable. He gave notice – 2½ weeks' notice – to the Port of London Authority that his Union men would not work with the non-unionists; making it clear that, if the Authority wanted to keep the Union men, they would have to dismiss the breakaway men. The Authority did dismiss the breakaway men, giving proper notice. One of them, Mr. Morgan, was out of work for six weeks and became a collector for the Gas Board at a less salary. He brought an action for damages against Mr. Fry. He failed because Mr. Fry's 'strike notice' was not unlawful. It was of proper length. If it has been a 'lightning strike', with notice of only an hour or two, or a day or two, it would have been unlawful. I will not give the judgment in full, but just these important extracts:

'. . . . It has been held for over 60 years that workmen have a right to strike (including therein a right to say that they will not work with non-unionists) provided that they give sufficient notice beforehand: and a notice is sufficient if it is at least as long as the notice required to terminate the contract.

'There have been many cases where trade-union officials have given "strike notices" of proper length, and no one has suggested there was anything illegal about them. And not a few of them have found their way into the Law Reports . . . . . . But if the "strike notice" is not of proper length – if it

1. [1968] 2 QB 762 at 781.
2. [1968] 2 QB 710.

is shorter than the legal period for termination – then it is unlawful . . . .

'What then is the legal basis on which a "strike notice" of proper length is held to be lawful? I think it is this: The men can leave their employment altogether by giving a week's notice to terminate it. That would be a strike which would be perfectly lawful. If a notice to terminate is lawful, surely a lesser notice is lawful: such as a notice that "we will not work alongside a non-unionist". After all, if the employers should retort to the men: "We will not accept this notice as lawful", the men can at once say: "Then we will give notice to terminate". The truth is that neither employer nor workmen wish to take the drastic action of termination if it can be avoided. The men do not wish to leave their work for ever. The employers do not wish to scatter their labour force to the four winds. Each side is, therefore, content to accept a "strike notice" of proper length as lawful. It is an implication read into the contract by the modern law as to trade disputes. If a strike takes place, the contract of employment is not terminated. It is suspended during the strike: and revives again when the strike is over.

'In my opinion, therefore, the defendants here did not use any unlawful means to achieve their aim. They were not guilty of intimidation: because they gave a "strike notice" of proper length. They were not guilty of conspiracy to use unlawful means: because they used none. They were not guilty of conspiracy to injure: because they acted honestly and sincerely in what they believed to be the true interests of their members'.

5 Direct interference with a contract

That case led to a distinction being drawn between acts which 'directly' prevent or hinder the performance of a contract – and those which do it 'indirectly'. It is a distinction which is illogical and difficult to apply, but it seems that it has to be done. This distinction was made in

Torquay Hotel Co Ltd v Cousins[1], the case where supplies to the Imperial Hotel at Torquay were 'blacked'. I said:

'The interference must be *direct*. Indirect interference will not do. Thus, a man who "corners the market" in a commodity may well know that it may prevent others from performing their contracts, but he is not liable to an action for so doing. A trade union official, who calls a strike on proper notice, may well know that it will prevent the employers from performing their contracts to deliver goods, but he is not liable in damages for calling it. *Indirect* interference is only unlawful if unlawful means are used . . . . This distinction must be maintained, else we should take away the right to strike altogether. Nearly every trade union official who calls a strike – even on due notice, as in *Morgan v Fry* [1968] 2 QB 710 – knows that it may prevent the employers from performing their contracts. He may be taken even to intend it. Yet no one has supposed hitherto that it was unlawful: and we should not render it unlawful today. A trade union official is only in the wrong when he procures a contracting party *directly* to break his contract, or when he does it indirectly *by unlawful means* . . . .

'I must say a word about unlawful means, because that brings in another principle. I have always understood that if one person deliberately interferes with the trade or business of another, and does so by unlawful means, that is, by an act which he is not at liberty to commit, then he is acting unlawfully, even though he does not procure or induce any actual breach of contract. If the means are unlawful, that is enough . . . .

'This point about unlawful means is of particular importance when a place is declared "black". At common law it often involves the use of unlawful means. Take the Imperial Hotel. When it was declared "black", it meant that the drivers of the tankers would not take oil to the hotel. The drivers would thus be induced to break their contracts of employment. That would be unlawful at common law. The

1. [1969] 2 Ch 106 at 138.

only case in which "blacking" of such a kind is lawful is when it is done "in contemplation or furtherance of a trade dispute". It is then protected by section 3 of the Trade Disputes Act 1906 . . . '.

6 Unlawful means

That last passage brings me to discuss 'unlawful means'. The circumstances vary so much that no definition can be attempted. But the Courts have shown themselves ready to extend the range of 'unlawful means' as occasion requires. The House of Lords did this in the great case of *Rookes v Barnard*[1] . They extended the wrong of 'intimidation' beyond anything that had been considered possible. Mr. Rookes was a skilled draughtsman employed by BOAC. The Union had expressly agreed with the employers that no lockout or strike should take place and that any disputes should be settled by arbitration. Mr. Rookes left the Union and refused to rejoin. The officials of the Union told the employers that, if Mr. Rookes was not removed within 3 days, they would withdraw their labour. The employers thereupon dismissed Mr. Rookes. They did it quite lawfully, giving him a week's salary in lieu of notice. The House of Lords held that the officials of the Union had been guilty of 'unlawful means'. Previously it had always been recognised that threats of violence were unlawful means. In *Rookes v Barnard* this was extended to threats of breach of contract — the threat there being to break their pledge 'not to strike'.

There are many other things which are unlawful means. Take first the kind of unlawful means used by industrial companies. It is quite lawful for one company to seduce a good man away from a rival firm — by paying him more — but it must be careful not to induce him to break his contract, or a covenant in restraint of trade (if it is reasonable), or to give away trade secrets or confidential information. All these are unlawful means. Speaking generally, unlawful means are

1. [1964] AC 1129.

184

any act or conduct which a company is not at liberty to commit (*Acrow v Rex*[1]).

7 Picketing and demonstrations

Take next the kind of unlawful means used by workmen. Anything in the nature of assault, trespass, violence, threats of violence, molestation or nuisance are all unlawful means. The only one which needs special mention is picketing. No doubt mass picketing is unlawful means. Pickets obstructing traffic, or preventing men going to work, is unlawful means. But is peaceful picketing itself unlawful means? Is a demonstration unlawful means? This came under discussion in *Hubbard v Pitt*[2]. A group of social workers thought that a firm of estate agents at Islington were 'harassing' the tenants. They peacefully picketed the offices of the estate agents. They made a demonstration. Was this unlawful at common law or not? The majority of the Court thought it was or might be. I thought it was not unlawful. As it is a matter of consequence, I would like to set out what I said:

'Now we come to the crunch of the case. The social workers, in pursuance of their campaign, have "picketed" the offices of Prebble & Co. The word "picket" is used, no doubt, because of the example shown by workers who, in a trade dispute, picket in support of their demands. But the "pickets" here consist of a small number of men and women, mostly young. There were sometimes four, and occasionally up to eight. They stood about on the pavement in front of Prebble's offices. They only did it for about three hours on Saturday mornings. Different persons on different Saturdays. They carried placards with the words: "Tenants Watch Out Prebbles About" and "If Prebbles In — You're Out"....
.... Picketing a person's premises (even if done with a view to compel or persuade) is not unlawful unless it is associated with other conduct such as to constitute the whole conduct

1. [1971] 1 WLR 1671.
2. [1976] QB 142.

185

a nuisance at common law. Picketing is not a nuisance in itself. Nor is it a nuisance for a group of people to attend at or near the plaintiff's premises in order to obtain or to communicate information or in order peacefully to persuade. It does not become a nuisance unless it is associated with obstruction, violence, intimidation, molestation, or threats.

. . . .

'The judge held that picketing was unlawful. He said:

"The sole issue before me has been whether or not the use of the highway for picketing which is not in contemplation or furtherance of a trade dispute is a lawful operation. I have concluded that it is not".

'This ruling is of such significance that I do not think it should be allowed to stand. I see no valid reason for distinguishing between picketing in furtherance of a trade dispute and picketing in furtherance of other causes. Why should workers be allowed to picket and other people not? I do not think there is any distinction drawn by the law save that, in the case of a trade dispute, picketing is governed by statutory provisions: and, in the case of other causes, it is left to the common law. But, broadly speaking, they are in line the one with the other. Picketing is lawful so long as it is done merely to obtain or communicate information, or peacefully to persuade; and is not such as to submit any other person to any kind of constraint or restriction of his personal freedom

. . . .

'The real grievance of the plaintiffs is about the placards and leaflets. To restrain these by an interlocutory injunction would be contrary to the principle laid down by the court 85 years ago in *Bonnard v Perryman* [1891] 2 Ch 269, and repeatedly applied ever since. That case spoke of the right of free speech. Here we have to consider the right to demonstrate and the right to protest on matters of public concern. These are rights which it is in the public interest that individuals should possess; and, indeed, that they should exercise without impediment so long as no wrongful act is done. It is often the only means by which grievances can be brought to the knowledge of those in authority — at any rate with such impact as to gain a remedy. Our history is full of warnings against suppression of these rights. Most notable was the demonstration at St. Peter's Fields, Manchester, in 1819 in support of universal suffrage. The magistrates sought to stop it. At least 12 were killed and hundreds injured. Afterwards the Court of Common Council of London affirmed "the undoubted right of Englishmen to assemble together for the purpose of deliberating upon public grievances". Such is the right of assembly. So also is the right to meet together, to go in procession, to demonstrate and to protest on matters of public concern. As long as all is done peaceably and in good order, without threats or incitement to violence or obstruction to traffic, it is not prohibited . . . . I stress the need for peace and good order. Only too often violence may break out: and then it should be firmly handled and severely punished. But so long as good order is maintained, the right to demonstrate must be preserved. In his recent inquiry on the Red Lion Square disorders, Scarman LJ was asked to recommend that "a positive right to demonstrate should be enacted". He said that it was unnecessary: "The right, of course exists, subject only to limits required by the need for good order and the passage of traffic" . . . . In the recent report on Contempt of Court [(1974) Cmnd. 5794], the committee considered the campaign of the "Sunday Times" about thalidomide and said that the issues were "a legitimate matter for public comment" . . . . It recognised that it was important to maintain the "freedom of protest on issues of public concern" . . . . It is time for the courts to recognise this too. They should not interfere by interlocutory injunction with the right to demonstrate and to protest any more than they interfere with the right of free speech; provided that everything is done peaceably and in good order. That is the case here. The only thing of which complaint can legitimately be made is the placards and leaflets. If it turned out at the trial that the words on the placards and leaflets were untrue, then an injunction should be granted. But not at present — when, for aught we know, the words may be true and justifiable.

And, if true, it may be very wholesome for the truth to be made known'.

8 Obligation to provide work

The latest way in which the law about 'inducing a breach of contract' may be extended is by stretching the terms of the contract of employment — so as to include by implication an obligation by the employer to provide work. This point was brought before the Court by Joseph Langston, a car welder. He came in person before us just as Raymond Blackburn had done. It was in the days of the Industrial Relations Act 1971. He was a man of 60 who had worked for Chryslers for years. He was a simple, honest man. He had written out his case well on paper. He declined to join the Union. He objected to the 'closed shop'. His workmates took strong objection. Owing to the impact of the 1971 Act, Chryslers did not dismiss him. They suspended him on full pay. When he went to collect his pay, there was a mass demonstration. 500 workers pelted him with stones, tin cans and mud. The question arose whether Chryslers were guilty of a breach of contract in suspending him on full pay. It was suggested that they might be. The case is *Langston v AUEW*[1]. I said:

'. . . . We have repeatedly said in this court that a man has a right to work, which the courts will protect: see *Nagle v Feilden* [1966] 2 QB 633 and *Hill v C.A. Parsons & Co Ltd* [1972] Ch 305. I would not wish to express any decided view, but simply state the argument which could be put forward by Mr. Langston. In these days an employer, when employing a skilled man, is bound to provide him with work. By which I mean that the man should be given the opportunity of doing his work when it is available and he is ready and willing to do it. A skilled man takes a pride in his work. He does not do it merely to earn money. He does it so as to make his contribution to the well-being of all. He does it so as to keep himself busy, and not idle. To use his skill, and to

1. [1974] 1 WLR 185.

improve it. To have the satisfaction which comes of a task well one. Such as Longfellow attributed to *The Village Blacksmith:*

"Something attempted, something done,
Has earned a night's repose".

'The *Code of Practice* (see S.I. 1972 No. 179) contains the same thought. It says, at paragraph 9:
". . . . management should recognise the employee's need to achieve a sense of satisfaction in his job and should provide for it so far as practicable".

'A parallel can be drawn in regard to women's work. Many a married woman seeks work. She does so when the children grow up and leave the home. She does it, not solely to earn money, helpful as it is: but to fill her time with useful occupation, rather than sit idly at home waiting for her husband to return. The devil tempts those who have nothing to do.

'To my mind, therefore, it is arguable that in these days a man has, by reason of an implication in the contract, a right to work. That is, he has a right to have the opportunity of doing his work when it is there to be done. If this be correct, then if any person knowingly induces the employer to turn the man away – and thus deprive him of the opportunity of doing his work – then that person induces the employer to break his contract. It is none the less a breach, even though the employer pays the man his full wages. So also when fellow workers threaten to walk out unless a man is turned off the job, they threaten to induce a breach of contract. At any rate, the man who is suspended has a case for saying that they have induced or threatened to induce the employer to break the contract of employment'.

9 The immunity of trade unions

Now I turn to the intervention of Parliament. Our legislative history is full of statutes by which trade unions, their officers and members have been granted considerable immunity from

189

actions at law. These statutes range from the Trade Disputes Act of 1906 to the latest Act in 1976. In between there was the Industrial Relations Act 1971. It was ill-fated. Important parts of it were repealed. We have now a comprehensive range of statutes which grant immunity for any act done by a union or by workers 'in contemplation or furtherance of a trade dispute'. It is not actionable for them to induce a breach of any contract — not only a contract of employment — but any contract. Nor is it actionable to interfere with its performance. Not only is it not actionable — it is also not unlawful. It is not to be regarded as the doing of an unlawful act or the use of unlawful means (see section 13 of the 1974 Act as amended by section 3 of the 1976 Act). The words 'trade dispute' are defined in comprehensive words so as to cover nearly every dispute in which a trade union is likely to be engaged. As a result of this legislation, some of the cases which I have described would today be decided differently. For instance, *Emerald Construction Co Ltd v Lowthian*[1], *Torquay Hotel Co Ltd v Cousins*[2] and *Rookes v Barnard*[3] would each be decided differently today.

10 In contemplation of a trade dispute

Since this legislation, there has, however, been one case in the Court of Appeal in which it was held that the conduct of the trade union was not 'in contemplation or furtherance of a trade dispute'. It is *BBC v Hearn*[4]. It arose out of the tele-vising of the Cup Final by means of a space satellite above the Indian Ocean. The Union objected to it being shown in South Africa — because they objected to its policy of apartheid. They threatened to cut off the satellite. The Court granted an injunction to ensure that the Cup Final should be televised. I said:

'It is not necessary today to go through all the legislation which we have had relating to trade unions. I would only say that in three recent Acts, the Trade Union and Labour

1. [1966] 1 WLR 691.
2. [1969] 2 Ch 106.
3. [1964] AC 1129.
4. [1977] ICR 685.

Relations Act 1974, the Employment Protection Act 1975, and the Trade Union and Labour Relations (Amendment) Act 1976, Parliament has conferred more freedom from restraint on trade unions than has ever been known to the law before. All legal restraints have been lifted so that they can now do as they will. Trade unions and their officers — and, indeed, groups of workmen, official or unofficial — are entitled to induce others to break their contracts — not only contracts of employment but other contracts as well — they are entitled to interfere and prevent the performance of contracts by others — all with impunity. Any such inducement or interference is not only not actionable at law. It is specifically declared to be "not unlawful". It is therefore proclaimed to be lawful, provided always this (and this is the one limit to the exemption which is conferred): it must be "in contemplation or furtherance of a trade dispute".

'Apply these considerations to this case. The officers of the union are going to call upon their members to break their contracts of employment with the BBC and to induce the BBC to break its contracts with all those countries overseas. That is what they are asking their members to do. It is, beyond doubt, lawful for the trade union, or its officers to do this, provided always it is in contemplation or furtherance of a trade dispute.

. . . .

'So I come to the words "in contemplation or furtherance of a trade dispute". There comes the rub. Was a trade dispute in contemplation? This has been discussed in the courts . . . .

'. . . . if shop stewards — who object to a man's religious belief — say to an employer, "Dismiss this man or we will go out on strike", that is not a trade dispute. It is coercive interference with the man's freedom of religion and with the employer's business. Take the case which I put in the course of argument: if printers in a newspaper office were to say: "We don't like the article which you are going to publish about the Arabs — or the Jews — or on this or that political issue — you must withdraw it. If you do not do so, we are not going to print your paper". That is not a trade dispute. It is coercive action unconnected with a trade dispute. It is an unlawful interference with the freedom of the press. It is a self-created power of censorship. It does not become a trade dispute simply because the men propose to break their contracts of employment in doing it. Even if the men have a strong moral case, saying, "We have a conscientious objection to this article. We do not want to have anything to do with it", that does not turn it into a trade dispute. The dispute is about the publication of the article, not about the terms and conditions of employment.

'Applying those considerations to this case, all that was happening was that the trade union, or its officers, were saying: "Stop this televising by the Indian Ocean satellite, stop it yourself. If you don't, we will ask our own people to stop it for you". That is not a trade dispute. They were hoping, I suppose, that the BBC would give in; but, if they did not give in, they were going to order their members to stop the broadcast. That does not seem to me to be a trade dispute'.

11 'Blacking' a ship

Quite recently the Court of Appeal indicated a further limit-ation on the statutory immunity. It was in the *Star Sea Transport Corporation of Monrovia v Slater and Others*, reported in *The Times* of 14 October 1978. A bulk carrier was about to sail from Glasgow to Antwerp. She had Greek officers and crew who were being paid the full rates of pay agreed by their own Greek Seamen's Union. If she had been flying the Greek flag, there could have been no objection taken to her. But she was flying the Liberian flag which was a 'flag of convenience'. On that account the officers of an international Federation of Seamen's Unions (which included the Greek Union as an affiliate) took objection to her. They demanded that the owners should pay the Greek officers and crew the Federation rates (which were higher than the Greek rates) and sign the Federation Articles. The Federation 'blacked' the vessel until their demands were met. The tug-men refused to take the vessel to sea. The owners were so anxious for the vessel to sail that they were themselves ready to comply with all the demands of the Federation. But the

Greek officers and crew refused to sign the Articles of the Federation, even though it would have given them more pay. They preferred to keep to their Greek Articles which they had signed and with which they were well acquainted. The Court of Appeal granted an interlocutory injunction to stop the 'blacking'. The order was obeyed. The ship sailed that very evening. It was the most expeditious of court hearings that ever was. I ventured to say:

'If we were to give the words "an act done by a person in contemplation or furtherance of a trade dispute" their full meaning, they would cover almost every difference or demand by a trade union. But judicial decisions starting with *Conway v Wade* [1909] AC 506 have put some limit on those words and said that the Court can look at the motives for which the action is taken.

'Take this very case. On this ship the crew are well treated and well paid and their own Union is content with their lot. If third persons — such as the officers of the Federation here — intermeddle by making threats or demands for some extraneous motive and not for any legitimate trade object, then it can be said that they are not acting in contemplation or furtherance of a trade dispute. It is suggested here that there was an extraneous motive in the officers of the Federation in that they disliked flags of convenience: and that they had no legitimate trade object, seeing that they were making demands which could not reasonably be fulfilled. This point is sufficiently strong that it merits full consideration at the trial. Meanwhile the balance of convenience is in favour of issuing an injunction'.

If this provisional view is accepted, it opens the way to the argument that the officers of a trade union may take themselves out of the statutory immunity if they make demands which are wholly extortionate or utterly unreasonable or quite impossible to fulfil — and then take industrial action to enforce those demands. I ask the question: Is this a good argument or not? No one has suggested it hitherto. But if it were accepted, it would go some way to restrain the abuse or misuse of power by a trade union.

Conclusion

This discussion shows that the common law has done a good deal to prevent the abuse of power by a powerful group of employers or employees. It has held that the members of the group and its officers are liable if they are guilty of some unlawful conduct, that is, use some unlawful means or pursue some unlawful end. But this does not apply to the trade unions. Parliament has granted them immunity. It is not for the Judges to cavil at this: or to criticise it. Parliament must think — and no doubt with reason — that the law should have nothing to do with trade disputes. They are to be solved by the good sense of the parties and not by the Judges. Any intervention by the law would provoke such resentment that it would only make matters worse. So be it. Such being the philosophy of the day, it behoves these powerful bodies to act with responsibility towards society at large and not out of any sectional interest of their own. The law can do nothing. Save in the very few cases when they step outside the pale of immunity granted by Parliament.

Part five

High Trees

Introduction

In the 19th century the law of England was dominated by the difference between Law and Equity. Law had its own strict rules. Equity was, or should have been, more flexible. It was the means by which the needs of the people could be met. As Sir Henry Maine said in his *Ancient Law* (page 24): 'Social necessities and social opinion are always more or less in advance of law. We may come indefinitely near to the closing of the gap between them, but it has a perpetual tendency to re-open. . . . The greater or less happiness of a people depends on the degree of promptitude with which the gap is narrowed'.

The importance of the *High Trees* case, as I see it, is this: During the 19th century the Courts of Common Law had laid down strict rules of law expressed in archaic terms such as 'consideration' and 'estoppel'. Those strict rules had survived the Judicature Act 1873 and were capable of causing injustice in many cases. There was a gap between those strict rules and the social necessities of the 20th century. The *High Trees* case helped to narrow that gap. Ever since the decision was given, it has been the subject of controversy. The extent of it is still under debate. It is therefore an appropriate theme for discussion in the Law Schools.

In this part I tell how it came to be decided and something of the sequels to it. I would ask: How far is it acceptable? Do you favour its extension?

197

The *High Trees* case

I The beginnings in 1921

Whenever I speak to students, someone is sure to call out –
'*High Trees*'. It is greeted with acclaim. This is very different
from the reception it used to get in days past from the higher
judiciary. Some of them treated it with reserve. Others with
suspicion, even with silent disapproval. To this day, there are
still traces of it.

But I will start with the latest pronouncement in the
House of Lords. In *Woodhouse Ltd v Nigerian Produce Ltd*[1],
the Lord Chancellor (Viscount Hailsham of St. Marylebone)
said:

'I desire to add that the time may soon come when the whole
sequence of cases based on promissory estoppel since the
war, beginning with *Central London Property Trust Ltd v
High Trees House Ltd* [1947] KB 130 may need to be
reviewed and reduced to a coherent body of doctrine by the
courts. I do not mean to say that they are to be regarded
with suspicion. But as is common with an expanding
doctrine, they do raise problems of coherent exposition
which have never been systematically explored'.

In these pages I will try to trace this 'expanding doctrine' and
to explore some of the problems of 'coherent exposition'.
Then you can say how far I have succeeded.

You will not appreciate the significance of *High Trees*
unless you have some understanding of the law as it was

1. [1972] AC 741.

when I started. Previously I had taught Mathematics at Winchester for one year. My first reading of law started in the holidays of September 1921. I bought *Anson on Contracts*. It is beside me now. In it I wrote 'A. T. Denning. September 1921'. I went back to Oxford in October 1921 and, after nine months, in June 1922 I took the Law School. One of the examiners was a young law don, Geoffrey Cheshire. He afterwards — together with Cecil Fifoot — wrote a book on Contract. It was much better than Anson. The examiners were kind at my viva and in marking my papers. They placed me in the first class. This was vital. It was the qualification for the Eldon Law Scholarship. This was £100 a year for three years. When I was dining in hall, the President of Magdalen sent me a little note telling me that I had been awarded the Eldon. He added: 'You are a marked man. Perhaps you will be a Lord of Appeal some day'. I was keen to start in practice. In October 1922 I became a pupil in chambers at No. 4 Brick Court in the Temple and worked for the Bar examination at the same time. There were no state grants then. My parents could not help. After nine months, in June 1923 I took the Bar examination. Again the examiners were kind. They placed me in the first class and I was awarded the Studentship. This too was £100 a year for three years. With this, I managed the first brief-less years. I stayed on in chambers at No. 4 Brick Court for the rest of my time at the Bar.

2 The 'broad rule of justice'

We did a lot of commercial work in No. 4 Brick Court, especially with sale of goods and charterparties of ships. Soon after I started I came upon a pathway which led to the *High Trees*. At that time one dominating factor was that every contract of sale of goods of £10 or more in value had to be in writing. The other dominating factor was that no promise was binding unless there was consideration for it. Those two factors caused injustices of all kinds. We used to resort to many subtleties to get round them. When I was still a pupil we came across a very useful case on the subject. It had just been reported, called *Hartley v Hymans*[1]. I noted it in pencil on my copy of Anson and added 'Suggest Estoppel'. It was a decision of Mr. Justice McCardie in which he had examined many authorities. He was the most diligent collector of cases that has ever been on the Bench. In it he made a passing reference to 'the broad rule of justice stated by Lord Cairns LC in *Hughes v Metropolitan Railway Co* [1877] 2 AC 439'. That case had been overlooked for 50 years. None of the textbooks had noticed it. I made a special note of it: and as it has had so much impact on subsequent developments, I will set it out:

'It is the first principle upon which all Courts of Equity proceed, that if parties who have entered into definite and distinct terms involving certain legal results — certain penalties or legal forfeiture — afterwards by their own act or with their own consent enter upon a course of negotiation which has the effect of leading one of the parties to suppose that the strict rights arising under the contract will not be enforced, or will be kept in suspense, or held in abeyance, the person who otherwise might have enforced those rights will not be allowed to enforce them where it would be inequitable having regard to the dealings which have thus taken place between the parties'.

I found also that that principle had been explained by Bowen LJ who said that it was not confined to penalties and forfeitures but extended to all cases of contractual rights. That was in a case in 1888 — *Birmingham and District Land Co v London and NW Railway Co*[2].

3 The fences in the way

As I went along the pathway towards the *High Trees,* I found many obstacles had been left in the way. I came across them

1. [1920] 3 KB 475.
2. (1888) 40 Ch D 268.

whilst I was waiting for briefs. They came slowly. It took me seven years before I was making £1,000 a year. During this time Sir Willes Chitty, the Senior Master and one of the most learned of men — coming from a long line of lawyers — asked me to join him as one of the editors of *Smith's Leading Cases*. It took up much of my time until it was published in 1929. Each editor took responsibility for the notes to a particular leading case. I learned more law in those years than I have done before or since. In particular I came across two fences barring the path. They had been put up 70 years before. One was that estopped applies only in respect of representations of fact, and not of statements of intention (*Jorden v Money*[1]). The other was that a representation, in order to work an estoppel, must be one of fact and not of law. Somehow or other these fences had to be overcome.

In order to leap these fences, I needed a good horse. It turned up. It was the Report of the Law Revision Committee on the Doctrine of Consideration. It came out in 1937 when I was in very busy practice as a junior. So I had no time to read it then. But on a significant day — All Fools' Day — 1 April 1938, I took silk. I had more time then for a year or two. I read the Report. It was made by the leading lawyers of the day. They included Lord Wright MR, Mr. Justice Goddard, Mr. Justice Asquith and Professor Goodhart. Even to this day it has not been implemented by the Legislature. But it was just the horse to get me over the fences. In particular it exposed the injustice of the rule that estoppel only applies to statements of fact, and of the rule that payment of a lesser sum is no consideration for the discharge of a larger sum. The Committee recommended the abolition of both those rules. They made this recommendation. It got me over the fences which obstructed the way to *High Trees:*

'We therefore recommend that a promise which the promisor knows, or reasonably should know, will be relied upon by the promisee, shall be enforceable if the promisee has altered his position to his detriment in reliance on the promise'.

1. (1845) 5 HL Cas 185.

Being now on the right path, I pointed it out to the Court of Appeal in my argument as King's Counsel in *Salisbury (Marquess) v Gilmore*[1]. Lord Justice Mackinnon was disposed to follow the path. But he did not feel able to do so. The fences were too high for him. In his usual pungent style, he said that the House of Lords — the 'voices of infallibility' — as they spoke in *Jorden v Money* — were binding on the Court of Appeal. So estoppel was still confined to representations of existing fact.

4 The *High Trees* case itself — promissory estoppel

At last I came in sight of *High Trees*. It was in July 1946. I had only been a Judge in the King's Bench for some six months. During that time I had been mostly out on circuit where it was all fact and no law. But in my first spell in London there came the *Central London Property Trust Ltd v High Trees House Ltd*[2]. It was argued by Mr. Robert Fortune on the one side — 'Frothy Bob' as we used to call him because of his spluttering — and Mr. Ronald Hopkins on the other, a sound and sensible advocate. They argued it well but they had not the reserves at their command as I had. I delivered judgment straight off the reel — with a tidying up afterwards for the Law Reports.

The facts were quite simple. During the war many people left London owing to the bombing. Flats were empty. In one block, where the flats were let on 99 year leases at £2,500 a year, the landlord had agreed to reduce it by half and to accept £1,250 a year. When the bombing was over, and the tenants came back, the landlord sought to recover the full £2,500 a year. I held that he could not recover it for the time when the flats were empty. I said:

'If I were to consider this matter without regard to recent developments in the law, there is no doubt that had the plaintiffs claimed it, they would have been entitled to recover ground rent at the rate of £2,500 a year from the beginning

1. [1942] 2 KB 38.
2. [1947] 1 KB 130.

203

of the term, since the lease under which it was payable was a lease under seal which, according to the old common law, could not be varied by an agreement by parol (whether in writing or not), but only by deed. Equity, however, stepped in, and said that if there has been a variation of a deed by a simple contract (which in the case of a lease required to be in writing would have to be evidenced by writing), the courts may give effect to it . . . . That equitable doctrine, however, could hardly apply in the present case because the variation here might be said to have been made without consideration. With regard to estoppel, the representation made in relation to reducing the rent, was not a representation of an existing fact. It was a representation, in effect, as to the future, namely, that payment of the rent would not be enforced at the full rate but only at the reduced rate. Such a representation would not give rise to an estoppel, because, as was said in *Jorden v Money*[1], a representation as to the future must be embodied as a contract or be nothing. But what is the position in view of developments in the law in recent years? The law has not been standing still since *Jorden v Money*[1]. There has been a series of decisions over the last fifty years which, although they are said to be cases of estoppel are not really such. They are cases in which a promise was made which was intended to create legal relations and which, to the knowledge of the person making the promise, was going to be acted on by the person to whom it was made, and which was in fact so acted on. In such cases the courts have said that the promise must be honoured . . . . As I have said they are not cases of estoppel in the strict sense. They are really promises – promises intended to be binding, intended to be acted on, and in fact acted on. *Jorden v Money*[1] can be distinguished, because there the promisor made it clear that she did not intend to be legally bound, whereas in the cases to which I refer the proper inference was that the promisor did intend to be bound. In each case the court held the promise to be binding on the party making it, even though under the old common law it might be difficult to find any consideration for it. The courts have not gone so far as to

1. (1854) 5 HL Cas 185.

give a cause of action in damages for the breach of such a promise, but they have refused to allow the party making it to act inconsistently with it. It is in that sense, and that sense only, that such a promise gives rise to an estoppel. The decisions are a natural result of the fusion of law and equity: for the cases of *Hughes v Metropolitan Rly Co, Birmingham and District Land Co v London & North Western Rly Co* and *Salisbury (Marquess) v Gilmore,* afford a sufficient basis for saying that a party would not be allowed in equity to go back on such a promise. In my opinion, the time has now come for the validity of such a promise to be recognised. The logical consequence, no doubt, is that a promise to accept a smaller sum in discharge of a larger sum, if acted upon, is binding notwithstanding the absence of consideration: and if the fusion of law and equity leads to this result, so much the better. That aspect was not considered in *Foakes v Beer.* At this time of day however, when law and equity have been joined together for over seventy years, principles must be reconsidered in the light of their combined effect. It is to be noticed that in the Sixth Interim Report of the Law Revision Committee, paras. 35, 40, it is recommended that such a promise as that to which I have referred, should be enforceable in law even though no consideration for it has been given by the promisee. It seems to me that, to the extent I have mentioned, that result has now been achieved by the decisions of the courts'.

There was no appeal. This was probably because the decision could be supported on other grounds. An appeal might have ruined everything.

The principle became known as promissory estoppel. Soon the time came for an extension of it. In the *High Trees* case there was an actual *promise* or *assurance*. In the next case there was only *conduct*. The law as to sale of goods had got tied into knots, especially when times for delivery had been extended by word of mouth. All these knots were untied in *Charles Rickards Ltd v Oppenhaim*[1]. Mr. Oppenhaim wanted a body built on a chassis of a Rolls Royce

1. [1950] 1 KB 616.

'Silver Wraith'. In July 1947 the coachbuilders promised to deliver it 'within six or at the most seven months'. They did not deliver it in that time. Mr. Oppenhaim still pressed them to deliver. Suppose they tendered delivery in June 1948 in accordance with his request, could Mr. Oppenhaim have refused to accept delivery? According to the old cases, he could have done. I pointed out the difficulty and gave the solution:

'. . . . It would have been said that there was no consideration; or, if the contract was for the sale of goods, that there was nothing in writing to support the variation. There is the well-known case of *Plevins v Downing,* coupled with what was said in *Besseler, Waechter, Glover & Co v South Derwent Coal Co Ltd,* which gave rise to a good deal of difficulty on that score; but all those difficulties are swept away now. If the defendant, as he did, led the plaintiffs to believe that he would not insist on the stipulation as to time, and that, if they carried out the work, he would accept it, and they did it, he could not afterwards set up the stipulation as to the time against them. Whether it be called waiver or forbearance on his part, or an agreed variation or substituted performance, does not matter. It is a kind of estoppel. By his conduct he evinced an intention to affect their legal relations. He made, in effect, a promise not to insist on his strict legal rights. That promise was intended to be acted on, and was in fact acted on. He cannot afterwards go back on it . . . . It is a particular application of the principle which I endeavoured to state in *Central London Property Trust Ltd v High Trees House Ltd'.*

In the sale of goods, *Charles Rickards Ltd v Oppenhaim* was a breakthrough. It was decided in 1950. At that time contracts for the sale of goods of £10 or more had to be in writing. That requirement was not abolished until 1954.

5 Did it abolish consideration?

During the years since 1946 there had been much discussion about *High Trees.* The question was asked: Had it done away with the doctrine of consideration? Was a promise now binding without consideration being given for it? This had been recommended by the Law Revision Committee for promises made in writing, but not for oral promises. The point came up for decision in *Combe v Combe*[1]. On getting a divorce, a husband, by a letter of his solicitor, agreed to pay his wife an allowance of £100 a year free of tax. The husband did not pay. She had a bigger income of her own than he did. After six years, she sued him for £600 arrears. The Judge at first instance had considered that the *High Trees* principle applied. But the Court of Appeal declined to extend it so. This is what I said:

'Much as I am inclined to favour the principle stated in the *High Trees* case, it is important that it should not be stretched too far, lest it should be endangered. That principle does not create new causes of action where none existed before. It only prevents a party from insisting upon his strict legal rights, when it would be unjust to allow him to enforce them, having regard to the dealings which have taken place between the parties. That is the way it was put in *Hughes v Metropolitan Railway*, the case in the House of Lords in which the principle was first stated, and in *Birmingham, etc., Land Company v London and North-Western Railway Co*, the case in the Court of Appeal where the principle was enlarged. It is also implicit in all the modern cases in which the principle has been developed. Sometimes it is a plaintiff who is not allowed to insist on his strict legal rights. Thus, a creditor is not allowed to enforce a debt which he has deliberately agreed to waive, if the debtor has carried on business or in some other way changed his position in reliance on the waiver.... A landlord, who has told his tenant that he can live in his cottage rent free for the rest of his life, is not allowed to go back on it, if the tenant stays in the house on that footing.... On other occasions it is a defendant who is not allowed to insist on his strict legal rights. His conduct may be such as to debar him from relying

1. [1951] 2 KB 215.

207

on some condition, denying some allegation, or taking some other point in answer to the claim. Thus a government department, which had accepted a disease as due to war service, were not allowed afterwards to say it was not, seeing that the soldier, in reliance on the assurance, had abstained from getting further evidence about it . . . . A buyer who had waived the contract date for delivery was not allowed afterwards to set up the stipulated time as an answer to the seller . . . . A tenant who had encroached on an adjoining building, asserting that it was comprised in the lease, was not allowed afterwards to say that it was not included in the lease . . . . A tenant who had lived in a house rent-free by permission of his landlord, thereby asserting that his original tenancy had ended, was not afterwards allowed to say that his original tenancy continued . . . . In none of these cases was the defendant sued on the promise, assurance, or assertion as a cause of action in itself: he was sued for some other cause; for example, a pension or a breach of contract, and the promise, assurance or assertion only played a supplementary role — an important role, no doubt, but still a supplementary role. That is, I think, its true function. It may be part of a cause of action, but not a cause of action in itself.

'The principle, as I understand it, is that, where one party has, by his words or conduct, made to the other a promise or assurance which was intended to affect the legal relations between them and to be acted on accordingly, then, once the other party has taken him at his word and acted on it, the one who gave the promise or assurance cannot afterwards be allowed to revert to the previous legal relations as if no such promise or assurance had been made by him, but he must accept their legal relations subject to the qualification which he himself has so introduced, even though it is not supported in point of law by any consideration but only by his word.

'Seeing that the principle never stands alone as giving a cause of action in itself, it can never do away with the necessity of consideration when that is an essential part of the cause of action. The doctrine of consideration is too firmly fixed to be overthrown by a side-wind. Its ill-effects have been largely mitigated of late, but it still remains a cardinal necessity of the formation of a contract, though not of its modification or discharge. I fear that it was my failure to make this clear which misled the Judge in the present case. He held that the wife could sue on the husband's promise as a separate and independent cause of action by itself, although, as he held, there was no consideration for it. That is not correct. The wife can only enforce it if there was consideration for it. That is, therefore, the real question in the case; was there sufficient consideration to support the promise?'

That case, however, led to a fall. Only a few years later Lord Simonds in the House of Lords in the *Tool Metal Manufacturing Co Ltd v Tungsten Electric Co Ltd*[1] gave a stern warning about it:

'.... I would not have it supposed, particularly in commercial transactions, that mere acts of indulgence are apt to create rights, and I do not wish to lend the authority of this House to the statement of the principle which is to be found in *Combe v Combe* and may well be far too widely stated'.

6 Extension to cover conduct

Despite this fall, the new extension of *High Trees* — so as to cover *conduct* — prospered rapidly, particularly in commercial transactions. The advance was most marked in two cases which do not appear in the Law Reports but only in Lloyd's List. I may say, in passing, that the Judges have no voice as to what is reported and where. That is left to the editors of the various series. In the first case, *Plasticmoda Societa per Azioni v Davidsons (Manchester) Ltd*[2], the new extension was used to get rid of the necessity for writing under the Sale

1. [1955] 1 WLR 761 at 764.
2. [1952] 1 Lloyd's Rep 527.

of Goods Act 1893. Some sellers of goods, by their conduct, led the buyers to believe that they would not insist on a letter of credit being established. I said:

'What is the effect of that conduct in law? Mr. Mocatta says with force that it is nothing else than an oral variation of a written contract, a contract which, under the Sale of Goods Act 1893, has to be in writing, and he says, therefore, under the authority of *Morris v Baron* [1918] AC 1, this variation must be disregarded. In my judgment, that principle does not apply to this case. Although this is a variation, nevertheless the requirement of writing, like the requirement of consideration, is overridden by the broad principle of "fair dealing and justice" which was laid down by the House of Lords in *Hughes v Metropolitan Railway Company* . . . and by this Court in . . . *Charles Rickards Ltd v Oppenhaim* . . . . It is this: If one party, by his conduct, leads another to believe that the strict rights arising under the contract will not be insisted upon, intending that the other should act on that belief, and he does act on it, then the first party will not afterwards be allowed to insist on the strict rights when it would be inequitable for him so to do'.

7 Extension of waiver

The second case was *Panchaud Freres SA v Et General Grain Co*[1] which is probably the case most frequently cited in the Commercial Court, although the text-book writers hardly notice it. In this case the new extension of estoppel by conduct was used to overcome the limitations of the old common law doctrine of 'waiver'. That doctrine only applied where the party waiving a breach had actual knowledge of it. *Panchaud Frères* extended it to cases where there was no knowledge but only conduct on which the other acted. Under a contract of sale on c.i.f. terms goods had to be shipped during the period June/July 1965. Whilst the goods were in transit, the shipping documents were tendered to the buyers. The buyers paid the price to the Bank and took up

1. [1970] 1 Lloyd's Rep 53.

the documents. If they had examined them closely, they would have discovered that the sellers had shipped the goods on 12 August 1965 — too late to satisfy the contract. But the buyers did not examine the documents closely. They missed the discrepancy. Yet when the ship actually arrived at the destination, the buyers refused to accept them, saying that they had been shipped too late. This defence was rejected. I said:

'. . . . When "waiver" is used in its legal sense, it only takes place when a man, with knowledge of a breach, does an unequivocal act which shows that he has elected to affirm the contract as still existing instead of disaffirming it as, for instance, in waiver of forfeiture . . . . In the present case Mr. Justice Roskill . . . held that these buyers had not waived the right to reject for late shipment because they had not got actual knowledge of that breach. At most they had constructive notice of it: and our commercial law sets its face resolutely against any doctrine of constructive notice . . . .

'The present case is not a case of "waiver" strictly so called. It is a case of estoppel by conduct. The basis of it is that a man has so conducted himself that it would be unfair or unjust to allow him to depart from a particular state of affairs which another has taken to be settled or correct . . . . Applied to the rejection of goods, the principle may be stated thus: If a man, who is entitled to reject goods on a certain ground, so conducts himself as to lead the other to believe that he is not relying on that ground, then he cannot afterwards set it up as a ground of rejection, when it would be unfair or unjust to allow him so to do. Mr. Lloyd gave a good illustration. Suppose, he said, in this case the bill of lading had contained the true date of shipment — Aug. 12 — (whereas the last date under the contract was July 31): so that, when the buyer took up the documents, he could have seen, if he had read it, that the date of shipment was Aug. 12. If he did not trouble to read it, but instead took up the documents and paid for them, he could not afterwards reject the goods on the ground of late shipment. Even though he had not read the bill of lading — and so was ignorant of the late shipment — he could not afterwards reject the goods on that ground: for the simple reason that he had the full opportunity of finding out from the contract documents what the real date of shipment was: and yet he did not trouble to do so. It would not be fair or just to allow him afterwards to reject the goods. Mr. Evans was inclined to accept this illustration as correct. Another instance can be given from the ordinary sale of goods. If a buyer does not choose to examine the goods when they arrive, and puts it off beyond a reasonable time, he loses his right to reject; see sect. 35 of the Sale of Goods Act 1893. Although he did not know they were not in conformity with the contract, nevertheless, by letting a reasonable time go by, he loses his right to reject.

'It seems to me that this case falls within that principle. If the buyers had read the shipping documents when they took them up and paid for them — as they could and should have done — they would have read this certificate of quality and seen that the date of shipment was really Aug. 12: and that someone had put July 31 on to the bill of lading so as to make it appear that the goods had been shipped in accordance with the contract, whereas, in fact they had not. If the buyers choose not to read the documents, they must put up with the consequences. They must be treated as if they had read them. This was clearly the view of the Committee of Appeal of the London Corn Trade Association Ltd: and, in a commercial matter like this, I like to hear the views of commercial men, just as Lord Mansfield did with his special jurymen. The Committee of Appeal held that the buyers "cannot be deemed to have been unaware" that the maize was loaded between Aug. 10 and 12, 1965. By taking up the documents and paying for them, they are precluded afterwards from complaining of the late shipment or of the defect in the bill of lading. That seems to me to be the finding of the Committee of Appeal, and I see no error of law in it. They used the word "waiver" but that does not matter. The buyers are precluded, by their conduct, from relying on the late shipment as a ground for rejecting the goods'.

Lord Justice Winn made it clear that this was an extension of the law as previously understood. He said:

'. . . . I too would deprecate any excessively scholastic approach to problems such as were presented to the commercial men in this Appeal Committee. I do not think they did use the word "waive" correctly, if the correctness of their use of it is to be judged by criteria which are familiar to and adopted by lawyers . . . . Their use of the word was not technically precisely correct, but their meaning seems to be reasonably clear.

'. . . . It does not seem possible in this case to say affirmatively that there was . . . anything which . . . could be described as an estoppel or a quasi-estoppel. I respectfully agree with my Lord that what one has here is something perhaps in our Law not yet wholly developed as a separate doctrine — which is more in the nature of a requirement of fair conduct — a criterion of what is fair conduct between the parties. There may be an inchoate doctrine stemming from the manifest convenience of consistency in pragmatic affairs, negativing any liberty to blow hot and cold in commercial conduct'.

It is a pity that this new concept of waiver was not put before the House of Lords in *Kammins Co v Zenith Investments*[1] . It would have supported the dissenting views of Lord Reid and Lord Pearson, and might have enabled Lord Diplock to overcome his reluctance.

The new concept of waiver was however applied by the House of Lords in *Bremer v Vanden*[2] , and by the Court of Appeal in *Toepfer v Cremer*[3] and *Intertradex v Lesieur*[4] . In each case the sellers served a notice of 'force majeure' which was defective. The buyers demanded delivery in such circumstances as to lead the sellers reasonably to believe that they buyers accepted it as a good notice. It was held that the buyers had 'necessarily waived any defect it might contain

1. [1971] AC 850.
2. [1978] 2 Lloyd's Rep 109.
3. [1975] 2 Lloyd's Rep 118 at 123.
4. (1978) 19th April (unreported).

whether they were aware of it or not'[1] : and this was applied by the majority of the Court of Appeal in *Bremer v Mack-prang*[2].

8 Detriment

Yet there was still one more fence to be surmounted. Was it necessary for there to be a 'detriment' in order for *High Trees* to operate? It had been so stated in the 1937 Report of the Law Revision Committee. But I ventured to suggest the contrary in *W. J. Alan & Co v El Nasar Export*[3]:

'What is the true basis of those decisions? is it a variation of the original contract? or a waiver of the strict rights thereunder? or a promissory estoppel precluding the seller from insisting on his strict rights? or what else?

. . . .

'The principle of waiver is simply this: if one party by his conduct, leads another to believe that the strict rights arising under the contract will not be insisted upon, intending that the other should act on that belief, and he does act on it, then the first party will not afterwards be allowed to insist on the strict legal rights when it would be inequitable for him to do so . . . . There may be no consideration moving from him who benefits by the waiver. There may be no detriment to him by acting on it. There may be nothing in writing. Nevertheless, the one who waives his strict rights cannot afterwards insist on them. His strict rights are at any rate suspended so long as the waiver lasts. He may on occasion be able to revert to his strict legal rights for the future by giving reasonable notice in that behalf, or otherwise making it plain by his conduct that he will thereafter insist upon them . . . . But there are cases where no withdrawal is possible. It may be too late to withdraw: or it cannot be done without injustice to the other party. In that event he is bound by his waiver.

1. By Lord Salmon [1978] 2 Lloyd's Rep at 127.
2. (1978) Times, 17th November.
3. [1972] 2 QB 189 at 212.

He will not be allowed to revert to his strict legal rights. He can only enforce them subject to the waiver he has made.

'Instances of these principles are ready to hand in contracts for the sale of goods. A seller may, by his conduct, lead the buyer to believe that he is not insisting on the stipulated time for exercising an option . . . . A buyer may, by requesting delivery, lead the seller to believe that he is not insisting on the contractual time for delivery . . . . A seller may, by his conduct, lead the buyer to believe that he will not insist on a confirmed letter of credit . . . but will accept an unconfirmed one instead . . . . A seller may accept a less sum for his goods than the contracted price, thus inducing him to believe that he will not enforce payment of the balance . . . . In none of these cases does the party who acts on the belief suffer any detriment. It is not a detriment, but a benefit to him, to have an extension of time or to pay less, or as the case may be. Nevertheless, he has conducted his affairs on the basis that he has that benefit and it would not be equitable now to deprive him of it.

The judge rejected this doctrine because, he said, "there is no evidence of the buyers having acted to their detriment". I know that it has been suggested in some quarters that there must be detriment. But I can find no support for it in the authorities cited by the judge . . . . If you study the cases in which the doctrine has been applied, you will see that all that is required is that the one should have "*acted* on the belief induced by the other party". That is how Lord Cohen put it in the *Tool Metal* case [1955] 1 WLR 761, 799, and that is how I would put it myself'.

This was accepted as correct by Mocatta J in *Bremer v Vanden*[1] with the approval of Lord Wilberforce in the House of Lords[2].

9 Must parties be contractually bound?

It has been suggested that the principle of *High Trees* is

1. [1977] 1 Lloyd's Rep 133 at 165.
2. [1978] 2 Lloyd's Rep 109 at 116.

limited to cases where the parties are contractually bound to one another. But this limitation was rejected in *Evenden v Guildford Football Club*[1]. A groundsman was employed at the football ground at Guildford. For some years he was employed by the Supporters' Club. Then he was transferred to the Football Club itself. The Football Club promised him that he would not suffer by the transfer. Was that promise binding so as to entitle him to redundancy pay for the whole period? The Court held that it was binding. I said:

'... Promissory estoppel ... applies whenever a representation is made, whether of fact or law, present or future, which is intended to be binding, intended to induce a person to act upon it and he does act upon it. That is the case here. Mr. Evenden entered into his employment with the football club on the faith of the representation that he would not be prejudiced and that his employment should be regarded as a continuous employment. Acting upon it, he has lost any rights against the supporters' club. The football club cannot be allowed to go back on it. His employment is to be treated as continuous for the whole 19 years. He is entitled to the full redundancy payment of £459'.

10 Proprietary estoppel

There remained one important field to be considered. It is what is now called 'proprietary estoppel'. It used to be called 'estoppel by acquiescence'. It was introduced by the Court of Equity long before the generalisation by Lord Cairns in *Hughes v Metropolitan Railway Co*[2]. But there has been a tendency in recent cases to combine the two doctrines. They are derived from the same source – namely, the interposition of equity to mitigate the rigours of the strict rules of law. But Sir Alexander Turner in the latest edition of his book on *Estoppel by Representation* considers that the two doctrines must be kept separate and distinct[3]. Everything he says is

1. [1975] 1 QB 917.
2. (1877) 2 AC 439.
3. Turner *Estoppel by Representation* (1977, 3rd Edn.), p. 307.

worthy of careful consideration: but I am on record as being in favour of combining them into one. In *Moorgate Ltd v Twitchings*[1] a car dealer bought a car from a man who brought it to his garage. The car dealer inquired of Hire-Purchase Information Ltd as to whether they had any record of the car being on hire-purchase. They said 'No'. Later on a finance company claimed that the car belonged to them. The Court of Appeal by a majority held that the car dealer acquired a good title but the House of Lords by 3 to 2 reversed this. I do not think, however, that there was any difference of view on this point. I said:

'There is no doubt that a buyer of goods can acquire a title by estoppel. This is recognised by section 21 (1) of the Sale of Goods Act 1893, which says:

"... the buyer acquires no better title to the goods than the seller had, unless the owner of the goods is *by his conduct* precluded from denying the seller's authority to sell".

'What conduct is sufficient for this purpose? To decide this, I go back to the general principles governing estoppel.

'Estoppel is not a rule of evidence. It is not a cause of action. It is a principle of justice and of equity. It comes to this: when a man, by his words or conduct, has led another to believe in a particular state of affairs, he will not be allowed to go back on it when it would be unjust or inequitable for him to do so. Dixon J put it in these words: "The principle upon which estoppel in pais is founded is that the law should not permit an unjust departure by a party from an assumption of fact which he has caused another party to adopt or accept for the purpose of their legal relations".

'Sir Owen (Dixon) said so in 1937 . . . .

'In 1947 after the *High Trees* case . . . , I had some correspondence with Sir Owen about it: and I think I may say that he would not limit the principle to an assumption of fact, but would extend it, as I would, to include an assumption of fact or law, present or future. At any rate, it applies to an

1. [1976] 1 QB 225.

assumption of ownership or absence of ownership. This gives rise to what may be called proprietary estoppel. There are many cases where the true owner of goods or of land has led another to believe that he is not the owner, or, at any rate, is not claiming an interest therein, or that there is no objection to what the other is doing. In such cases it has been held repeatedly that the owner is not to be allowed to go back on what he has led the other to believe. So much so that his own title to the property, be it land or goods, has been held to be limited or extinguished, and new rights and interests have been created therein. And this operates by reason of his conduct – what he has led the other to believe – even though he never intended it'.

11 Combining the estoppels

The matter, however, arose further for consideration in *Crabb v Arun DC*[1]. A man owned a piece of land in a field. The local council were building a new road near the field. The owner of the land wanted to get access to the new road. The surveyor to the local council led him to believe that he would be granted access. He actually left a gap in the fence for it, and the man acted on it. Later on the council blocked up the gap and refused him access. The Court held that the man had acquired a right of way by estoppel. I put it this way:

'When Mr. Millett, for the plaintiff, said that he put his case on an estoppel, it shook me a little: because it is commonly supposed that estoppel is not itself a cause of action. But that is because there are estoppels and estoppels. Some do give rise to a cause of action. Some do not. In the species of estoppel called proprietary estoppel, it does give rise to a cause of action. We had occasion to consider it a month ago in *Moorgate Mercantile Co Ltd v Twitchings* where I said that the effect of estoppel on the true owner may be that
".... his own title to the property, be it land or goods, has

1. [1976] 1 Ch 179.

been held to be limited or extinguished, and new rights and interests have been created therein. And this operates by reason of his conduct — what he has led the other to believe — even though he never intended it".

'The new rights and interests, so created by estoppel, in or over land, will be protected by the courts and in this way give rise to a cause of action . . . .

'The basis of this proprietary estoppel — as indeed of promissory estoppel — is the interposition of equity. Equity comes in, true to form, to mitigate the rigours of strict law. The early cases did not speak of it as "estoppel". They spoke of it as "raising an equity". If I may expand what Lord Cairns LC said in *Hughes v Metropolitan Railway Co:* "it is the first principle upon which all courts of equity proceed", that it will prevent a person from insisting on his strict legal rights — whether arising under a contract, or on his title deeds, or by statute — when it would be inequitable for him to do so having regard to the dealings which have taken place between the parties.

'What then are the dealings which will preclude him from insisting on his strict legal rights? If he makes a binding contract that he will not insist on the strict legal position, a court of equity will hold him to his contract. Short of a binding contract, if he makes a promise that he will not insist upon his strict legal rights — then, even though that promise may be unenforceable in point of law for want of consideration or want of writing — then, if he makes the promise knowing or intending that the other will act upon it, and he does act upon it, then again a court of equity will not allow him to go back on that promise . . . . Short of an actual promise, if he, by his words or conduct, so behaves as to lead another to believe that he will not insist on his strict legal rights — knowing or intending that the other will act on that belief — and he does so act, that again will raise an equity in favour of the other; and it is for a court of equity to say in what way the equity may be satisfied. The cases show that this equity does not depend on agreement but on words or conduct. In *Ramsden v Dyson* . . . Lord Kingsdown spoke of a verbal agreement "or what amounts to the same thing, an expectation, created or encouraged". In *Birmingham and District Land Co v London and North Western Railway Co* ... Cotton LJ said that ". . . what passed did not make a new agreement, but . . . what took place . . . raised an equity against him". And it was the Privy Council in *Plimmer v Wellington Corporation* ... who said that ". . . . the court must look at the circumstances in each case to decide in what way the equity can be satisfied" giving instances.

'Recent cases afford illustrations of the principle. In *Inwards v Baker* ... it was held that, despite the legal title being in the plaintiffs, the son had an equity to remain in the bungalow "as long as he desired to use it as his home". Danckwerts LJ said: "equity protects him so that an injustice may not be perpetrated". In *E. R. Ives Investment Ltd v High* . . . , it was held that Mr. High and his successors had an equity which could only be satisfied by allowing him to have a right of access over the yard, "so long as the block of flats has its foundations on his land". In *Siew Soon Wah v Yong Tong Hong* ... the Privy Council held that there was an "equity or equitable estoppel protecting the defendant in his occupation for 30 years". In *Bank Negara Indonesia v Hoalim* ... the Privy Council held that, despite the fact that the defendant had no protection under the Rent Acts, he had an equity to remain "so long as he continued to practise his profession" '.

To this I may add the words of Lord Justice Scarman:

'. . . . The plaintiff and the defendants are adjoining land-owners. The plaintiff asserts that he has a right of way over the defendants' land giving access from his land to the public highway. Without this access his land is in fact landlocked, but, for reasons which clearly appear from the narration of the facts already given by my Lords, the plaintiff cannot claim a right of way by necessity. The plaintiff has no grant. He has the benefit of no enforceable contract. He has no prescriptive right. His case has to be that the defendants are estopped by their conduct from denying him a right of access over their land to the public highway. If the plaintiff has any right, it is an equity arising out of the conduct and relationship of the parties. In such a case I think it is now well settled law that the court, having analysed and assessed the conduct and relationship of the parties, has to answer three questions. First, is there an equity established? Secondly, what is the extent of the equity, if one is established? And, thirdly, what is the relief appropriate to satisfy the equity? .... Such therefore I believe to be the nature of the inquiry that the courts have to conduct in a case of this sort. In pursuit of that inquiry I do not find helpful the distinction between promissory and proprietary estoppel. This distinction may indeed be valuable to those who have to teach or expound the law; but I do not think that, in solving the particular problem raised by a particular case, putting the law into categories is of the slightest assistance'.

This ruling was recently applied by the Court of Appeal of Kenya[1]. They have, as yet, no Law Reports there. So this book is the only place where their wisdom can be made known.

12 Payment of a lesser sum

Lastly, I would return to a doctrine which was mentioned in the *High Trees* case. It is the doctrine that payment of a lesser sum is no discharge for a larger. The opportunity to remedy this did not arise for nearly 20 years. Then in *D and C Builders Ltd v Rees*[2] it did arise. This is what I said:

'This case is of some consequence: for it is a daily occurrence that a merchant or tradesman, who is owed a sum of money, is asked to take less. The debtor says he is in difficulties. He offers a lesser sum in settlement, cash down. He says he cannot pay more. The creditor is considerate. He accepts the proffered sum and forgives him the rest of the debt. The

1. *Chase International Corpn v Oliver*, (1978) 11th July (unreported).
2. [1966] 2 QB 617.

221

question arises: Is the settlement binding on the creditor? The answer is that, in point of law, the creditor is not bound by the settlement. He can the next day sue the debtor for the balance: and get judgment. The law was so stated in 1602 by Lord Coke in *Pinnel's Case* – and accepted in 1889 by the House of Lords in *Foakes v Beer*.

. . . .

'This doctrine of the common law has come under heavy fire. It was ridiculed by Sir George Jessel . . . . It was said to be mistaken by Lord Blackburn . . . . It was condemned by the Law Revision Committee [(1945) Cmnd. 5449], paras. 20 and 21. But a remedy has been found. The harshness of the common law has been relieved. Equity has stretched out a merciful hand to help the debtor. The courts have invoked the broad principle stated by Lord Cairns in *Hughes v Metropolitan Railway Co.* . . . It is worth noticing that the principle may be applied, not only so as to suspend strict legal rights, but also so as to preclude the enforcement of them.

'This principle has been applied to cases where a creditor agrees to accept a lesser sum in discharge of a greater. So much so that we can now say that, when a creditor and a debtor enter upon a course of negotiation, which leads the debtor to suppose that, on payment of the lesser sum, the creditor will not enforce payment of the balance, and on the faith thereof the debtor pays the lesser sum and the creditor accepts it as satisfaction: then the creditor will not be allowed to enforce payment of the balance when it would be inequitable to do so. This was well illustrated during the last war. Tenants went away to escape the bombs and left their houses unoccupied. The landlords accepted a reduced rent for the time they were empty. It was held that the landlords could not afterwards turn round and sue for the balance, see *Central London Property Trust Ltd v High Trees House Ltd.* This caused at the time some eyebrows to be raised in high places. But they have been lowered since. The solution was so obviously just that no one could well gainsay it'.

Conclusion

Looking back over the last 32 years since the *High Trees* case, it is my hope that the principles then stated – and the extensions of them – will come to be accepted in the profession. The effect has been to do away with the doctrine of consideration in all but a handful of cases. During the 16 years whilst I have been Master of the Rolls I do not recall any case in which it has arisen or been discussed. It has been replaced by the better precept: 'My word is my bond', irrespective of whether there is consideration to support it. Once a man gives a promise or assurance to his neighbour – on which the neighbour relies – he should not be allowed to go back on it. In stating the principle, and its extensions, the lawyers use the archaic word 'estoppel'. I would prefer to put it in language which the ordinary man understands:

It is a principle of justice and of equity. It comes to this: When a man, by his words or conduct, has led another to believe that he may safely act on the faith of them – and the other does act on them – he will not be allowed to go back on what he has said or done when it would be unjust or inequitable for him to do so.

Part six

Negligence

Introduction

Of all the developments in the 20th century — by the Judges — the greatest has been in the law of negligence. At the beginning of the 19th century the rules of law were all derived from the forms of action. These were old and technical and expressed in Norman-French, such as trespass, case, trover, assumpsit, and so forth. During that century, the Judges did a great deal to bring them up to date. But they did it, naturally enough, by using English words to express the same underlying concepts as the old forms of action. As Maitland at the time said in his book, *Equity* (page 296): 'The forms of action we have buried, but they still rule us from their graves'. In the result the Judges of the 19th century formulated a series of particular rules as to when the defendant was under a duty to the plaintiff and what was the extent of that duty. These particular rules did not satisfy the social necessities and social opinion of the 20th century. In a series of decisions from 1932 onwards the Courts evolved negligence as an independent and vigorous wrong. It has come to dominate the whole field of civil liability. In particular there has been a remarkable extension of the liability of professional men and of public authorities.

In this part I tell of this extension and also of the problems that are still left unsolved. I hope that the Law Schools will help to provide the solution to these problems.

1 Leading up to *Candler v Crane, Christmas*

1 The law before 1932

Few can go back 50 years as I can. Few can appreciate the law as to negligence as it then stood. It was altogether different from what it is now. To understand the present position, I would invite you to look back before *Donoghue v Stevenson*[1]. I remember that case well from helping to edit the 13th edition of *Smith's Leading Cases* which was published three years before. There was a difference between a negligent *act*, and a negligent *statement;* that is, between something you *did* carelessly, and something you *said* carelessly. You could often recover damages for a negligent act, but you could rarely recover damages for a negligent statement. In either case your way would be beset with pitfalls. Let me give you two illustrations.

Take a negligent *act*. Suppose a client came to you and said: 'I was driving a van. The wheel came off. I was badly injured. It was all the fault of the wheelwright. It had been sent to him to repair and he did his work badly'. In advising the driver, you would have to ask him: 'Did you make the contract with the wheelwright?' He would reply: 'No. The firm did'. You would then have to reply: 'I am sorry but you can recover no compensation at all. The wheelwright was under no duty to you. His only duty was to the firm'. No one can sue a contracting party except the person who made the contract with him. That had been decided in *Earl v Lubbock*[2].

1. [1932] AC 562.
2. [1905] 1 KB 253.

Take a negligent *statement*. Suppose a client came to you and said: 'I am a rubber merchant. I knew that a firm of promoters were bringing out a new Company. I asked them, "Is it a Rubber Company?" The partner in the firm said "Yes". So I invested £5,000 in it. It turned out not to have been a Rubber Company at all: and I lost all my money. The promoters ought to have known better. If they had made the slightest inquiry, they would have found out that the Company had very few rubber trees and these had all been damaged by natives'. In advising the investor, you would have had to tell him: 'I am sorry but you have no claim against the promoters'. No one can bring an action for a negligent statement. He must show either fraud or a warranty: and this was neither. That had been decided in *Heilbut Symons & Co v Buckleton*[1].

2 *Donoghue v Stevenson*

Such was the state of the law in 1929. In looking into the cases, I discovered that Lord Esher MR in 1883 had tried to alter the law about negligent acts. He had done it in a case called *Heaven v Pender*[2]. But he had not succeeded in persuading his colleagues to his point of view. (Other Masters of the Rolls have found the same.) It was only 50 years later that his efforts were recognised – by the House of Lords with a majority of 3 to 2. It was in *Donoghue v Stevenson*[3]. Some manufacturers of ginger-beer had been careless and left a snail in the bottle. A lady drank it and was made ill. According to the previous law she had no claim against the manufacturers. They had made their contract with the wholesalers, not with her. So they were under no duty to her. Lord Aitken persuaded two Scotsmen to agree with him. They held the manufacturers liable. But two Englishmen dissented. They had been brought up in Chancery. Lord Atkin approved of Lord Esher. He said: 'Who then is my neighbour?

1. [1913] AC 30.
2. (1883) 11 QBD 503.
3. [1932] AC 562.

The answer seems to be — persons who are so closely and directly affected by my act that I ought reasonably to have them in mind as being so affected when I am directing my mind to the acts or omissions which are called in question. This appears to me to be the doctrine of *Heaven v Pender* as laid down by Lord Esher'.

But Lord Buckmaster dissented. He thought it better that the 'dicta in *Heaven v Pender* should be buried so securely that their perturbed spirits shall no longer vex the law'.

I well remember the impact of that case on the profession. Scrutton LJ, at the very first opportunity he had, said that the general proposition of Lord Atkin was wider than necessary and needed qualification — see *Farr v Butters*[1]. The proposition was, in the opinion of many, to be confined to manufacturers of products. It did not extend to builders and landlords and others. For instance, if a builder was employed to build a house — and he built it so badly that the ceiling fell down and injured someone — the builder was not liable to the injured person. He was only under a duty to the man who employed him. He had no duty to the injured person. The injured person could recover no compensation from anyone. It was so held in 1936 — *Otto v Bolton*[2].

In addition everyone held that *Donoghue v Stevenson*[3] was confined to negligent *acts*. It did not extend to negligent *statements*. If a professional man made a negligent statement or gave negligent advice, he could only be made liable when he made it to or for a client who employed him. It often happened that a third person acted on it and suffered loss by it, but he could recover nothing. That had been decided in 1893 in *Le Lievre v Gould*[4]. That was a case of a surveyor. In it Lord Esher himself had said: 'Such negligence, in the absence of a contract with the plaintiff, can give no right of action at law or in equity'. And Lord Atkin himself threw no doubt upon it in *Donoghue v Stevenson*[3].

1. [1932] 2 KB 606 at 614.
2. [1936] 2 KB 46.
3. [1932] AC 562.
4. [1893] 1 QB 491.

3 *Candler v Crane, Christmas*

Such was the state of affairs when *Candler v Crane, Christmas & Co*[1] came before us. It brought up the whole question of the liability of professional men for negligent statements. An accountant had been employed to prepare the accounts of a company. He was employed by the company itself to do it. He knew that the accounts were to be shown to a man who was thinking of investing money in the company. On the faith of the accounts, the man invested £2,000 and lost all of it. The Judge found the accountant was extremely careless but he dismissed the action because, in the absence of fraud, there was no duty of care owed by the accountant to the plaintiff.

On the appeal, the case for the investor was argued by Junior Counsel, Mr. Neil Lawson. There was no legal aid in those days. But Mr. Lawson was very knowledgeable. Although only a junior then, he made his mark in this case. He afterwards became a member of the Law Commission and later a Judge. His argument convinced me, though not my colleagues. We reserved our decision. I worked on it during the Christmas vacation. It was a dissenting opinion but it was worth giving because it had a good deal of impact. I may perhaps be forgiven for quoting some of it:

'Now I come to the great question in the case: did the accountants owe a duty of care to the plaintiff? If the matter were free from authority, I should have said that they clearly did owe a duty of care to him. They were professional accountants who prepared and put before him these accounts, knowing that he was going to be guided by them in making an investment in the company. On the faith of those accounts he did make the investment, whereas if the accounts had been carefully prepared, he would not have made the investment at all. The result is that he has lost his money. In the circumstances, had he not every right to rely on the accounts being prepared with proper care; and is he not entitled to redress from the accountants on whom he relied?

1. [1951] 2 KB 164.

I say that he is, and I would apply to this case the words of Knight Bruce LJ, in an analogous case ninety years ago: "A country whose administration of justice did not afford redress in a case of the present description would not be in a state of civilization". . . .

. . . .

'In my opinion these decisions of the House of Lords in *Donoghue v Stevenson* and *Nocton v Ashburton* are sufficient to entitle this court to examine afresh the law as to negligent statements, and that is what I propose to do.

'Let me first be destructive and destroy the submissions put forward by Mr. Foster. His first submission was that a duty to be careful in making statements arose only out of a contractual duty to the plaintiff or a fiduciary relationship to him. Apart from such cases, no action, he said, had ever been allowed for negligent statements, and he urged that this want of authority was a reason against it being allowed now. This argument about the novelty of the action does not appeal to me in the least. It has been put forward in all the great cases which have been milestones of progress in our law, and it has always, or nearly always, been rejected. If you read the great cases of *Ashby v White, Pasley v Freeman* and *Donoghue v Stevenson* you will find that in each of them the judges were divided in opinion. On the one side there were the timorous souls who were fearful of allowing a new cause of action. On the other side there were the bold spirits who were ready to allow it if justice so required. It was fortunate for the common law that the progressive view prevailed. Whenever this argument of novelty is put forward I call to mind the emphatic answer given by Pratt CJ nearly two hundred years ago in *Chapman v Pickersgill* when he said: "I wish never to hear this objection again. This action is for a tort: torts are infinitely various; not limited or confined, for there is nothing in nature but may be an instrument of mischief". The same answer was given by Lord Macmillan in *Donoghue v Stevenson* when he said: "The criterion of judgment must adjust and adapt itself to the changing circumstances of life. The categories of negligence are never closed". I beg leave to quote those cases and those passages against those who would emphasise the paramount importance of certainty at the expense of justice. It needs only a little imagination to see how much the common law would have suffered if those decisions had gone the other way.

'The second submission of Mr. Foster was that a duty to take care only arose where the result of a failure to take care will cause physical damage to persons or property. It was for this reason that he did not dispute two illustrations of negligent statements which I put in the course of the argument, the case of an analyst who negligently certifies to a manufacturer of food that a particular ingredient is harmless, whereas it is in fact poisonous, or the case of an inspector of lifts who negligently reports that a particular lift is safe, whereas it is in fact dangerous. The analyst and the lift inspector would, I should have thought, be liable to any person who was injured by consuming the food, or using the lift, at any rate if there was no likelihood of intermediate inspection . . . . Mr. Foster said that that might well be so because the negligence there caused physical damage, but that the same would not apply to negligence which caused financial loss . . . . I must say, however, that I cannot accept this as a valid distinction. I can understand that in some cases of financial loss there may not be a sufficiently proximate relationship to give rise to a duty of care; but, if once the duty exists, I cannot think that liability depends on the nature of the damage.

'The third submission of Mr. Foster was that the duty owed by the accountants was purely a contractual duty and therefore they were not liable for negligence to a person to whom they were under no contractual obligation. This seems to me to be simply a repetition of the nineteenth century fallacy which was . . . exploded by *Donoghue v Stevenson*.

'Let me now be constructive and suggest the circumstances in which I say that a duty to use care in statement does exist apart from a contract in that behalf. First, what persons are under such duty? My answer is those persons such as accountants, surveyors, valuers and analysts, whose profession and occupation it is to examine books, accounts, and other things, and to make reports on which other people – other than their clients – rely in the ordinary course of business. Their duty is not merely a duty to use care in their reports. They have also a duty to use care in their work which results in their reports . . . .

'The same reasoning has been applied to medical men who make reports on the sanity of others . . . . It is, I think, also applicable to professional accountants. They are not liable, of course, for casual remarks made in the course of conversation, nor for other statements made outside their work, or not made in their capacity as accountants . . .; but they are, in my opinion, in proper cases, apart from any contract in the matter, under a duty to use reasonable care in the preparation of their accounts and in the making of their reports.

'Secondly, to whom do these professional people owe this duty? I will take accountants, but the same reasoning applies to the others. They owe the duty, of course, to their employer or client; and also I think to any third person to whom they themselves show the accounts, or to whom they know their employer is going to show the accounts, so as to induce him to invest money or take some other action on them. But I do not think the duty can be extended still further so as to include strangers of whom they have heard nothing and to whom their employer without their knowledge may choose to show their accounts. Once the accountants have handed their accounts to their employer they are not, as a rule, responsible for what he does with them without their knowledge or consent.
. . . .

'Thirdly, to what transactions does the duty of care extend? It extends, I think, only to those transactions for which the accountants knew their accounts were required. For instance, in the present case it extends to the original investment of £2,000 which the plaintiff made in reliance on the accounts, because the accountants knew that the accounts were required for his guidance in making that investment; but it does not extend to the subsequent £200 which he made after he had been two months with the company . . . . It will be noticed that I have confined the duty to cases where the accountant prepares his accounts and makes his report for the guidance of the very person in the very transaction in question. That is sufficient for the decision of this case. I can well understand that it would be going too far to make an accountant liable to any person in the land who chooses to rely on the accounts in matters of business, for that would expose him to "liability in an indeterminate amount for an indeterminate time to an indeterminate class": see *Ultramares Corporation v Touche*, per Cardozo CJ'.

It was Lord Justice Asquith, however, who had the last word. He pierced my *ballon d'essai* with a courteous and disarming thrust:

'In the present state of our law different rules still seem to apply to the negligent misstatement on the one hand and to the negligent circulation or repair of chattels on the other; and *Donoghue's* case does not seem to me to have abolished these differences. I am not concerned with defending the existing state of the law or contending that it is strictly logical — it clearly is not. I am merely recording what I think it is. If this relegates me to the company of "timorous souls", I must face that consequence with such fortitude as I can command'.

2 Doctors at law

1 Medical malpractice

Fourteen years later my dissent in *Candler v Crane, Christmas* was approved by the House of Lords. But during the intervening time, the Courts gave much consideration to the position of medical men and hospitals. They were held liable to patients for negligent acts and negligent statements, even though they had no contract with the parties. So I will fill in this discourse by telling the story. It shows the law at its most progressive. But in addition it is a good guide to the standard of care required of a professional man. At one time the Courts held that a professional man was not liable for ordinary negligence but only for gross negligence, *Crassa Negligentia*. Later on it was said that there is no difference between negligence and gross negligence. 'It is the same thing with the addition of a vituperative epithet'. But there is a tendency today to draw the distinction again. It is done so as to protect a professional man from having his reputation unjustly besmirched. A medical man, for instance, should not be found guilty of negligence unless he has done something of which his colleagues would say: 'He really did make a mistake there. He ought not to have done it'.

So I turn to the medical cases. When I was at the Bar — soon after I took silk — I was instructed on behalf of a little girl of five. It was a poor person's case. So none of us got any fee. The child had warts on her face. Her mother had taken her to the Essex County Hospital for treatment. It was free. She had not to pay anything. The radiologist was negligent, and as a result the child was badly burned and disfigured. The

237

case was tried by Tucker J. There was a decision of the Court of Appeal in 1909, called *Hillyer v St. Bartholomew's Hospital*[1], saying that a hospital was not liable for the negligence of its professional staff. The Judge felt bound to decide against us. We took it to appeal. I found an article which Professor Goodhart had written in the Law Quarterly Review in which he suggested that the 1909 decision was wrong. The Court of Appeal were so impressed by the reasoning of it that they allowed our appeal. The little girl was awarded damages. It is reported as *Gold v Essex County Council*[2]. My clients were so pleased that they presented me with a table lamp for my room in chambers.

2 Two stiff fingers

Later on, when I was in the Court of Appeal, there was a case when a man went into the Walton Hospital at Liverpool to be treated for two stiff fingers. His hand was put in a splint. But when the splint was removed, his hand was useless. Instead of two stiff fingers, he had four stiff fingers. The trial Judge found for the hospital. He said that the plaintiff had failed to prove negligence on the part of any particular individual on the staff. The Court reversed his decision. It is *Cassidy v Ministry of Health*[3]. It has been the leading authority on the subject ever since. I said:

'If a man goes to a doctor because he is ill, no one doubts that the doctor must exercise reasonable care and skill in his treatment of him: and that is so whether the doctor is paid for his services or not. But if the doctor is unable to treat the man himself and sends him to hospital, are not the hospital authorities then under a duty of care in their treatment of him? I think they are. Clearly, if he is a paying patient, paying them directly for their treatment of him, they must take reasonable care of him; and why should it make any

1. [1909] 2 KB 820.
2. [1942] 2 KB 293.
3. [1951] 2 KB 343.

difference if he does not pay them directly, but only indirectly through the rates which he pays to the local authority or through insurance contributions which he makes in order to get the treatment? I see no difference at all. Even if he is so poor that he can pay nothing, and the hospital treats him out of charity, still the hospital authorities are under a duty to take reasonable care of him just as the doctor is who treats him without asking a fee. In my opinion authorities who run a hospital, be they local authorities, government boards, or any other corporation, are in law under the selfsame duty as the humblest doctor; whenever they accept a patient for treatment, they must use reasonable care and skill to cure him of his ailment. The hospital authorities cannot, of course, do it by themselves: they have no ears to listen through the stethoscope, and no hands to hold the surgeon's knife. They must do it by the staff which they employ; and if their staff are negligent in giving the treatment, they are just as liable for that negligence as is anyone else who employs others to do his duties for him. What possible difference in law, I ask, can there be between hospital authorities who accept a patient for treatment, and railway or shipping authorities who accept a passenger for carriage? None whatever. Once they undertake the task, they come under a duty to use care in the doing of it, and that is so whether they do it for reward or not.

'It is no answer for them to say that their staff are professional men and women who do not tolerate any interference by their lay masters in the way they do their work. The doctor who treats a patient in the Walton Hospital can say equally with the ship's captain who sails his ship from Liverpool, and with the crane driver who works his crane in the docks, "I take no orders from anybody". That "sturdy answer", as Lord Simonds described it, only means in each case that he is a skilled man who knows his work and will carry it out in his own way; but it does not mean that the authorities who employ him are not liable for his negligence . . . . The reason why the employers are liable in such cases is not because they can control the way in which the work is

239

done — they often have not sufficient knowledge to do so — but because they employ the staff and have chosen them for the task and have in their hands the ultimate sanction for good conduct, the power of dismissal.

'This all seems so clear on principle that one wonders why there should ever have been any doubt about it. Yet for over thirty years — from 1909 to 1942 — it was the general opinion of the profession that hospital authorities were not liable for the negligence of their staff in the course of their professional duties. This opinion was based on a judgment given by Kennedy LJ in *Hillyer v St. Bartholomew's Hospital.* I cannot help thinking that this error — for it was undoubtedly an error — was due to a desire to relieve the charitable hospitals from liabilities which they could not afford. They were dependent on voluntary contributions and their work would be seriously impeded if they were exposed to heavy claims of this sort . . . .

. . . .

'Turning now to the facts in this case, this is the position: the hospital authorities accepted the plaintiff as a patient for treatment, and it was their duty to treat him with reasonable care. They selected, employed, and paid all the surgeons and nurses who looked after him. He had no say in their selection at all. If those surgeons and nurses did not treat him with proper care and skill, then the hospital authorities must answer for it, for it means that they themselves did not perform their duty to him. I decline to enter into the question whether any of the surgeons were employed only under a contract for services, as distinct from a contract of service. The evidence is meagre enough in all conscience on that point. But the liability of the hospital authorities should not, and does not, depend on nice considerations of that sort. The plaintiff knew nothing of the terms on which they employed their staff: all he knew was that he was treated in the hospital by people whom the hospital authorities appointed; and the hospital authorities must be answerable for the way in which he was treated.

'This conclusion has an important bearing on the question

of evidence. If the plaintiff had to prove that some particular doctor or nurse was negligent, he would not be able to do it. But he was not put to that impossible task: he says, "I went into the hospital to be cured of two stiff fingers. I have come out with four stiff fingers, and my hand is useless. That should not have happened if due care had been used. Explain it, if you can". I am quite clearly of opinion that that raises a prima facie case against the hospital authorities . . . . They have nowhere explained how it could happen without negligence. They have busied themselves in saying that this or that member of their staff was not negligent. But they have called not a single person to say that the injuries were consistent with due care on the part of all the members of their staff. They called some of the people who actually treated the man, each of whom protested that he was careful in his part; but they did not call any expert at all, to say that this might happen despite all care. They have not therefore displaced the prima facie case against them and are liable to damages to the plaintiff'.

3 Anxieties relieved

As a result of that case, the medical profession became alarmed. It seemed to have opened the door to many groundless charges of negligence. This became known to us — from articles in journals and periodicals and so forth. The Courts are, I find, always sensitive to criticism. So in the next case we sought to relieve the anxieties of the medical men. It was *Roe v Minister of Health*[1]. In it I said:

'One final word. These two men have suffered such terrible consequences that there is a natural feeling that they should be compensated. But we should be doing a disservice to the community at large if we were to impose liability on hospitals and doctors for everything that happens to go wrong. Doctors would be led to think more of their own safety than of the good of their patients. Initiative would be

1. [1954] 2 QB 66.

stifled and confidence shaken. A proper sense of proportion requires us to have regard to the conditions in which hospitals and doctors have to work. We must insist on due care for the patient at every point, but we must not condemn as negligence that which is only a misadventure'.

4 A summing up

More particularly I should like to give an extract from a summing up which I gave to a jury. The case was *Hatcher v Black and others*[1] . Although I was a Lord Justice of Appeal, I did occasionally sit as a Judge of first instance. It is a useful thing to do – like a staff officer going back to the regiment for a spell in the line. Mrs. Hatcher was a lady who occasionally broadcast for the BBC. She went into St. Bartholomew's Hospital suffering from a toxic thyroid gland. An operation was advised. She asked if there was any risk to her voice. She was reassured by the doctors. The operation was performed. In the course of it, the nerve was so badly damaged that she could not speak properly. She could not broadcast again. This is what I told the jury:

'Before I consider the individual facts, I ought to explain to you the law on this matter of negligence against doctors and hospitals. Mr. Marven Everett sought to liken the case against a hospital to a motor-car accident or to an accident in a factory. That is the wrong approach. In the case of an accident on the road, there ought not to be any accident if everyone used proper care; and the same applies in a factory; but in a hospital, when a person who is ill goes in for treatment, there is always some risk, no matter what care is used. Every surgical operation involves risks. It would be wrong, and, indeed, bad law, to say that simply because a misadventure or mishap occurred, the hospital and the doctors are thereby liable. It would be disastrous to the community if it were so. It would mean that a doctor examining a patient, or a surgeon operating at a table, instead

1. (1954) Times, 2nd July.

of getting on with his work, would be for ever looking over his shoulder to see if someone was coming up with a dagger — for an action for negligence against a doctor is for him like unto a dagger. His professional reputation is as dear to him as his body, perhaps more so, and an action for negligence can wound his reputation as severely as a dagger can his body. You must not, therefore, find him negligent simply because something happens to go wrong; if, for instance, one of the risks inherent in an operation actually takes place or some complication ensues which lessens or takes away the benefits that were hoped for, or if in a matter of opinion he makes an error of judgment. You should only find him guilty of negligence when he falls short of the standard of a reasonably skilful medical man, in short, when he is deserving of censure — for negligence in a medical man is deserving of censure.

Let me illustrate this by the vexed question which has been discussed in this case: What should the doctor tell his patient? Mr. Tuckwell admitted that on the evening before the operation he told the plaintiff that there was no risk to her voice, when he knew that there was some slight risk, but that he did it for her own good because it was of vital importance that she should not worry. In short, he told a lie, but he did it because he thought in the circumstances it was justifiable. If this were a court of morals, that would raise a nice question on which moralists and theologians have differed for centuries. Some hold that it is never permissible to tell a lie even for a just cause: a good end, they say, does not justify a bad means. You must not do a little wrong in order to do a great right. Others, however, hold that it is permissible, if the justification is strong enough, and they point to the stratagems used in war to deceive the enemy. This, however, is not a court of morals but a court of law, and the law leaves this question of morals to the conscience of the doctor himself — though I may perhaps remark that if doctors have too easy a conscience on this matter they may in time lose the confidence of the patient, which is the basis of all good medicine. But so far as the law is concerned, it does not condemn the doctor when he only does that which

243

many a wise and good doctor so placed would do. It only condemns him when he falls short of the accepted standards of a great profession; in short, when he is deserving of censure. No one of the doctors that have been called before you has suggested that Mr. Tuckwell did wrong. All agree that it was a matter for his own judgment. They did not condemn him; nor should we'.

I remember how anxious the doctors and nurses were. It showed on their faces. I remember how long the jury were out. It was 3 or 4 hours. They came back and found a verdict for the defendants. I was relieved. The law was on the right course. It has remained so. It is, I believe, very different in the United States of America. 'Medical malpractice' suits there have become the curse of the medical profession. The legal profession get 'contingency fees'. So they take up cases on speculation. The jury gives enormous damages. Insurance premiums are high. The doctors charge large fees to cover them. It is all very worrying.

3 The impact of *Hedley Byrne*

1 *Hedley Byrne*

After that interlude on medical men, I return to the sequel to *Candler v Crane, Christmas & Co*[1]. It came about in a case which has become as famous as *Donoghue v Stevenson*[2]. It was *Hedley Byrne & Co Ltd v Heller & Partners Ltd*[3]. Whereas *Donoghue v Stevenson* dealt with negligent acts, *Hedley Byrne* dealt with negligent statements. I was invited to sit in the Lords on the appeal, but I knew that my dissenting judgment in *Candler* would come under review. So I declined. Hedley Byrne were advertising agents who were about to enter into a contract with a customer. They wanted a bankers' reference as to the customer's credit. Their own bankers passed on their request to a firm of merchant bankers. These reported that the customer was considered good for ordinary business arrangements. Relying on this report, the advertising agents gave the customer credit in a sum of £17,000. The customer was in fact very unsound. The advertising agents lost the £17,000. They sued the merchant bankers for negligence in giving the report. The merchant bankers had headed their report 'Without responsibility'. On that account they were held not liable. But the House of Lords, in a series of *obiter dicta*, considered the decision in *Candler*. I was gratified to find that they approved of my dissent and gave reasoning on the same lines. They held that a professional man was liable for negligent statements when

1. [1951] 2 KB 164.
2. [1952] AC 562.
3. [1964] AC 465.

245

he knew they were going to be acted upon: and they were acted upon. I will not pause here to quote from their judgments. Their influence will be apparent from the succeeding cases.

2 Barristers

Very soon it was sought to extend *Hedley Byrne* to make barristers liable for negligence. They never had been — but were they now?

It arose in *Rondel v Worsley*[1]. Mr. Rondel was charged with causing grievous bodily harm. He was defended by counsel, Mr. Michael Worsley. He was convicted and sentenced. He appealed and his appeal was dismissed. He then sued Mr. Worsley. He said that Mr. Worsley had not cross-examined sufficiently, and had not called the witnesses whom Mr. Rondel wanted. In every Court it was held that the action should be struck out. *Hedley Byrne* did not apply to a barrister. The reason was because, as a matter of public policy, a barrister could not be held liable for negligence in the conduct of a case. It may be presumptuous of me but I venture to set out what I said about the duty of a barrister:

'I will first consider the law as it was understood by the profession up till May of 1963 when the House of Lords decided *Hedley Byrne & Co Ltd v Heller & Partners Ltd.* Beyond doubt the barrister was treated differently from other professional men. He could not sue for his fees. He could not even make a contract for them with his client. Nor with the solicitor who represented the client. The obligation to pay him was an obligation which was binding in honour, not in law. Such was the position of the advocate in the Roman law. Such was the position of the barrister in our English law. It was the tradition of centuries that what he received from the client was a gift or honorarium, and not a stipulated wage. To this day his very robe bears witness. At the back of it there is still the flap of the little pocket

1. [1967] 1 QB 443.

where the client could place his gratuity. In the pretence that the barrister did not know he was being given a reward! Over 200 years ago Sir William Blackstone compared our serjeants at law and barristers with the ancient Roman orators:

"These indeed practised gratis, for honour merely, or at most for the sake of gaining influence: and so likewise it is established with us, that a counsel may maintain no action for his fees; which are given, not as a salary or hire, but as a mere gratuity, which a counsellor cannot demand without doing wrong to his reputation".

. . . .

'. . . . The rule itself was an anomaly. No other professional man was exempt from liability. A medical man was liable for negligence. So was a solicitor. Only a barrister was exempt. In addition, the reason given for the rule was bad. Both judges and text-writers said it was because he could not sue for his fees . . . . Yet in other professions it had been held ever since 1789 that, if a professional man undertook a task involving his skill, without any fee at all, he was liable if he performed it negligently . . . .

Although the rule was an anomaly, and the reason for it was bad, nevertheless it was regarded as so well settled that it could not be overturned . . . .

'This brings me to *Hedley Byrne & Co Ltd v Heller & Partners Ltd*. The facts are far removed. But in the speeches the House enunciated a principle which I take from the speech of Lord Morris of Borth-y-Gest:

"if someone possessed of a special skill undertakes, quite irrespective of contract, to apply that skill for the assistance of another person who relies upon such skill, a duty of care will arise".

I need hardly say that I greatly welcome this principle, seeing that I said somewhat the same in *Candler v Crane, Christmas & Co*.

'As soon as the House in May, 1963, stated this principle, the profession were quick to see that it was wide enough to apply to a barrister in all his work, both in court and out of it. So at once they asked whether the barrister's immunity

247

had gone. No one suggested that the House had given any thought to it. The speeches contain no word about a barrister. Nevertheless the principle was there. It made plain that the immunity can no longer be justified on the ground that a barrister cannot sue for his fees. If the rule is to be justified, it must be on some better ground. I turn to see if it exists.

'There is, in my judgment, a sure ground on which to rest the immunity of a barrister. At any rate, so far as concerns his conduct of a case in court. It is so that he may do his duty fearlessly and independently as he ought: and to prevent him being harassed by vexatious actions such as this present one now before us. It is like the ground on which a judge cannot be sued for an act done in his judicial capacity, however corrupt . . ., and on which a witness cannot be sued for what he says in giving evidence, however perjured . . ., and on which an advocate cannot be sued for slander for what he says in court however malicious . . . .

'All the reasons given in those cases apply as well to a suit against a barrister for negligence. As an advocate he is a minister of justice equally with the judge. He has a monopoly of audience in the higher courts. No one save he can address the judge, unless it be a litigant in person. This carries with it a corresponding responsibility. A barrister cannot pick or choose his clients. He is bound to accept a brief for any man who comes before the courts. No matter how great a rascal the man may be. No matter how given to complaining. No matter how undeserving or unpopular his cause. The barrister must defend him to the end. Provided only that he is paid a proper fee, or in the case of a dock brief, a nominal fee. He must accept the brief and do all he honourably can on behalf of his client. I say "all he *honourably* can" because his duty is not only to his client. He has a duty to the court which is paramount. It is a mistake to suppose that he is the mouthpiece of his client to say what he wants: or his tool to do what he directs. He is none of these things. He owes allegiance to a higher cause. It is the cause of truth and justice. He must not consciously mis-state the facts. He must not knowingly conceal the truth. He must not unjustly make a charge of fraud, that is, without evidence to support it. He must produce all the relevant authorities, even those that are against him. He must see that his client discloses, if ordered, the relevant documents, even those that are fatal to his case. He must disregard the most specific instructions of his client if they conflict with his duty to the court. The code which requires a barrister to do all this is not a code of law. It is a code of honour. If he breaks it, he is offending against the rules of the profession and is subject to its discipline. But he cannot be sued in a court of law.

'Such being his duty to the court, the barrister must be able to do it fearlessly. He has time and time again to choose between his duty to his client and his duty to the court. This is a conflict often difficult to resolve: and he should not be under pressure to decide it wrongly. Mr. Zander says that when a barrister puts first his duty to the court, he has nothing to fear. He has not been negligent and cannot be made liable. But that is too simple by far. It is a fearsome thing for a barrister to have an action brought against him. To have his reputation besmirched by a charge of negligence. To have the case tried all over again but this time with himself, the counsel, as the defendant. To be put to all the anxiety and, I would add, all the cost of defending himself. Even though in the end he should win. Faced with this prospect, a barrister would do all he could to avoid it. Rather than risk it, he would forever be looking over his shoulder to forestall it. He would be tempted to ask every question suggested by the client, however irrelevant; to call every witness desired by the client, however useless; to take every point, however bad; to prolong the trial inordinately: in case the client should be aggrieved and turn round on him and sue him for negligence. If a barrister is to be able to do his duty fearlessly and independently, he must not be subject to the threat of an action for negligence.

. . . .

'Finally, on public policy I would say this: If this action were to be permitted, it would open the door to every disgruntled client. You have only to read the applications made daily to the Criminal Division of this court. They are filled with complaints against the judge, against the counsel, against the witnesses, against everyone who has had a hand in bringing the man to justice. If this action is to go for trial, it will lead to dozens of like cases . . . . Every convicted prisoner who blamed his counsel could at once bring an action for negligence. Rather than open the door to him, I would bolt it'.

This immunity was upheld when the case reached the House of Lords[1]. Four, at least, of the Law Lords said that it extended, not only to the actual conduct of a case in Court, but also to the conduct and management of litigation. But 11 years later, in *Saif Ali v Sidney Mitchell*[2], a new set of Law Lords disagreed with their predecessors. They restricted the immunity greatly. It was by a narrow majority of 3 to 2. They confined the immunity virtually to the actual conduct of a case in Court. Lord Keith of Kinkel, in a persuasive dissent, thought this went 'some length towards defeating the purpose of the immunity' and the considerations of public interest on which it was based.

3 Borstal boys

In *Rondel v Worsley*, public policy was invoked to exempt the barrister. But soon afterwards public policy was invoked to extend *Hedley Byrne* and make many people liable for negligence, who had not been liable before. It was a new thing to use public policy in this way. Previously the Judges fought shy of invoking public policy. It was thought that public policy and law did not mix well together: no more than water and wine. In *Dorset Yacht Co v Home Office*[3], public policy was invoked so as to make the Home Office itself liable in respect of its statutory duties. Seven Borstal boys escaped at night from a camp. They boarded a yacht in Poole Harbour, cast her adrift and damaged her. The owners said that the three officers in charge of the boys had failed to supervise them properly. They had gone to bed and

1. [1969] 1 AC 191.   3. [1969] 2 QB 412.
2. [1978] 3 WLR 849.

250

left the boys at large. The owners of the yacht sued the
Home Office. I remember that we felt great difficulty about
the case. At the end of the argument I felt so uncertain that
I could have written a judgment either way. But after much
thought we held that the Home Office could be made liable:
(and the House of Lords — by 4 to 1 — upheld this
decision[1]). This is what I said:

'Although the issue is only stated in regard to Borstal
training, it involves the wider question of whether the Home
Office are liable for damage done by prisoners who escape
from custody or done by them while on parole. Strangely
enough there is no authority upon it in any of our books.
Nor is there much light thrown on it by the judges of the
great countries overseas which follow the common law . . . .
. . . .

These recent developments compel us to examine the whole
question. It is, I think, at bottom a matter of public policy
which we, as judges, must resolve. This talk of "duty" or
"no duty" is simply a way of limiting the range of liability
for negligence . . . .

'What then is the right policy for the judges to adopt?
On whom should the risk of negligence fall? Up till now it
has fallen on the innocent victim. Many, many a time has a
prisoner escaped — or been let out on parole — and done
damage. But there is never a case in our law books when the
prison authorities have been liable for it. No householder
who has been burgled, no person who has been wounded by
a criminal, has ever recovered damages from the prison
authorities such as to find a place in the reports. The householder has claimed on his insurance company. The injured
man can now claim on the compensation fund. None has
claimed against the prison authorities.

'Should we alter all this? I should be reluctant to do so if,
by so doing, we should hamper all the good work being done
by our prison authorities. "Open" prisons are the order of
the day. So is the parole system. The men are allowed their
freedom as much as possible. It helps to fit them better for

1. See [1970] AC 1004.

251

their return to society. This is especially the case with Borstal institutions. The Attorney-General, speaking for the Home Office, said:

"We want to train these boys to become good citizens. We put them under no restraint quite deliberately. We trust them. We leave them free to escape. It is the way in which they learn responsibility".

'The Attorney-General went so far as to suggest that, if the Home Office were to be liable for their escape, they might have to close these open Borstals. That would be a great disservice to society at large.

'I can see the force of this argument. But I do not think it should prevail. I think that the officers of Borstal institutions should be liable for negligence. And the reason I say this is because of the people who live in the neighbourhood. When the authorities open a Borstal institution, those living nearby are surely entitled to expect that reasonable care will be taken to protect them. Their confidence in the law would be undermined if the judges were to declare that the authorities owed no duty of care to them. Test it by a possible case which is by no means extravagant. Suppose the authorities know that some of the boys, with house-breaking records, are planning to escape, and have collected implements to break into houses, and yet they do nothing to stop the boys. They do not even take away the implements. Everybody in the neighbourhood would say that the authorities had failed in their duty and ought to pay for the damage. So would I.
. . . .

'The Attorney-General said something about the Borstal institutions being set up under statute: and that, as the statute did not give a remedy, an injured person had none. I cannot agree with this at all. The statute may be the basis of a Borstal system but it is the common law which builds on the statute. It says that those in authority are to use due care to train the boys, to discipline and control them, and to supervise them. If they fail, in circumstances in which it could reasonably be foreseen that the boys might escape and do damage, they must pay for the damage.

'But I wish to say this: an action does not lie except on

proof of negligence. It is not negligence to keep an open Borstal, or to let the boys have a great deal of freedom. The prison authorities are only negligent if, within that system, they do not take such care and supervision as a reasonable person, operating such a system, would take. It is one of the risks of the system — a conscious and deliberate risk — that boys will sometimes escape and do damage. So the fact that boys escape and do damage is no evidence of negligence. There must be proof of something more. An error of judgment will not do. There must be something which can genuinely be regarded as blameworthy. Knowing the high standard of the officers and staff of the Borstal system, I do not think there will be many claims of this sort: or, at any rate, not many which will succeed'.

4 Policy or operational

I would ask you to notice the last paragraph, especially when I said: 'It is not negligence to keep an open Borstal, or to let the boys have a great deal of freedom'. That is a decision made by the Home Office within their statutory powers — in making a policy or planning decision. For such decisions they will not normally be liable to an action. People who make such decisions have to consider, not only what is the right policy, but also what are the resources and means at their disposal to implement it. They are not to be accused of negligence simply because in the result someone is injured or damaged in consequence of it. It is very different when there is negligence at the operational level; that is, when men in the field do something negligent in carrying out their operations. Such as in the *Dorset Yacht* case when the three officers in charge of the boys went to bed instead of keeping proper supervision over the boys. For negligence at the operational level a government department or public authority should certainly be liable. But for negligence at the policy or planning level they will rarely be, though the possibility of it may not be excluded. That seems to be the way in which the law is moving, at any rate since the speech of Lord Wilberforce in *Anns v Merton Borough Council*[1].

1. [1977] 2 WLR 1024.

After that case, there came a run of cases against public authorities. The negligence in each case was at the operational level. The negligence was of men in the field. Each case showed *Hedley Byrne* in operation and incidentally brought up the question of economic loss – which is beginning to loom large nowadays.

In *Ministry of Housing v Sharp*[1] there was a register of land charges kept by a local authority. A purchaser asked for a search to be made to see if there was any charge on the land. The registrar's clerk was negligent. He certified that there was no charge on the land. On the faith of the certificate, the purchaser bought the land – only to find that there was a charge on it. As a result, he was much worse off financially. It was a case of a negligent statement by a clerk to a public authority which caused financial damage. I felt no difficulty about it. This is what I said:

'I have no doubt that the clerk is liable. He was under a duty at common law to use due care. That was a duty which he owed to any person – incumbrancer or purchaser – whom he knew, or ought to have known, might be injured if he made a mistake. The case comes four square within the principles which are stated in *Candler v Crane, Christmas & Co* [1951] 2 KB 164, 179–185, and which were approved by the House of Lords in *Hedley Byrne & Co Ltd v Heller & Partners Ltd* [1964] AC 465.

. . . .

'. . . . the duty to use due care in a statement arises, not from any voluntary assumption of responsibility, but from the fact that the person making it knows, or ought to know, that others, being his neighbours in this regard, would act on the faith of the statement being accurate. That is enough to bring the duty into being. It is owed, of course, to the person to whom the certificate is issued and whom he knows is going to act on it . . . . But it also is owed to any person whom he knows, or ought to know, will be injuriously affected by a mistake, such as the incumbrancer here'.

1. [1970] 2 QB 223.

4 Houses falling down

1 *Dutton's* case

The next case was one of the most important of modern times. It brought in everything — negligent statement, economic loss, public authorities, and previous decisions. It is *Dutton v Bognor Regis UDC*[1] . Some builders in Bognor Regis built a house on a rubbish tip. They did not make a proper concrete foundation. It was too thin — no doubt so as to save money. The Council's surveyor made his inspection. Either he did not notice the thinness or he turned a blind eye to it. Beyond doubt he was negligent. The first buyer bought it in ignorance. He sold it to Mrs. Saidee Dutton. No cracks had appeared then. During her time the walls and ceilings cracked. It would cost £2,240 to repair. She had not got the money to do it. The builder paid £625 to settle the claim against him. She sued the Council for the balance, saying that their surveyor was negligent.

This case gave us much anxiety. It was exceedingly well argued. A new silk, Mr. Tapp, did it for the Council. His early death was a great loss to the Bar. We gave judgment for Mrs. Dutton against the Council. We expected that the Council would appeal to the House of Lords, but they did not do so. Later on the House did consider it in *Anns v Merton Borough Council*[1] and approved it subject to one or

1. [1972] 1 QB 373.
2. [1977] 2 WLR 1024.

two qualifications which I will mention later. But I will
set out the matters in *Dutton* which were approved:

'*The Position of the builder*

Mr. Tapp submitted that the inspector owed no duty to a
purchaser of the house. He said that on the authorities the
builder, Mr. Holroyd, owed no duty to a purchaser of the
house. The builder was not liable for his negligence in the
construction of the house. So also the council's inspector
should not be liable for passing the bad work.

. . . .

'In the 19th century, and the first part of this century,
most lawyers believed that no one who was not a party to a
contract could sue on it or anything arising out of it. They
held that if one of the parties to a contract was negligent in
carrying it out, no third person who was injured by that
negligence could sue for damages on that account. The reason
given was that the only duty of care was that imposed by the
contract. It was owed to the other contracting party, and to
no one else . . . .

'That 19th century doctrine may have been appropriate in
the conditions then prevailing. But it was not suited to the
20th century. Accordingly it was done away with in
Donoghue v Stevenson [1932] AC 562. But that case only
dealt with the manufacturer of an article. *Cavalier v Pope* (on
landlords) and *Bottomley v Bannister* (on builders) were
considered by the House in *Donoghue v Stevenson*, but they
were not overruled. It was suggested that they were distin-
guishable on the ground that they did not deal with chattels
but with real property . . . . Hence they were treated by the
courts as being still cases of authority. So much so that in
1936 a judge at first instance held that a builder who builds
a house for sale is under no duty to build it carefully. If a
person was injured by his negligence, he could not recover . .

'The distinction between chattels and real property is quite
unsustainable. If the manufacturer of an article is liable to a
person injured by his negligence, so should the builder of a
house be liable. After the lapse of 30 years this was
recognised (in one or two cases). But the judges in those cases

confined themselves to cases in which the builder was only a contractor and was not the owner of the house itself. When the builder is himself the owner, they assumed that *Bottomley v Bannister* [1932] 1 KB 458 was still authority for exempting him from liability for negligence.

'There is no sense in maintaining this distinction. It would mean that a contractor who builds a house on another's land is liable for negligence in constructing it, but that a speculative builder, who buys land and himself builds houses on it for sale, and is just as negligent as the contractor, is not liable. That cannot be right. Each must be under the same duty of care and to the same persons. If a visitor is injured by the negligent construction, the injured person is entitled to sue the builder, alleging that he built the house negligently. The builder cannot defend himself by saying: "True I was the builder; but I was the owner as well. So I am not liable". The injured person can reply: "I do not care whether you were the owner or not, I am suing you in your capacity as builder and that is enough to make you liable".

. . . .

'I hold, therefore, that a builder is liable for negligence in constructing a house — whereby a visitor is injured — and it is no excuse for him to say that he was the owner of it. In my opinion *Bottomley v Bannister* [1932] 1 KB 458 is no longer authority. Nor is *Otto v Bolton and Norris* [1936] 2 KB 46. They are both overruled. *Cavalier v Pope* [1906] AC 428 has gone too. It was reversed by the Occupiers' Liability Act 1957, section 4 (1).

'The Position of the Professional Adviser
Mr. Tapp then submitted another reason for saying that the inspector owed no duty to a purchaser. He said that an inspector is in the same position as any professional man who, by virtue of his training and experience, is qualified to give advice to others on how they should act. He said that such a professional man owed no duty to one who did not employ him but only took the benefit of his work: and that an inspector was in a like position . . . .

'Nowadays since *Hedley Byrne & Co Ltd v Heller &*

Partners Ltd [1964] AC 465 it is clear that a professional man who gives guidance to others owes a duty of care, not only to the client who employs him, but also to another who he knows is relying on his skill to save him from harm. It is certain that a banker or accountant is under such a duty. And I see no reason why a solicitor is not likewise. The essence of this proposition, however, is the *reliance*. . . . . The professional man must know that the other is *relying* on his skill and the other must in fact rely on it.

'Reliance

Mr. Tapp made a strong point here about reliance. He said that even if the inspector was under a duty of care, he owed that duty only to those who he knew would rely on this advice – and who did rely on it – and not to those who did not. He said that Mrs. Dutton did not rely on the inspector and, therefore, he owed her no duty.

'It is at this point that I must draw a distinction between the several categories of professional men. I can well see that in the case of a professional man who gives advice on financial or property matters – such as a banker, a lawyer or an accountant – his duty is only to those who rely on him and suffer financial loss in consequence. But in the case of a professional man who gives advice on the safety of buildings, or machines, or material, his duty is to all those who may suffer injury in case his advice is bad. In *Candler v Crane, Christmas & Co* [1951] 2 KB 164, 179, I put the case of an analyst who negligently certifies to a manufacturer of food that a particular ingredient is harmless, whereas it is, in fact, poisonous: or the case of an inspector of lifts who negligently reports that a particular lift is safe, whereas it is in fact dangerous. It was accepted that the analyst and the lift inspector would be liable to any person who was injured by consuming the food or using the lift. Since that case the courts have had the instance of an architect or engineer. If he designs a house or a bridge so negligently that it falls down, he is liable to every one of those who are injured in the fall: see *Clay v A. J. Crump & Sons Ltd* [1964] 1 QB 533. None of those injured would have relied on the architect

258

or the engineer. None of them would have known whether an architect or engineer was employed, or not. But beyond doubt, the architect and engineer would be liable. The reason is not because those injured relied on him, but because he knew, or ought to have known, that such persons might be injured if he did his work badly.

. . . .

'Proximity

Mr. Tapp submitted that in any case the duty ought to be limited to those immediately concerned and not to purchaser after purchaser down the line. There is a good deal in this, but I think the reason is because a subsequent purchaser often has the house surveyed. This intermediate inspection, or opportunity of inspection, may break the proximity. It would certainly do so when it ought to disclose the damage. But the foundations of a house are in a class by themselves. Once covered up, they will not be seen again until the damage appears. The inspector must know this, or, at any rate, he ought to know it. Applying the test laid down by Lord Atkin in *Donoghue v Stevenson,* I should have thought that the inspector ought to have had subsequent purchasers in mind when he was inspecting the foundations. He ought to have realised that, if he was negligent, they might suffer damage.

'Economic Loss

Mr. Tapp submitted that the liability of the council would, in any case, be limited to those who suffered bodily harm: and did not extend to those who only suffered economic loss. He suggested, therefore, that although the council might be liable if the ceiling fell down and injured a visitor, they would not be liable simply because the house was diminished in value . . . . I cannot accept this submission. The damage done here was not solely economic loss. It was physical damage to the house. If Mr. Tapp's submission were right, it would mean that if the inspector negligently passes a house as properly built and it collapses and injures a person, the council are liable: but if the owner discovers the defect in time to repair it — and he does repair it — the council are not liable. That is an impossible distinction. They are liable in either case.

'I would say the same about the manufacturer of an article. If he makes it negligently, with a latent defect (so that it breaks to pieces and injures someone), he is undoubtedly liable. Suppose that the defect is discovered in time to prevent the injury. Surely he is liable for the cost of repair.
. . . .

'*Policy*
This case is entirely novel. Never before has a claim been made against a council or its surveyor for negligence in passing a house. The case itself can be brought within the words of Lord Atkin in *Donoghue v Stevenson:* but it is a question whether we should apply them here . . . . It seems to me that it is a question of policy which we, as judges, have to decide. The time has come when, in cases of new import, we should decide them according to the reason of the thing.

'In previous times when faced with a new problem, the judges have not openly asked themselves the question: what is the best policy for the law to adopt? But the question has always been there in the background. It has been concealed behind such questions as: Was the defendant under any duty to the plaintiff? Was the relationship between them sufficiently proximate? Was the injury direct or indirect? Was it foreseeable, or not? Was it too remote? And so forth.
. . . .
What are the considerations of policy here? I will take them in order.

'First, Mrs. Dutton has suffered a grievous loss. The house fell down without any fault of hers. She is in no position herself to bear the loss. Who ought in justice to bear it? I should think those who were responsible. Who are they? In the first place, the builder was responsible. It was he who laid the foundations so badly that the house fell down. In the second place, the council's inspector was responsible. It was his job to examine the foundations to see if they would take the load of the house. He failed to do it properly. In the third place, the council should answer for his failure. They were entrusted by Parliament with the task of seeing that houses were properly built. They received public funds for the purpose. The very object was to protect purchasers and occupiers of houses. Yet they failed to protect them. Their shoulders are broad enough to bear the loss.

. . . .

'Next, I ask: Is there any economic reason why liability should not be imposed on the council? In some cases the law has drawn the line to prevent recovery of damages. It sets a limit to damages for economic loss, or for shock, or theft by escaping convicts. The reason is that if no limit were set there would be no end to the money payable. But I see no such reason here for limiting damages. In nearly every case the builder will be primarily liable. He will be insured and his insurance company will pay the damages. It will be very rarely that the council will be sued or found liable. If it is, much the greater responsibility will fall on the builder and little on the council.

'Finally, I ask myself: If we permit this new action, are we opening the door too much? Will it lead to a flood of cases which neither the council nor the courts will be able to handle? Such considerations have sometimes in the past led the courts to reject novel claims. But I see no need to reject this claim on this ground. The injured person will always have his claim against the builder. He will rarely allege – and still less be able to prove – a case against the council.

'All these considerations lead me to the conclusion that the policy of the law should be, and is, that the council should be liable for the negligence of their surveyor in passing work as good when in truth it is bad'.

2 Valuers

Dutton's case was the precursor of many developments. Take the liability of professional men. For over 100 years there was one class of professional men who were thought to be immune from suit. These were valuers, auditors and architects. When they were deciding matters as between two parties, they were held to owe no duty of care to anyone: because they were quasi-arbitrators. If an architect gave a certificate for payment negligently — giving too much or too little — he could not be sued by either party. If a valuer negligently assessed the value of the property and put it too high or too low, he again could not be sued by either party. These decisions were considered by the Court of Appeal in *Arenson v Arenson*[1]. The majority of the Court felt bound to give immunity to those professional men. But I dissented. And later on the House of Lords took the same view as I had done. This was in *Sutcliffe v Thackrah*[2] and *Arenson v Cassan Beckman Rutley & Co*[3]. So perhaps I may be forgiven if I set out my reasoning:

'The liability of the auditors
As experts and not arbitrators

At the outset I would stress that the auditors were expressly engaged to act "as experts and not as arbitrators". So they cannot claim the immunity from liability which attaches to arbitrators. Nevertheless they say that, as experts, they are entitled to immunity. They rely on a long line of cases which appear to decide that, when a professional man is employed to decide a matter as between two others, fairly and impartially, using his own skill and judgment, then he is not liable for negligence in coming to his decision . . . . The judge felt impelled by those cases to strike out the claim against the auditors. He said that "short of fraud" they were not liable.

'Mr. Muir Hunter challenged that line of cases. He suggested that they should be reconsidered in the light of *Hedley Byrne & Co Ltd v Heller & Partners Ltd* [1964] AC 465. I agree with him. Those cases proceeded on the footing that a professional man, employed to decide between two others, was an arbitrator or in the position of an arbitrator, or was a quasi-arbitrator. He was so described in every one of those cases. But in our present case he was nothing of the

1. [1973] Ch 346.
2. [1974] AC 727.
3. [1977] AC 405.

kind. He was an expert, and not an arbitrator. The parties so
stipulated. There is this great difference between the two. If
an arbitrator makes a mistake of law, or is about to make it,
it can be corrected. If he makes his award, or is about to
make it, on the wrong basis, it can be put right. If he is guilty
of misconduct, his award can be set aside. But if a professional man, acting as an expert and not as an arbitrator,
makes a mistake, it cannot be corrected. At any rate, if he
gives no reasons. As between the two parties, they are bound
by it. Short of fraud or collusion, they are stuck with it. So
I ask this question: If a professional man, acting as an expert,
is guilty of gross negligence – whereby one of the parties is
greatly damnified – why should he not be liable to
damages? . . . .

'A professional duty and not a clerkly duty
In *Stevenson v Watson* (1879) 4 CPD 148, 157, Lord Coleridge
CJ drew a distinction between a professional duty and a clerkly
duty. If a professional man was called upon to give a certificate or make a valuation, which was to be binding as
between two others, using his professional judgment and
skill, he was not to be liable for negligence in doing it. But,
if a professional man was called upon to do work which was
purely a matter of arithmetical calculation, or was merely a
ministerial or clerkly duty, he would be liable for negligence
in doing it. This distinction was endorsed in *Chambers v
Goldthorpe* [1901] 1 KB 624, 635, by A. L. Smith MR, and
at p. 641 by Collins LJ.
. . . .

'Seeing that a clerk is liable for negligence in doing a clerkly
duty, why should not a professional man be likewise? Much
of a professional man's duties are purely matters of arithmetical calculation. A quantity surveyor has to measure the
area of a room and multiply it by the cost per square foot.
An accountant has to get out figures from the books, add up
the income and deduct the expenses. What is that but arith-
metic? He may leave it to his clerk or he may do it himself. If
the clerk does it and gets it wrong – due to his negligence –
the clerk is liable. So is his principal . . . . If the professional

263

man does it himself and likewise gets it wrong — due to the selfsame negligence — why should not he himself be liable?

'It may be said that the difference is between a certificate which requires skill and judgment and one which does not. But if so, where do you draw the line? A public weigher must know his weights and measures and be accurate in his observations. A clerk in the land registry must be able to read maps, search files and note entries. Each of those has to undergo a course of instruction before entering upon the work. Each of those is liable for negligence in exercising his skills. And his principal is answerable for it too. So should the professional man be liable for negligence in his skills, higher though they be'.

3 Economic loss

Another matter in which *Dutton v Bognor Regis UDC*[1] led the way was one which is giving rise to much discussion nowadays. It is economic loss. Mrs. Dutton was not injured herself. The ceiling did not fall down on her. The damage to her was simply financial damage. She had not repaired the house but it would cost £2,240 to do the repairs; and the house was diminished in value by £500. Was she entitled to recover that economic loss? It was held that she was so entitled. Later, Lord Wilberforce in *Anns v Merton Borough Council*[2] took the same view when he classified the damages recoverable as 'material physical damages'.

But to show the problems which arise about economic loss, I would have you consider a hypothetical case. Suppose that Mrs. Dutton was a dressmaker and that she could not do her dressmaking whilst the house was being repaired. Could she have recovered her loss of profit? It is difficult to see any good reason why she should not do so. Suppose now that the danger was discovered before there was any physical damage to the house, but it was reasonably anticipated that damage

1. [1972] 1 QB 373.
2. [1977] 2 WLR 1024.

would be done. Mrs. Dutton would be justified in spending money to avert that danger, and such expenditure would be recoverable. But could she recover the loss of business whilst the work was being done? It would seem difficult to refuse it. In *Dutton's* case, however, there was only damage to one person. In contrast, there are cases of negligent acts when there is damage to a large number of people – as when an electric cable or water main is severed by the negligence of a contractor. So also in cases of negligent statements, damage may be caused to a large number of investors, who are induced to act on it. In those cases those damaged or injured may recover the damage or expenses actually incurred, or anticipated, to remedy the damage or danger; but can they recover the loss of profit? This is a distinction which was drawn by the majority of the Court in the next case, *Spartan Steel v Martin & Co*[1] :

'At bottom I think the question of recovering economic loss is one of policy. Whenever the courts draw a line to mark out the bounds of *duty,* they do it as matter of policy so as to limit the responsibility of the defendant. Whenever the courts set bounds to the *damages* recoverable – saying that they are, or are not, too remote – they do it as matter of policy so as to limit the liability of the defendant.

. . . .

'The more I think about these cases, the more difficult I find it to put each into its proper pigeonhole. Sometimes I say: "There was no duty". In others I say: "The damage was too remote". So much so that I think the time has come to discard those tests which have proved so elusive. It seems to me better to consider the particular relationship in hand, and see whether or not, as a matter of policy, economic loss should be recoverable, or not . . . .

'So I turn to the relationship in the present case. It is of common occurrence. The parties concerned are: the electricity board who are under a statutory duty to maintain supplies of electricity in their district; the inhabitants of the

1. [1973] QB 27.

district, including this factory, who are entitled by statute to a continuous supply of electricity for their use; and the contractors who dig up the road. Similar relationships occur with other statutory bodies, such as gas and water undertakings. The cable may be damaged by the negligence of the statutory undertaker, or by the negligence of the contractor, or by accident without any negligence by anyone; and the power may have to be cut off whilst the cable is repaired. Or the power may be cut off owing to a short-circuit in the power house: and so forth. If the cutting off of the supply causes economic loss to the consumers, should it as matter of policy be recoverable? And against whom?

. . . .

. . . . in such a hazard as this, the risk of economic loss should be suffered by the whole community who suffer the losses — usually many but comparatively small losses — rather than on the one pair of shoulders, that is, on the contractor on whom the total of them, all added together, might be very heavy. . . . . If the defendant is guilty of negligence which cuts off the electricity supply and causes actual physical damage to person or property, that physical damage can be recovered . . . . ; and also any economic loss truly consequential on the material damage . . . .

'These considerations lead me to the conclusion that the plaintiffs should recover for the physical damage to the one melt (£368), and the loss of profit on that melt consequent thereon (£400): but not for the loss of profit on the four melts (£1,767), because that was economic loss independent of the physical damage'.

4 Limitation Acts

I now come to one matter in *Dutton*'s case in which I was wrong. It was about the Limitation Acts. When did time run against Mrs. Dutton so as to bar a claim by her? In *Dutton*'s case I said[1] : 'The damage was done when the foundations were badly constructed. The period of limitation (six years)

1. [1972] 1 QB 373 at 396.

then began to run'. But in the later case of *Sparham-Souter v Town Developments*[1] I recanted on these grounds:

'In recent years the law of negligence has been transformed out of all recognition. This is the first case in which we have had to consider the effect of this transformation on the Statute of Limitations. One thing is quite clear. A cause of action for negligence accrues not at the date of the negligent act or omission but at the date when the damage is sustained by the plaintiff . . . .

'Another thing is quite clear: "A Statute of Limitations cannot begin to run unless there are two things present – a party capable of suing and a party liable to be sued". . . . There is good sense in it. It would be most unjust that time should run against a plaintiff when there is no possibility of bringing an action to enforce it.

'Starting with these two propositions. I would now ask: when does the time start to run in actions against the manu-facturer of defective goods? For this may afford a guide in seeing when it starts to run against the builder of a defective house, or the surveyor who passes it.

'Take a case which has happened in the past. A motor manufacturer makes a motor car so negligently that there is a latent defect in the braking system. The car is sold by one person to another down a chain of buyers. Some time later the brakes fail owing to the defect. There is an accident. Persons are injured. Property is damaged. Each person who suffers damage to person or property has a cause of action against the manufacturer under *Donoghue v Stevenson* . . . . The cause of action accrues not at the time when the latest owner bought the car but at the time when the accident took place and the damage was sustained . . . .

'Now apply that to a case like *Dutton v Bognor Regis Urban District Council* [1972] 1 QB 373 . . . and you will see that the parallel is very close. A builder negligently makes foundations for a house which are quite insufficient and in breach of the byelaws. The council's inspector negligently

1. [1976] QB 858.

267

passes them as sufficient. The house is built and is sold by the builder to a purchaser, who sells it to another, and so on down a chain of purchasers. Some time later the house begins to sink and cracks appear in the structure owing to the insufficient foundations. The man who is the owner at that time has a cause of action against the builder and the council under *Dutton v Bognor Regis Urban District Council*. The cause of action accrues, not at the time of the negligent making or passing of the foundations, nor at the time when the latest owner bought the house, but at the time when the house began to sink and the cracks appeared. That was the first time that any damage was sustained. None of the previous owners had sustained any damage. Each had bought and sold the house at a full price in the belief that the foundations were sound. The only person to sustain the damage was the man who owned the house at the time when the house sank and the cracks appeared. It is only at that time that he can reasonably be expected to know that he may have a cause of action. It would be most unfair that time should run against him before he knows – or has any possibility of knowing – that he has a cause of action. Time should not begin to run against him until he knows of the defective foundations, or could, with reasonable diligence, have discovered it . . . .

'That principle underlies the Limitation Acts of 1963 and 1975: and it is, I think, the principle which we should adopt in regard to this new cause of action introduced by *Dutton v Bognor Regis Urban District Council*.

. . . .

'And again: what about *Bagot v Stevens Scanlan & Co Ltd* [1966] 1 QB 197, 203, when Diplock LJ expressed the view that the damage occurred "when the drains were improperly built": and I followed him in *Dutton v Bognor Regis Urban District Council* [1972] 1 QB 373, 396. This does make me pause. But now, having thought it over time and again – and been converted by my brethren – I have come to the conclusion that, when building work is badly done – and covered up – the cause of action does not accrue, and time does not begin to run, until such time as the plaintiff discovers that it has done damage, or ought, with reasonable diligence, to have discovered it.

'One word more: the only owner who has a cause of action is the owner in whose time the damage appears. He alone can sue for it unless, of course, he sells the house with its defects and assigns the cause of action to his purchaser.

'It may seem hard on the builder or the council surveyor that he may find himself sued many years after he left the work: but it would be harder on the householder that he should be without remedy, seeing that the surveyor passed the bad work and the builder covered it up, and thus prevented it being discovered earlier. And, when one finds such cases as *Dutton v Bognor Regis Urban District Council* (where the house was built on a rubbish tip), or *Higgins v Arfon Borough Council* (where it was built on bare earth), or *Anns v Walcroft Property Co Ltd* (where the foundations were too thin) — and the inspector was alleged negligently or conveniently to have overlooked it — it is only fair that the plaintiff should have a remedy'.

In *Anns v Merton Borough Council*[1] the House of Lords approved *Sparham-Souter* in substance, but Lord Wilberforce said that the cause of action only arose when there was 'present or imminent danger to the health or safety of persons occupying it'. I hope that, in practice, this will produce the same result as my own formulation.

1. [1977] 2 WLR 1024.

5 Innocent representation made actionable

1 Representations inducing a contract

At this point I will leave *Dutton* and its consequences. There remains one important question: Does *Hedley Byrne* apply to representations made in order to induce a contract? At the beginning of this discourse, I told you of the case in 1913 about the so-called 'Rubber Company' in which the House of Lords laid it down that no action lay for damages for an innocent misrepresentation, no matter how negligent it was of the man who made it.

In 1963, when *Hedley Byrne* was decided, no one thought that it had altered that state of the law. Whenever a representation was made to induce a contract, people still thought that the other party had to show either fraud or a collateral warranty. There were observations of good judges, including Lord Reid himself, to that effect. Moreover, Parliament itself acted on that assumption in passing the Misrepresentation Act 1967. They remedied it partially but that Act did not come into force until 22nd April 1967. It so happened that the common law was taking the matter in hand itself. The Judges, in a series of decisions, held that *Hedley Byrne* did apply to representations made in order to induce a contract.

The first was *McInerny v Lloyds Bank*[1]. A banker sent a telex to Mr. McInerny as a result of which he sold valuable

1. [1974] 1 Lloyd's Rep 246.

assets to a purchaser who defaulted. It was a representation made to induce a contract with a third party. The case was eventually decided on the facts but I tried to state the law. The case was only reported in *Lloyd's Law Reports.* So I will set out the principal part:

'Before 1963 it was thought that no action lay for negligent words. If a person was induced to enter into a contract by fraudulent misrepresentation, he could sue the deceiver in fraud . . . . But, if the misrepresentation was innocent, then he had no action for damages at all, unless he could raise it into a warranty or a collateral contract . . . . It mattered not whether the misrepresentation was negligent, or not. It was regarded as innocent unless tainted with fraud. Nor did it matter whether the misrepresentation was made by the other party to the contract or by a third person. No action lay.

'That has all been altered now. Since the decision in 1963 of *Hedley Byrne & Co v Heller & Partners* . . . It seems to me that, if one person, by a negligent mis-statement, induces another to enter into a contract — with himself or with a third person — he may be liable in damages. This is quite independent of the Misrepresentation Act 1967, which deals only with misrepresentation made by a party to the contract. It does not deal with negligent misrepresentations made by a third person, such as were made in *Candler v Crane, Christmas* . . .; *Hedley Byrne v Heller* . . ., which induce a party to enter into a contract with another.

'In order to make a person liable for a negligent mis-statement, he must in some way or other have voluntarily undertaken to assume responsibility for the statements. Not responsible for it in the sense that he *warrants* its accuracy, but responsible in the sense that he must use due care in making it . . . . But "voluntary" in this context does not mean that he has consciously agreed to accept responsibility. It is sufficient if he has impliedly agreed. That is, if in all the circumstances a reasonable person would take it that he had agreed to accept responsibility. This implication . . . is like an implied term in a contract. It is implied or imposed by

271

the law itself. It can be excluded by express words, such as by heading a letter "without responsibility"; but, unless so excluded, it is implied wherever the circumstances require it.

'Since *Hedley Byrne* the courts have gradually been formulating the circumstances in which the implication will be made. It certainly will be made when a professional man, like an accountant, a solicitor, or a banker, is employed to give skilled advice knowing that it will be passed on to one who will rely upon it . . . . But those are not the only circumstances. The implication is not confined to professional men doing skilled tasks. It has been found where ordinary men are doing quite mundane tasks. A good instance is the decision of Mr. Justice Cardozo in New York where a weighman was employed to weigh goods and certify the quantity . . . . Recent instances in this court are the clerk in a Registry who makes a search for entries in the register and certifies the result . . .; or a Council Inspector who inspects work and passes it as satisfactory . . . . Each of those persons is under a duty to use care in making his statement. He owes this duty to those whom he knows, or ought to know, will rely on it, or will be injuriously affected by a mistake. Similarly, it seems to me that when one man makes a statement to another with the intention of inducing him to enter into a contract with him – or with someone else, on the faith of it, the maker must be regarded as accepting responsibility for the statement. It is not necessary that it should be made directly to the contracting party. It is sufficient if the statement is made to a third person to be passed on to the contracting party, or in such circumstances that the maker knew or ought to know that it would or might be passed on to the contracting party and acted on by him. That is sufficient when the statement is made fraudulently . . . . It is sufficient when it is made negligently.

'On the other hand, the case do show that there are circumstances when the party cannot be supposed to have accepted responsibility for the statement. Such as . . . . when a solicitor meets a friend in a railway train and casually gives him advice on a point of law. Similarly, *Mutual Life Ltd v*

Evatt [1971] AC 793 ... when one of the officers of an insurance company gave advice to a policy-holder about investments. It was no part of the business of the insurance company to advise policy-holders on their investments: and there was nothing on the pleadings to warrant the implication that they had accepted any responsibility in the matter. In every case the circumstances must be examined to see whether the defendant must be regarded as accepting responsibility for the statement to the person who relied on it'.

2 *Esso Petroleum*

The next case was *Esso Petroleum v Mardon*[1]. Esso wanted to get a tenant for their filling station at Southport. They represented to Mr. Mardon that they had made a forecast of the estimated annual consumption of petrol. It was 200,000 gallons a year. On the faith of it, Mr. Mardon took a tenancy. The estimate was entirely wrong. The Esso Company honestly but foolishly made 'a fatal error'. The throughput of the filling station was only about 60,000 gallons a year. Mr. Mardon sued for damages. He succeeded before the trial Judge, who was Lawson J. As a junior, he had argued *Candler*'s case[2] before us. So he knew all about the law on the subject. The Court of Appeal affirmed him. I said:

'. . . . It seems to me that *Hedley Byrne & Co Ltd v Heller & Partners Ltd* [1964] AC 465, properly understood, covers this particular proposition: if a man, who has or professes to have special knowledge or skill, makes a representation by virtue thereof to another – be it advice, information or opinion – with the intention of inducing him to enter into a contract with him, he is under a duty to use reasonable care to see that the representation is correct, and that the advice, information or opinion is reliable. If he negligently gives unsound advice or misleading information or expresses an

1. [1976] 1 QB 801.
2. [1951] 2 KB 164.

273

erroneous opinion, and thereby induces the other side to enter into a contract with him, he is liable in damages. This proposition is in line with what I said in *Candler v Crane, Christmas & Co* [1951] 2 KB 164, 179–180, which was approved by the majority of the Privy Council in *Mutual Life and Citizens' Assurance Co Ltd v Evatt* [1971] AC 793. And the judges of the Commonwealth have shown themselves quite ready to apply *Hedley Byrne* [1964] AC 465, between contracting parties: in Canada . . . and in New Zealand. . . .

'Applying this principle, it is plain that Esso professed to have — and did in fact have — special knowledge or skill in estimating the throughput of a filling station. They made the representation — they forecast a throughput of 200,000 gallons — intending to induce Mr. Mardon to enter into a tenancy on the faith of it. They made it negligently. It was a 'fatal error'. And thereby induced Mr. Mardon to enter into a contract of tenancy that was disastrous to him. For this misrepresentation they are liable in damages'.

3 The Misrepresentation Act 1967

The third case was *Howard Marine Ltd v A. Ogden & Sons*[1]. The case contained a new element. It invoked not only the common law as to negligent misrepresentation but also the Misrepresentation Act 1967. Howards made a representation by word of mouth that their barges would carry 1,600 tonnes of material: but it was wrong. They would only carry 1000 tonnes. On the faith of it, Ogdens hired the barges. They could not do the work required of them. So Ogdens claimed damages. They succeeded in part. There was some difference in the Courts as to the correct interpretation of the facts, but not, I think, in the law. This is what I said:

'Ogdens contended next that the representations by Howards, as to the carrying capacity of the barges, were made negligently: and that Howards are liable in damages for negligent misrepresentation on the principles laid down in

1. [1978] 2 WLR 515.

Hedley Byrne & Co Ltd v Heller & Partners Ltd [1964] AC 465.

'This raises the vexed question of the scope of the doctrine of *Hedley Byrne* . . . . To my mind one of the most helpful passages is to be found in the speech of Lord Pearce in *Hedley Byrne & Co Ltd v Heller & Partners Ltd* [1964] AC 465, 539:

". . . . To import such a duty (of care) the representation must normally, I think, concern a business or professional transaction whose nature makes clear the gravity of the inquiry and the importance and influence attached to the answer . . . . A most important circumstance is the form of the inquiry and of the answer".

'To this I would add the principle stated by Lord Reid and Lord Morris of Borth-y-Gest in the Privy Council case, *Mutual Life and Citizens' Assurance Co Ltd v Evatt* [1971] AC 793, 812, which I would adopt in preference to that stated by the majority:

". . . . when an inquirer consults a business man in the course of his business and makes it plain to him that he is seeking considered advice and intends to act on it in a particular way . . . his action in giving such advice . . . (gives rise to) . . . a legal obligation to take such care as is reasonable in the whole circumstances".

'Those principles speak of the "gravity of the inquiry" and the seeking of "considered advice". Those words are used so as to exclude representations made during a casual conversation in the street; or in a railway carriage; or an impromptu opinion given offhand; or "off the cuff" on the telephone. To put it more generally, the duty is one of honesty and no more whenever the opinion, information or advice is given in circumstances in which it appears that it is unconsidered and it would not be reasonable for the recipient to act on it without taking further steps to check it . . . .

. . . .

'*The Misrepresentation Act 1967*
This enactment imposes a new and serious liability on anyone

275

who makes a representation of fact in the course of negotiations for a contract. If that representation turns out to be
mistaken — then however innocent he may be — he is just as
liable as if he made it fraudulently. But how different from
times past! For years he was not liable in damages at all for
innocent misrepresentation: see *Heilbut, Symons & Co v
Buckleton* [1913] AC 30. Quite recently he was made liable
if he was proved to have made it negligently: see *Esso Petroleum Co Ltd v Mardon* [1976] QB 801. But now with this
Act he is made liable — unless he proves — and the burden is
on him to prove — that he had reasonable ground to believe
and did in fact believe that it was true'.

The majority of the Court held that Howards had failed to
discharge the burden of proof imposed by the Act. So
Ogdens won on that point. There were so many interesting
points that we hoped that the case would be taken to the
Lords. But the parties settled it. So for the time being, the
Court of Appeal holds the field.

6 Surprising consequences

1 Contract or tort

I have not yet done — because I must yet draw attention to a matter of much importance which was discussed in *Esso Petroleum v Mardon*[1]. Before that case it was generally accepted that when a solicitor or an architect was negligent in advising his client, the remedy against him was in contract and not in tort. This had important consequences, both as to the measure of damages and as to the limitation period. In *Esso Petroleum v Mardon* this belief was challenged. This is what I said:

'Assuming that there was no warranty, the question arises whether Esso are liable for negligent mis-statement under the doctrine of *Hedley Byrne & Co Ltd v Heller & Partners Ltd* [1964] AC 465. It has been suggested that *Hedley Byrne* cannot be used so as to impose liability for negligent pre-contractual statements: and that, in a pre-contract situation, the remedy (at any rate before the Act of 1967) was only in warranty or nothing . . . .

'In arguing this point, Mr. Ross-Munro took his stand in this way. He submitted that when the negotiations between two parties resulted in a contract between them, their rights and duties were governed by the law of contract and not by the law of tort. There was, therefore, no place in their relationship for *Hedley Byrne* [1964] AC 465, which was solely on liability in tort . . . . But I venture to suggest that those cases are in conflict with other decisions of high

1. [1976] 1 QB 801.

authority which were not cited in them. These decisions show that, in the case of a professional man, the duty to use reasonable care arises not only in contract, but is also imposed by the law apart from contract, and is therefore actionable in tort. It is comparable to the duty of reasonable care which is owed by a master to his servant, or vice versa. It can be put either in contract or in tort . . . .

. . . .

. . . . A professional man may give advice under a contract for reward; or without a contract, in pursuance of a voluntary assumption of responsibility, gratuitously without reward. In either case he is under one and the same duty to use reasonable care . . . . In the one case it is by reason of a term implied by law. In the other, it is by reason of a duty imposed by law. For a breach of that duty he is liable in damages: and those damages should be, and are, the same, whether he is sued in contract or in tort'.

2 The duty of solicitors

If that view is correct, it has serious consequences for solicitors. If their client sues them in tort for negligence, the time will begin to run – not from the date of the negligent conduct – but from the time the damage was discovered, or should, with reasonable diligence, have been discovered. This very point came before Oliver J in *Midland Bank Trust Co Ltd v Hett, Stubbs and Kemp*[1]. He held that under the *Hedley Byrne* principle as interpreted in *Esso Petroleum v Mardon,* a solicitor could be made liable in tort for negligence and that on that account, the claim was not barred by the Limitation Act. I summarised the point in *Photo Production Ltd v Securicor Ltd*[2]:

'. . . . But I hasten to say that in the 19th century it would have been different. At that time it was thought – and held – that if a duty to use care arose out of a contract, no one

1. [1978] 3 WLR 167.
2. [1978] 1 WLR 856 at 862.

could sue for a breach of that contract except a party to it,
and he could only sue in contract and not in tort . . . . But,
during the last few years, it has become plain that, if the facts
disclose the self-same duty of care arising both in contract
and in tort – and a breach of that duty – then the plaintiff
can sue either in contract or in tort, as he pleases . . . . The
self-same consequences apply both as to remoteness of
damage . . . and statutes of limitation . . . . The result should
not, and does not, depend on the legal classification in which
the plaintiff put his case'.

Conclusion

During this discussion I have tried to show you how much the law of negligence has been extended; especially in regard to the negligence of professional men. This extension would have been intolerable for all concerned — had it not been for insurance. The only way in which professional men can safeguard themselves — against ruinous liability — is by insurance. In most of the cases that come before the Courts today, the parties appear at first sight to be ordinary persons or industrial companies or public authorities. But their true identity is obscured by masks. If you lift up the mask, you will usually find the legal aid funds or an insurance company or the taxpayer — all of whom are assumed to have limitless funds. In theory the Courts do not look behind the masks. But in practice they do. That is the reason why the law of negligence has been extended so as to embrace nearly all activities in which people engage. That is the reason the awards of damages have escalated so as to exceed anything that even the wealthiest individual could pay. The policy behind it all is that, when severe loss is suffered by any one singly, it should be borne, not by him alone, but be spread throughout the community at large. Nevertheless, the moral element does come in. The sufferer will not recover any damages from anyone except when it is that person's fault. It is only by retaining that moral element that society can be kept solvent. To award compensation without fault would make society bankrupt. No one could pay the premium needed to get cover. I sometimes wonder whether the time has not come — may indeed be already with us — when the Courts should cry Halt!

Enough has been done for the sufferer. Now remember the man who has to foot the bill — even though he be only one of many.

Part seven

The doctrine of precedent

Introduction

In the latter part of the 19th century, the law held firmly to the doctrine of *stare decisis;* that is, a previous decision on the point was binding even though it was found afterwards to be wrong. How far has this doctrine been carried into the 20th century?

To a student of jurisprudence this doctrine of precedent exercises a peculiar fascination. He is hypnotised by it. To a practising lawyer it is *Mr. Facing-both-ways.* He is attracted or repelled by it according as to whether it is for him or against him. He can argue either way, as you please. To a Judge it comes, if he chooses, as a way of escape. He does not have to think for himself or to decide for himself. It has already been decided by the previous authority. But not so for most Judges. Whilst ready to applaud the doctrine of precedent when it leads to a just and fair result, they become restless under it when they are compelled by it to do what is unjust or unfair. This restlessness leads them to various expedients to get round a previous authority. But never to depart from it altogether — except for an absolution recently granted by the House of Lords to themselves, though not vouchsafed by them to others. Even when a Judge is so bound by a previous authority that he cannot depart from it, the question arises: Ought he to express his own opinion as to its correctness or not?

In this part I consider these jurisprudential questions and give instances of their practical consequences. With what effect, I leave you to judge.

The doctrine of precedent

Many a time I have been asked: 'Why did you step down from the House of Lords?' My answer is: 'I was too often in a minority. In the Lords it is no good to dissent'. In the Court of Appeal it is some good. On occasion a head-note there says: 'Lord Denning dissenting'. Let me recall a few which have pointed to the way ahead, and have led to decisions by the Lords which might never have taken place except for my dissenting from previous precedents; such as *Candler v Crane, Christmas* about negligent statements, *Bonsor v Musicians' Union* about trade unions, *Conway v Rimmer* about Crown privilege, *Padfield's* case about ministerial discretion, and *Schorsch GmbH v Hennin* about judgments in foreign currency.

1 Dissenting in the Lords

You must remember, too, that during the five years that I was there – from 1957 to 1962 – the House held itself to be absolutely bound by the doctrine of *stare decisis*. If a previous decision was wrong – and caused injustice – nobody could put it right except Parliament, and they were not interested in reforming the law. There were no votes in it.

In my very first case in the Lords, I dissented – on a point of principle. It was of much importance in international law – *Rahimtoola v Nizam of Hyderabad*[1] . There was a sum of

1. [1958] AC 379.

287

£1,000,000 in the Westminster Bank in London. It had been placed there by the Nizam of Hyderabad. It was claimed by the Government of Pakistan. The question was whether Pakistan could claim sovereign immunity. To my mind the past precedents were out of date. During the long vacation — by the Helford river — I spent much time on the case. I came to the conclusion that, when sovereign states engaged in commercial transactions, they should not be entitled to claim immunity; and as I said so, I realised that this would not be acceptable to my colleagues. So I concluded with these words:

'My Lords, I acknowledge that, in the course of this opinion, I have considered some questions and authorities which were not mentioned by counsel. I am sure they gave all the help they could and I have only gone into it further because the law on this subject is of great consequence and, as applied at present, it is held by many to be unsatisfactory. I venture to think that if there is one place where it should be reconsidered on principle — without being tied to particular precedents of a period that is past — it is here in this House: and if there is one time for it to be done, it is now, when the opportunity offers, before the law gets any more enmeshed in its own net. This I have tried to do. Whatever the outcome, I hope I may say, as Holt CJ once did after he had done much research on his own: "I have stirred these points, which wiser heads in time may settle" '.

But my reward for doing all this work was this rebuke by Viscount Simonds with which all the others said they wholeheartedly agreed:

'My Lords, I must add that, since writing this opinion, I have had the privilege of reading the opinion which my noble and learned friend, Lord Denning, is about to deliver. It is right that I should say that I must not be taken as assenting to his views upon a number of questions and authorities in regard to which the House has not had the benefit of the arguments of counsel or of the judgment of the courts below'.

Thus rebuked, I may as well make a confession. On many occasions I have done my own researches and given an opinion on matters on which the Court has not had the benefit of the arguments of counsel or of the judgment of the Court below. I have done this because counsel vary much in their ability and I do not think that their clients should suffer by any oversight or mistake of counsel. If it is a new point or new matter which could alter the outcome of the case, then the right course is to inform counsel and put the case in the list for further hearing. But if it is just the elaboration of existing points or matters, there is no such need – although I do know of one authority where the defendants failed on every point argued on their behalf, but succeeded on a new point which was taken by the Judges themselves after the argument was concluded. It was *Shaw v Great Western Rly*[1].

In spite of that rebuke it was, I think, worth while that I did do all that work on the *Rahimtoola* case. Twenty years later it was of much use in *Trendtex v Bank of Nigeria*[2] and has now the satisfaction of being given statutory effect in the State Immunity Act 1978.

There was another case in the Lords when I dissented on a point of principle. It was a great disappointment to me. It was *Midland Silicones Ltd v Scruttons Ltd*[3]. Previously, whilst in the Court of Appeal, I had suggested in several cases that it was open to the Judges to hold that, when a contract was made for the benefit of a third party, then it could be enforced for the benefit of that party. This had the merit that it had been recommended by the Law Revision Committee in 1937. Lord Simonds condemned my efforts in this resounding passage:

'.... (There is) a principle which is, I suppose, as well established as any in our law, a "fundamental" principle, as Lord Haldane called it in *Dunlop Pneumatic Tyre Co Ltd v Selfridge & Co Ltd,* an "elementary" principle, as it has been called times without number, that only a person who is a

1. [1894] 1 QB 373.
2. [1977] QB 529.
3. [1962] AC 446.

party to a contract can sue upon it. "Our law", said Lord Haldane, "knows nothing of a jus quaesitum tertio arising by way of contract". Learned counsel for the respondents claimed that this was the orthodox view and asked your Lordships to reject any proposition that impinged upon it. To that invitation I readily respond. For to me heterodoxy, or, as some might say, heresy, is not the more attractive because it is dignified by the name of reform. Nor will I easily be led by an undiscerning zeal for some abstract kind of justice to ignore our first duty, which is to administer justice according to law, the law which is established for us by Act of Parliament or the binding authority of precedent. The law is developed by the application of old principles to new circumstances. Therein lies its genius. Its reform by the abrogation of those principles is the task not of the courts of law but of Parliament. Therefore I reject the argument for the appellants under this head and invite your Lordships to say that certain statements (of Denning LJ) which appear to support it in recent cases . . . must be rejected. If the principle of jus quaesitum tertio is to be introduced into our law, it must be done by Parliament after a due consideration of its merits and demerits. I should not be prepared to give it my support without a greater knowledge than I at present possess of its operation in other systems of law'.

Was my dissent worth while? I am inclined to think so: because it paved the way for two cases which show that in many ways – by adroit procedural steps – the strict rule can be avoided. They are *Beswick v Beswick*[1] and *Jackson v Horizon Holidays*[2].

In my last case in the Lords, as in the first, I dissented. But this time in good company with Lord Reid. It was *Griffiths v J. P. Harrison (Watford) Ltd*[3]. Dividend-strippers manipulated share dealings so as to show a trading loss; and used it to get repayment of tax. I put it bluntly:

'There are occasions when a reasonable man may turn a blind

1. [1966] Ch 538, [1968] AC 58.
2. [1975] 1 WLR 1468.
3. [1963] AC 1 at 22.

eye to the facts, but this is not one of them. To my mind, the commissioners were entitled to see these people as they really are, prospectors digging for wealth in the subterranean passages of the Revenue, searching for tax repayments. They are not simple traders dealing in stocks and shares'.

Even this did not shake Lord Simonds. He with the other two let the dividend-strippers keep their ill-gotten gains. But this dissent was worth while. In subsequent cases, the House went out of its way to 'distinguish' *Griffiths v Harrison* and Lord Dilhorne positively declined to follow it — see *Lupton v FA and AB Ltd*[1].

2 The Romanes Lecture

Thus rebuffed in my judicial efforts at that time — on these and other occasions — to persuade my colleagues in the Lords; I looked for other ways. I went for an afternoon to my own University of Oxford. I was invited to deliver the Romanes Lecture. It was in the Sheldonian Theatre on 21 May 1959. I gave it the title, *From Precedent to Precedent.* My theme was that the House of Lords should not be bound by a previous precedent if it should be found to be wrong. It had, I believe, some influence on the ensuing reform. So I will, if I may, set out some parts of it:

'This land of ours, this England, has been spoken of by the poet as the land where —

"A man may speak the thing he will;
  A land of settled government,
    A land of just and old renown,
      Where Freedom broadens slowly down
  From precedent to precedent"[2].

'Some lawyers take pride in those words of Lord Tennyson, "from precedent to precedent". They think he gives the

1. [1972] AC 634.
2. Tennyson, *You ask me, Why?*

impress of a noble mind to the doctrine of *stare decisis* which, according to their interpretation, means: "Stand by your decisions and the decisions of your predecessors, however wrong they are and whatever injustice they inflict". But I take leave to point out that, so interpreted, the doctrine of precedent does nothing to *broaden* the basis of freedom, rather to *narrow* it. If lawyers hold to their precedents too closely, forgetful of the fundamental principles of truth and justice which they should serve, they may find the whole edifice comes tumbling down about them. They will be lost in -

"That codeless myriad of precedent,
   That wilderness of single instances"[1].

The common law will cease to grow. Like a coral reef, it will become a structure of fossils[2]. If it is to avoid this fate, the law cannot afford to be a "lawless science" but should be a science of law. Just as the scientist seeks for truth, so the lawyer should seek for justice. Just as the scientist takes his instances and from them builds up his general propositions, so the lawyer should take his precedents and from them build up his general principles. Just as the propositions of the scientist fall to be modified when shown not to fit all instances, or even discarded when shown to be in error, so the principles of the lawyer should be modified when found to be unsuited to the times or discarded when found to work injustice.

'Many a lawyer will dispute this analogy with science. "I am only concerned", he will say, "with the law as it is, not with what it ought to be". For him the rule is the thing. Right or wrong does not matter. That approach is all very well for the working lawyer who applies the law as a working mason lays bricks, without any responsibility for the building which he is making. But it is not good enough for the lawyer who is concerned with his responsibility to the community at

1. Ibid. *Aylmer's Field.*
2. Mr. Justice Jackson (US Supreme Court), *The Struggle for Judicial Supremacy*, p. 295.

large. He should ever seek to do his part to see that the principles of the law are consonant with justice. If he should fail to do this, he will forfeit the confidence of the people. The law will fall into disrepute; and if that happens the stability of the country will be shaken. The law must be certain. Yes, as certain as may be. But it must be just too.

'I am a lawyer myself and I hope that in what I have to say I will not bite the hand that fed me; for, with Lord Bacon, I hold every man a debtor to his profession[1] . All I wish to do is to throw out some thoughts on the proper use of precedents: and to give a friendly warning too. For I observe that, in the past, when the lawyer's precedents have been found to work injustice, they have been corrected, as often as not, by the actions of juries; or by the Lords of Parliament who were, for the most part, not lawyers. It is these ordinary folk who have broadened the basis of freedom, not by sticking to bad old precedents, but by making good new ones. Let me prove this, and afterwards see what lessons we may draw from it.

. . . .

'You will have noticed how progressive the House of Lords has been when the lay peers have had their say, or at any rate, their vote on the decisions. They have insisted on the true principles and have not allowed the conservatism of lawyers to be carried too far. Even more so when we come to the meaning of words. Lawyers are here the most offending souls alive. They will so often stick to the letter and miss the substance. The reason is plain enough. Most of them spend their working lives drafting some kind of document or another – trying to see whether it covers this contingency or that. They dwell upon words until they become mere precisians in the use of them. They would rather be accurate than be clear. They would sooner be long than short. They seek to avoid two meanings, and end – on occasion – by having no meaning. And the worst of it all is that they claim to be the masters of the subject. The meaning of words, they say, is a matter of law for them and not a matter for the

1. Bacon, *The Elements of the Common Law*, Preface.

ordinary man. Like Humpty Dumpty, they seem to say, in rather a scornful tone: "When I use a word, it means what I choose it to mean — neither more nor less", and like Humpty Dumpty they sometimes have a great fall. At any rate, the House of Lords, when manned by lay peers, have always insisted on the natural meaning of words and not their literal meaning . . . .

. . . .

'I have spoken so far only of cases where the judges below went wrong. There is no difficulty in the House correcting their errors. But now comes the question: Can the House correct its own errors? Can it correct the precedents of its predecessors which the course of time has shown to be erroneous? Most of the supreme tribunals in the world hold themselves at liberty to reconsider the previous decisions of themselves or their predecessors. They will not, of course, reopen a previous decision without the greatest hesitation, but they will do so if convinced that it is erroneous. The Judicial Committee of the Privy Council — with its great and extensive jurisdiction — takes this view[1]. So does the Supreme Court of the United States. When it recently held that black children were to be taught in schools side by side with white children, the decision was a notable step forward, but it meant a departure from a previous doctrine of the Supreme Court[2]. Likewise with the Indian Supreme Court[3]. Likewise with the Supreme Court of South Africa. When it held that the coloured people in Cape Province were entitled to vote equally with the white people, it had to overrule a previous decision of its own to do so. And the whole world approved[4]. Quite recently in Israel the Legislature has actually enacted that the Supreme Court is not bound by its previous decisions[5]. What is the position in England?

1. *Gideon Nkambule v R* [1950] AC 379 at 397.
2. *Brown v Board of Education of Topeka* 34 7 US 483 departing from the doctrine of 'separate but equal' in *Plessey v Ferguson* 163 US 537.
3. *Bengal Immunity Co Ltd v State of Bihar* [1955] 2 Sup Ct R 603.
4. *Harris v Donges* [1952] 1 TLR 1245 overruling *Ndlwana v Hofmeyr* [1937] AD 229.
5. The Judicial Courts Law 1957, art. 33.

'Here, again, let me tell you what happened when lay peers sat and voted on judicial matters. They undoubtedly reserved power to reverse their own decisions. Sir Matthew Hale, the great Lord Chief Justice, whose knowledge of the subject was greater than any man before or since, writing about 1676, says that "if a judgment of attainder *or affirmation or reversal* be given in the lords house in parliament, a writ of petition of error lies at another session in the same lords house to reverse their own judgment; and possibly it may be done even the same session". . . .

. . . .

'Many years later Lord Denman — whose father had been Lord Chief Justice but was not himself qualified as a Law Lord — sat at the decision of an appeal and attempted to vote but his vote was not counted[1]. At any rate, since 1850 lay peers have taken no part in judicial business. It has been left to the Law Lords: and it is during this time that the greatest contrast of all has taken place. Whereas previously the House could and did reverse its rulings on points of law when found to be erroneous, now it cannot do so, or rather does not do so . . . .

. . . . Lord Campbell declared that "the rule of law which your Lordships lay down as the ground of your judgment sitting judicially, . . . must be taken for law till altered by an Act of Parliament, agreed to by the Commons and the Crown, as well as by your Lordships". Since that time it has been generally accepted that the House cannot reverse a ruling of its own on a point of law.

'But is this state of affairs bound to continue? Is it not open to the House to reconsider the question of how far it is bound by its own decisions? Sir Frederick Pollock seems to have thought so. He said that "The members of the Court at a given time cannot make its usage a strict law for those who

---

1. It was in *Bain v Fothergill* (1874) LR 7 HL 158 decided on 22 June 1874. See his speech on 25 Feb. 1876 in the House of Lords. Only two Law Lords had heard the arguments. The other peers present had not. He again sat on 9 April 1883 in *Bradlaugh v Clarke,* as appears from *The Times* and is said to have voted, but the Law Reports ignore him, see 8 App Cas 354.

succeed to their authority hereafter[1]. The modern convention has only grown up during the last 100 years and can be departed from just as any other practice of the House can be . . . .

'I have almost done. And what does it all come to? I have shown you how in times past the House of Lords used to correct errors into which the lower courts had fallen – and indeed errors into which the House itself or its predecessors had fallen – and how it used to create new precedents so as to meet new situations. If the law is to develop and not to stagnate, the House must, I think, recapture this vital principle – the principle of growth. The House of Lords is more than another court of law. It is more than another court of appeal. It is the Court of Parliament itself. It acts for the Queen as the fountain of justice in our land. It must, of course, correct errors that have been made by the courts below: but it should do more. It lays down, or should lay down, the fundamental principles of the law to govern the people; and, whilst adhering firmly to those principles, it should overrule particular precedents that it finds to be at variance therewith. Then only shall we be able to claim that "freedom broadens slowly down from precedent to precedent" '.

Nothing was done on those lines whilst I was still a Lord of Appeal – not so long as Lord Simonds was there. But later on Lord Gardiner became Lord Chancellor. He was the foremost of his time on law reform. He took the leading part in the discussions on precedent. He made a statement in the House on 26 July 1966. All the then Lords of Appeal in Ordinary were there. In addition, Lord Parker and I because we had taken part in the discussions. This was the key paragraph:

'Their Lordships nevertheless recognise that too rigid adherence to precedent may lead to injustice in a particular case and also unduly restrict the proper development of the law. They propose, therefore, to modify their present

1. Pollock, *First Book of Jurisprudence*, p. 334.

practice and, while treating former decisions of this House as normally binding, to depart from a previous decision when it appears right to do so'.

Every word thus far was much to my liking. But what about the Court of Appeal? There was this sentence at the end of the announcement:

'This announcement is not intended to affect the use of precedent elsewhere than in this House'.

I understood that sentence to mean simply: 'We are only considering the doctrine of precedent in the Lords. We are not considering its use elsewhere'. But it has been read as saying much more. As if to say: The Court of Appeal is absolutely bound by its own decisions subject only to the three exceptions stated in *Young v Bristol Aeroplane Co Ltd*[1]. So read, it has been used as a bar to any reform of the doctrine of precedent in the Court of Appeal. To my dismay.

3 Is the Court of Appeal bound by its own decisions?

But before that pronouncement, I had already returned in 1962 to the Court of Appeal. Here there was a chance of doing good. I realised, of course, that most of my colleagues treated *Young v Bristol Aeroplane Co* as binding on them. But even so, there were ways and means of getting round a previous decision that was wrong. The conventional means was by 'distinguishing' it, that is, finding some distinction on the facts or on the law – maybe a minor distinction. But still it would serve the turn. Another means was by 'pouring cold water' on the reasoning given in the previous case; by saying that it was unnecessary for the decision of the case; or it was too widely stated; or the Judges cannot have had such cases as this in mind. If those means failed, it was often possible to find some ground for 'departing' from a previous decision: such as by saying that things were different now that equity and law were fused, or by relying on one of the exceptions to

1. [1944] KB 718.

the rule in *Young v Bristol Aeroplane Co.* But if all those means failed, the Court of Appeal was powerless. Or so it seemed. That is why I embarked on my most extravagant dissent and met my most humiliating defeat. I tried to persuade my colleagues to do what the House of Lords had done — that is, whilst treating a previous decision as normally binding, to depart from it if it appeared right to do so.

My plea was treated with sympathy by my colleagues but with no encouragement. I put forward my arguments in full in the recent case of *Davis v Johnson*[1] . Two recent decisions on a new statute — the Domestic Violence Act 1976 — had given rise to much concern. So I thought it right to convene a special Court to hear an appeal. It was a Court of five and included Sir George Baker, the President, who was especially knowledgeable on the subject. This is what I said:

'I turn to the second important point: Can we depart from those two cases? Although convinced that they are wrong, are we at liberty to depart from them? What is the correct practice for this court to follow?

'On principle, it seems to me that, while this court should regard itself as normally bound by a previous decision of the court, nevertheless it should be at liberty to depart from it if it is convinced that the previous decision was wrong. What is the argument to the contrary? It is said that if an error has been made, this court has no option but to continue the error and leave it to be corrected by the House of Lords. The answer is this: the House of Lords may never have an opportunity to correct the error: and thus it may be perpetuated indefinitely, perhaps for ever. That often happened in the old days when there was no legal aid. A poor person had to accept the decision of this court because he had not the means to take it to the House of Lords . . . . Even today a person of moderate means may be outside the legal aid scheme, and not be able to take his case higher: especially with the risk of failure attaching to it. That looked as if it would have been the fate of Mrs. Farrell when the case was decided in this court . . . . But she afterwards did manage to

1. [1978] 2 WLR 182.

collect enough money together and by means of it to get the decision of this court reversed by the House of Lords . . . . Apart from monetary considerations, there have been many instances where cases have been settled pending an appeal to the House of Lords: or, for one reason or another, not taken there, especially with claims against insurance companies or big employers. When such a body has obtained a decision of this court in its favour, it will buy off an appeal to the House of Lords by paying ample compensation to the appellant. By so doing, it will have a legal precedent on its side which it can use with effect in later cases. I fancy that such may have happened in cases following *Oliver v Ashman* . . . . By such means an erroneous decision on a point of law can again be perpetuated for ever. Even if all those objections are put on one side and there is an appeal to the House of Lords, it usually takes 12 months or more for the House of Lords to reach its decision. What then is the position of the lower courts meanwhile? They are in a dilemma. Either they have to apply the erroneous decision of the Court of Appeal, or they have to adjourn all fresh cases to await the decision of the House of Lords. That has often happened. So justice is delayed — and often denied — by the lapse of time before the error is corrected . . . .'.

But I received a crushing rebuff from the House of Lords. My efforts were described as a 'one-man crusade' to free the Court of Appeal from the shackles of *stare decisis*[1]. My arguments were rejected by the Lords. So my plea failed. But I am consoled to find that there are many intermediate Courts of Appeal in the Commonwealth which adopt the course which I advocated. So this has made my dissent worth while. These are the Courts of Appeal in New South Wales, Victoria, South Australia, and New Zealand. In particular, in *Bennett v Orange City Council*[2] Wallace P said:

'Giving full credit to the desirability of certainty in the law (which occasionally appears to be a pious aspiration) I consider that even an intermediate Court of Appeal may, on

1. See [1978] 2 WLR 553 at 559.
2. [1967] 1 NSW 502.

special occasions and in the absence of higher authority on the subject in hand, play its part in the development of the law and in ensuring that it keeps pace with modern conditions and modern thought, and accordingly, in an appropriate case, I do not think that an earlier decision of the Court (including this Court) should be allowed to stand when justice seems to require otherwise'.

Those words from New South Wales prompt the reflection: What is an intermediate Court of Appeal in England now to do when it is faced with a previous decision of the same Court which is directly in point? It has, I suppose, to say to the appellant: 'We cannot consider whether the previous decision was right or wrong. We are bound by it. So do not waste your time or ours by canvassing it'.

This means that, whenever a party wishes to challenge a previous decision of the Court of Appeal, the Lords will not hear the views of the present Court of Appeal on it. I know many Law Lords place great value on the views of the Court of Appeal. It was why Lord Simonds objected so strongly to the introduction of the 'leap-frog' procedure. It has always seemed to me a great pity that there was a 'leap frog' in *Daymond v South-West Water Authority*[1]. It was a case with staggering financial and legislative consequences. I do not suppose many will have time to read it: but, when you find that Lord Wilberforce and Lord Diplock dissented, you may think that the Court of Appeal might have been able to contribute something of value.

Despite my disappointment on precedent in the Court of Appeal, nevertheless I would draw your attention to some cases of outstanding importance in which a departure from precedent – even from a previous decision in the House of Lords – proved to be well worth while.

4 Crown privilege

The first concerned Crown privilege. It was *Conway v Rimmer*[2]. Michael Conway was a young lad training to

1. [1976] AC 609.
2. [1967] 1 WLR 1031.

become a police-constable. Each of the lads in training bought his own electric torch. There was a mix-up about the torches. The Police Superintendent — with no sufficient grounds — charged Conway with stealing another lad's torch. The jury stopped the case. They took a poor view of the Superintendent's conduct. Conway was acquitted with nothing against him. The Police Superintendent afterwards called Conway in and dismissed him from the Force. Conway sued the Police Superintendent for damages. Conway's lawyers wanted to see the reports which the Superintendent had made on Conway from time to time — so as to see if he had an unreasonable prejudice against Conway. The Home Secretary then stepped in and claimed what was called 'Crown privilege'. They were a class of documents which were to be kept confidential. They were not to be disclosed, said the Home Secretary, and his decision could not be overruled by the Courts. There was a decision of the House of Lords which fully supported the claim of the Home Secretary. It was a case in 1942 — *Duncan v Cammell Laird*[1]. It was of the highest authority. The Lord Chancellor had presided with all six Lords of Appeal. The House had unanimously declared that a Minister had the right to object to the production of any document to the Court 'when the practice of keeping a class of document secret is necessary for the proper functioning of the public service'. If the Minister objected, the Courts could not override his objection. The House had so declared.

My colleagues in *Conway v Rimmer* felt bound by that authority but I ventured to dissent. Conway had no means. He could not appeal to the House of Lords unless he got legal aid. In order to get legal aid, it is helpful to have a dissenting judgment in your favour. So a dissent is worth while. This is what I said:

'This is a suit between two private litigants. One of them has in his possession or power documents which are relevant to the case. They are necessary to do justice between the parties. But the Attorney-General has come to this court and

1. [1942] AC 624.

asserted a claim of Crown privilege. He says that the court shall not have access to these documents. At once the question arises: Have the courts any power to look into this claim of Crown privilege? And to override it?

'On three occasions lately this court has considered the matter . . . . On each occasion the court was constituted of my brothers Harman and Salmon LJJ and myself. We held with one accord that the court has a residual power in a proper case to override the objections of a Minister. I will not recite again all the arguments. They will be found in the judgments. Suffice to state the upshot as I put it in the *Grosvenor Hotel* case:

"The objection of a Minister, even though taken in proper form, should not be conclusive. If the court should be of opinion that the objection is not taken in good faith, or that there are no reasonable grounds for thinking that the production of the documents would be injurious to the public interest, the court can override the objection and order production. It can, if it thinks fit, call for the documents and inspect them itself so as to see whether there are reasonable grounds for withholding them: ensuring, of course, that they are not disclosed to anyone else. It is rare indeed for the court to override the Minister's objection, but it has the ultimate power, in the interests of justice, to do so. After all, it is the judges who are the guardians of justice in this land: and if they are to fulfil their trust, they must be able to call upon the Minister to put forward his reasons so as to see if they outweigh the interests of justice".

In so holding, we were encouraged by the fact that we were in accord with the countries of the Commonwealth. They start, of course, with the classic judgment of the Privy Council in *Robinson v State of South Australia (No. 2)* . . . .

'I know that in *Duncan v Cammell, Laird & Co Ltd* the House of Lords dissented from *Robinson*'s case. But the courts of the Commonwealth, being free to choose, have unanimously followed *Robinson*'s case, and have endorsed the views of this court in the *Grosvenor Hotel* case, or in other cases acted on like principles. Let me recite the cases.

They are a veritable roll-call. The Supreme Court of Canada
. . . . The Supreme Court of Victoria . . . . The Court of
Appeal of New South Wales . . . . The Court of Appeal of
New Zealand . . . . The Supreme Court of India . . . . The
Supreme Court of Ceylon . . . . The Court of Appeal of
Jamaica . . . . To say nothing of the Court of Session in
Scotland, backed in this respect by the House of Lords itself
in *Glasgow Corporation v Central Land Board.*

'Despite this impressive array, my brethren today feel that
we are still bound by the observations of the House of Lords
in *Duncan v Cammell, Laird & Co Ltd* . . . . I do not agree.
The doctrine of precedent has been transformed by the
recent statement of Lord Gardiner LC [Practice Statement
(Judicial Precedent)]. This is the very case in which to throw
off the fetters. Crown privilege is one of the prerogatives of
the Crown. As such, it extends only so far as the common
law permits. It is for the judges to define its ambit, and not
for any government department, however powerful. And
when I say "the judges", I mean not only the judges of
England. I include the judges of the countries of the
Commonwealth. The Queen is their Queen, as she is ours.
Crown prerogative is the same there as here. At least it should
be. When we find that the Supreme Courts of those
countries, after careful deliberation, decline to follow the
House of Lords — because they are satisfied it was wrong —
that is excellent reason for the House to think again. It is not
beneath its dignity, nor is it now beyond its power, to
confess itself to have been in error. Likewise with this court.
We should draw on the wisdom of those overseas, as they in
the past have drawn on ours. Thus we shall do our part to
keep the common law a just system — yes, a just and uniform
system — throughout its broad domain.
. . . .

'The Home Secretary does not suggest that the "contents"
of the documents are in any way injurious to the public
interest. So much so that the Attorney-General agreed that if
a judge looked at them he would not think them in the least
injurious to the public interest. But the Home Secretary

303

asserts Crown privilege for the "classes" to which they apply. The probationary reports, he says, belong to the class of "confidential reports by police-officers to chief officers of police relating to the conduct, efficiency and fitness for employment of individual police-officers under their command". That, he claims, is a privileged class. The report to the chief constable, he says, falls within the class of "reports by police-officers to their superiors concerning investigations into the commission of crime". That too, he claims, is a privileged class. The Home Secretary in his affidavit says that the production of documents of each such "class" would be injurious to the public interest. He does not condescend to say why it would be injurious. But the Attorney-General did. He quoted Lord Simon in *Duncan v Cammell, Laird & Co Ltd* and said that the "candour and completeness of such communications might be prejudiced if they were ever liable to be disclosed in litigation". Accordingly, he contended that every document in the class must be kept back. No matter how harmless any particular document might be. No matter how necessary to the cause of justice. No matter whether it helps the Crown or hinders it, the document must be withheld from production. No exception can be made. The class must be kept intact, inviolate, undisclosed. I do not accept this line of reasoning, at any rate for the classes of documents here in question'.

In the result the case was taken to the Lords where the Home Secretary was unanimously overridden. The House looked at the documents and found no reason why they should not be disclosed. The case was afterwards settled.

I may perhaps add a further word. In the *NSPCC* case[1] it was strongly argued that 'Crown privilege' was restricted to the Crown and did not apply to other bodies. My colleagues accepted this submission. I dissented. The House of Lords upheld my dissent on a narrow ground. But it appears that the tendency now is to replace the words 'Crown privilege' by the words 'Public Interest privilege'. In all cases now the

1. [1978] AC 171.

question seems to be whether it is in the public interest that documents should be disclosed or not. That is the test applied by the Court of Appeal in *Science Research Council v Nasse*[1].

5 Judgments in foreign currency

The next case where a departure — even from a decision of the House of Lords — proved its worth was the case of foreign currency. It arose in *Schorsch GmbH v Hennin*[2]. A German company in 1971 supplied goods to a firm in England and stipulated for payment of the price to be made in German Deutschmarks. The English firm did not pay. After two years the German company sued the English firm in an English Court and asked for judgment for the price to be awarded in German Deutschmarks. The Judge refused. He said that he could only give judgment for the price in sterling — and the rate of exchange had to be taken at the 1971 figure when the goods were supplied. That would mean a great loss for the German company because during the two years sterling had gone down very greatly in value. The German company appealed to the Court of Appeal and asked for judgment in German Deutschmarks. Now there was a decision of the House of Lords only fourteen years before in 1961 (*Re United Railways of Havana*[3]) by which it was held that an English Court could only give judgment in sterling. The Court of Appeal ought to have followed the *Havana* case and refused the German company's appeal. But I am afraid we did what a great sailor once did. We turned a blind eye to the *Havana* case. We were guilty of what Lord Wilberforce afterwards described as 'some distortion of the judicial process'. We gave judgment for the German company in German Deutschmarks. I tried to justify it in this way:

'. . . . A German company comes to an English court and asks for judgment — not in English pounds sterling, but, if you please, in German Deutschmarks. The judge offered a sterling

1. [1978] 3 WLR 754.
2. [1975] QB 416.
3. [1961] AC 1007.

judgment. But the German company said "No. Sterling is no good to us. It has gone down much in value. If we accepted it, we would lose one-third of the debt. The debt was payable in Deutschmarks. We want Deutschmarks. We will accept no other". The judge refused their request. He had no power, he said, in English law to give any judgment but in sterling. The German company appeal to this court.

. . . .

'. . . . It has always been accepted that an English court can only give judgment in sterling. Judges and text-book writers have treated it as a self-evident proposition. No advocate has ever submitted the contrary. The modern cases start with *Manners v Pearson & Son* . . ., in which Sir Nathaniel Lindley MR said, "speaking generally, the courts of this country have no jurisdiction to order payment of money except in the currency of this country". In 1961 I was myself quite confident about it. In the *Havana* case . . . . I said: "And if there is one thing clear in our law, it is that the claim must be made in sterling and the judgment given in sterling". . . .

'In several other countries they have no such rule. Dr. F.A. Mann in his book *The Legal Aspect of Money,* 3rd ed. (1971), p. 351 gives a list of many countries, including Germany, in which a plaintiff can claim payment of a sum of money in a foreign currency and get judgment for it.

'Why have we in England insisted on a judgment in sterling and nothing else? It is, I think, because of our faith in sterling. It was a stable currency which had no equal. Things are different now. Sterling floats in the wind. It changes like a weathercock with every gust that blows. So do other currencies. This change compels us to think again about our rules. I ask myself: Why do we say that an English court can only pronounce judgment in sterling? Lord Reid thought that it was "primarily procedural": see the *Havana* case [1961] AC 1007, 1052. I think so too. It arises from the form in which we used to give judgment for money. From time immemorial the courts of common law used to give judgment in these words: "It is adjudged that the plaintiff *do recover* against the defendant £X" in sterling. On getting such a judgment the plaintiff could at once issue out a writ of execution for £X. If it was not in sterling, the sheriff would not be able to execute it. It was therefore essential that the judgment should be for a sum of money in sterling: for otherwise it could not be enforced.

. . . .

'Seeing that the reasons no longer exist, we are at liberty to discard the rule itself. *Cessante ratione legis cessat ipsa lex.* The rule has no support amongst the juridical writers. It has been criticised by many. Dicey . . . says:
"Such an encroachment of the law of procedure upon substantive rights is difficult to justify from the point of view of justice, convenience or logic".

'Only last year we refused to apply the rule to arbitrations. We held that English arbitrators have jurisdiction to make their awards in a foreign currency, when that currency is the currency of the contract . . . . The time has now come when we should say that when the currency of a contract is a foreign currency – that is to say, when the money of account and the money of payment is a foreign currency – the English courts have power to give judgment in that foreign currency; they can make an order in the form: "It is adjudged this day that the defendant do pay to the plaintiff" so much in foreign currency (being the currency of the contract) "or the sterling equivalent at the time of payment". If the defendant does not honour the judgment, the plaintiff can apply for leave to enforce it. He should file an affidavit showing the rate of exchange at the date of the application and give the amount of the debt converted into sterling at that date. Then leave will be given to enforce payment of that sum'.

Although we have since been told we were wrong to give that judgment, it nevertheless had a dramatic effect. There was, as it happened, another case about to come before the High Court. It was *Miliangos v Geo. Frank*[1] . A Swiss company in 1971 had supplied goods to an English firm and

1. [1975] 1 QB 487.

stipulated for payment in Swiss Francs. The English firm did not pay. Two years later the Swiss firm sued the English firm in an English Court for the price. The Swiss firm were advised that they could only get judgment in sterling. They accepted this advice and were ready to take judgment accordingly. The case was just about to come into the list for hearing — for judgment to be given in sterling — when the Swiss firm saw the report in *The Times* of the *Schorsch v Hennin* case. Their counsel immediately amended his claim and asked for judgment in Swiss Francs. After several adventures, the case reached the House of Lords, and the House gave judgment for the Swiss firm in Swiss Francs. The House themselves overruled the *Havana* case for it was only by so doing that they could give judgment in Swiss Francs.

It was a decision of the greatest importance. But it only came about because we were guilty of a 'distortion of the judicial process'. If in the *Schorsch GmbH v Hennin* case we had held ourselves bound by the *Havana* case, we would have given judgment in sterling. In that event, in the *Miliangos* case the Swiss firm would automatically have taken judgment in sterling also — because they had already been advised that that was the only course. The Swiss firm would not have appealed. The House of Lords would never have had the opportunity of overruling the *Havana* case. The law today would still have been that an English Court could only give judgment in sterling. That would have been a disaster for our trade with countries overseas.

6 Exemplary damages

In the end, therefore, a good end was attained but by a bad means. If that be regarded as some mitigation for our 'turning a blind eye' to the House of Lords, the same cannot be said of the case of *Broome v Cassell & Co*[1]. It was a disaster for me. It arose out of a disaster of war. A convoy of 35 merchant ships was being escorted by a destroyer force under the command of Commander Broome RN. Owing to a

1. [1971] 2 QB 354, [1972] AC 1027 at 1036.

308

mistake in the Admiralty, the convoy was ordered to scatter. The destroyer force was unable to give them protection. They were annihilated by the enemy. Twenty years later a young author wrote a book putting the blame on Commander Broome. It accused him of shameful conduct. It was a gross libel on a courageous naval officer. Cassells published it. Captain Broome (as he now was) brought a libel suit. It was tried by Lawton J and a jury. (Incidentally, it was in the course of it that a group of Welsh students invaded the Court and staged a demonstration in support of the Welsh language. You will find the story of it in *Morris v Crown Office*[1].) The Judge had a difficult task in his summing up. He tried loyally to follow the advice given by the House of Lords in the recent case of *Rookes v Barnard*[2]. The jury in turn followed his advice. They awarded Captain Broome £15,000 as compensatory damages and £25,000 as exemplary damages. The Judge gave judgment for those sums. Cassells appealed. They submitted that the award of £25,000 exemplary damages was erroneous. They said that the Judge had not directed the jury properly in accordance with the doctrine in *Rookes v Barnard*[2]. In the course of the argument it seemed to me that the doctrine in *Rookes v Barnard* caused more problems than it solved. So I threw some doubt on the validity of that doctrine and invited Mr. David Hirst QC to argue it. He is a most able and learned counsel who is now Chairman of the Bar Council. He did argue the validity of *Rookes v Barnard*. In the end we upheld the verdict of the jury and the award of £25,000 exemplary damages on two grounds: first, that accepting the doctrine of *Rookes v Barnard*, the judge's summing up was correct; alternatively, that the doctrine of *Rookes v Barnard* was erroneous. For some time it was thought that Cassells were not going to appeal to the House of Lords. If they had not appealed, the law would have remained as we declared it. Such is the uncertainty of the doctrine of precedent. But they did appeal.

1. [1970] 2 QB 114.
2. [1964] AC 1129.

In my judgment[1] I had ventured to criticise some of the reasoning in the House in *Rookes v Barnard* about exemplary damages. I put it much too strongly. After detailing my reasons, I said (at page 382):

'All this leads me to the conclusion that, if ever there was a decision of the House of Lords given per incuriam, this was it. The explanation is that the House, as a matter of legal theory, thought that exemplary damages had no place in the civil code, and ought to be eliminated from it; but as they could not be eliminated altogether, they ought to be confined within the strictest possible limits, no matter how illogical those limits were'.

I am sorry that I ever said it. It earned for me a severe rebuke by the House of Lords. They specially convened seven Law Lords to hear the appeal[2]. But, in mitigation, I may say that they appreciated the difficulties which had been presented by *Rookes v Barnard*. Viscount Dilhorne went so far as to dissent from it. He thought it was in conflict with a previous decision of the House of Lords and that the *Rookes v Barnard* approach was wrong (page 1111). In addition Lord Wilberforce gave convincing reasons for thinking that the legal theory underlying *Rookes v Barnard* was wrong. He said (at page 1114):

'. . . . It cannot lightly be taken for granted, even as a matter of theory, that the purpose of the law of tort is compensation, still less that it ought to be . . . or that there is something inappropriate or illogical or anomalous (a question-begging word) in including a punitive element in civil damages, . . .'.

and (at page 1116) he said:

'My Lords, I think there was much merit in what I understand was the older system, before *Rookes v Barnard* [1964] AC 1129. I agree with the Court of Appeal that in substance, though not perhaps philosophically or linguistically, this was

1. [1971] 2 QB 354.
2. [1972] AC 1027.

clear and as explained above I doubt if there was any confusion as to what the jury should do'.

Added to those wise words, there is the fact that Canada, Australia and the United States have retained the doctrine of exemplary damages as previously understood and have not been led away along the path of *Rookes v Barnard*.

The difficulties of *Rookes v Barnard* are high-lighted by the effect it had on the summing up of the Judge and of the division it produced in the House of Lords. In the end the House decided in favour of Captain Broome. He retained the award of £25,000 exemplary damages. But only by a majority of 4 to 3. The minority thought that the award of £25,000 exemplary damages was excessive. They would have ordered a new trial. That would have been a disaster for Captain Broome. He could not have faced the expense of it. But, as it was, he suffered a disaster about the costs. The House had a special hearing about them[1]. Mr. Roger Parker QC for Cassells submitted that Captain Broome had had a 'windfall' in being awarded £25,000 — and there was no injustice in depriving him of part of it. He suggested that, because Mr. Hirst had argued the validity of *Rookes v Barnard*, Captain Broome should pay the costs of that issue. Mr. Hirst said that he had not argued the *Rookes v Barnard* issue until the Court of Appeal invited him to do so. That was true. The House gave no reasons. They simply deprived Captain Broome of half his costs in the Court of Appeal and in the House of Lords. This meant that he would have to pay these out of the £25,000. It would make a great hole in it. This gives me much cause for regret: for it was really my fault that the issue was raised and argued. Neither Captain Broome nor his legal advisers were at fault.

Yet was I at fault? If you read the speeches of the seven in *Cassell & Co Ltd (No. 2) v Broome* you will see that they saw the difficulties presented by *Rookes v Barnard*. Yet all but one of them felt they were bound by it. Was it not right for the Court of Appeal to point out those difficulties? So that

1. [1972] AC 1136.

the House might, if it thought fit, escape from them. I am afraid that my fault lay in my insubordination to the authority of the House. This is what Lord Hailsham of St. Marylebone, the Lord Chancellor, had to say about it[1]:

'.... I am driven to the conclusion that when the Court of Appeal described the decision in *Rookes v Barnard* as decided "per incuriam" or "unworkable" they really only meant that they did not agree with it. But, in my view, even if this were not so, it is not open to the Court of Appeal to give gratuitous advice to judges of first instance to ignore decisions of the House of Lords in this way and, if it were open to the Court of Appeal to do so, it would be highly undesirable. The course taken would have put judges of first instance in an embarrassing position, as driving them to take sides in an unedifying dispute between the Court of Appeal or three members of it (for there is no guarantee that other Lords Justices would have followed them and no particular reason why they should) and the House of Lords. But, much worse than this, litigants would not have known where they stood. None could have reached finality short of the House of Lords, and, in the meantime, the task of their professional advisers of advising them either as to their rights, or as to the probable cost of obtaining or defending them, would have been, quite literally, impossible. Whatever the merits, chaos would have reigned until the dispute was settled, and, in legal matters, some degree of certainty is at least as valuable a part of justice as perfection.

'The fact is, and I hope it will never be necessary to say so again, that, in the hierarchical system of courts which exists in this country, it is necessary for each lower tier, including the Court of Appeal, to accept loyally the decisions of the higher tiers. Where decisions manifestly conflict, the decision in *Young v Bristol Aeroplane Co Ltd* [1944] KB 718 offers guidance to each tier in matters affecting its own decisions. It does not entitle it to question considered decisions in the upper tiers with the same freedom . . .'.

1. [1972] AC 1027.

Yes — I had been guilty — of lese majesty. I had impugned the authority of the House. That must never be done by anyone save the House itself. Least of all by the turbulent Master of the Rolls[1].

---

1. *'Who will free me from this turbulent priest?'* (Henry II of Thomas à Becket).

Conclusion

Let it not be thought from this discourse that I am against the doctrine of precedent. I am not. It is the foundation of our system of case law. This has evolved by broadening down from precedent to precedent. By standing by previous decisions, we have kept the common law on a good course. All that I am against is its too rigid application — a rigidity which insists that a bad precedent must necessarily be followed. I would treat it as you would a path through the woods. You must follow it certainly so as to reach your end. But you must not let the path become too overgrown. You must cut out the dead wood and trim off the side branches, else you will find yourself lost in thickets and brambles. My plea is simply to keep the path to justice clear of obstructions which would impede it.

Epilogue

Nothing must be left undone

Writing in *The Times* of 5 January 1977, Sir Leslie Scarman said: 'The past 25 years will not be forgotten in our legal history. They are the age of legal aid, law reform and Lord Denning'. I am gratified by the tribute but I feel that many of my endeavours have failed — at any rate so far. The strict constructionists still hold their fortress. The officious by-stander still dominates the field. The Court of Appeal is still bound hand and foot. The powerful still abuse their powers without restraint.

Something has, however, been attempted. Something done. You will find it in the previous pages. If I had time, I would have told you more. I would have told how the deserted wife was given shelter by equity only to find it rudely torn from her by the House of Lords. I would have told how the unfair exemption clauses were wiped out by means of fundamental breach only to be restored by the supreme tribunal. I would have told how the press were free to comment on matters of public interest but shouted down by the 'voices of infallibility'. I would have told how the law of real property has been revolutionised by finding the hidden wealth of licences and constructive trusts — and not up to now condemned by higher authority.

All these and other matters I must leave you to find out for yourselves. You can read them in law books. I have no time to write more now. This book was my 'holiday task' for the long vacation. Usually we travel much overseas. But this year we stayed at home. In the country. In the place where I was born. Specially to write this book for you. Done in so short a time, there are bound to be imperfections. So please forgive me.

Now we are back again at work. We have been to the Services which mark the beginning of the legal year. Such as the Judges of England have done from time immemorial. In Westminster Abbey, in Winchester Cathedral and in the Temple Church. There we have prayed for 'the spirit of discernment, the spirit of uprightness, the spirit of understanding'. During the legal term we are fully occupied. I sit in Court every day of the week. Five days a week. I spend my weekends writing reserved judgments. And get lots of outside things to attend to.

Now we have got to the middle of November. We hope that the book will be published in time for my 80th birthday. It is on 23 January 1979. I am one of the few Judges left who have a freehold. Others leave at 75.

It is something to have lived through this century – the most dangerous century in the history of the English people. Our family has done its part. All five of us brothers fought in the wars. Two were lost. They were the best of us. Three survive. One to become a General. One an Admiral. And me, the Master of the Rolls. Some day, if I have time, I will tell the family story. But that must wait. I must get on with the next case. Nothing must be left undone.

Index

324